DOES IT RAIN
IN OTHER
DIMENSIONS?

Mike Oram

Jayne
Enjoy the Journey
Love & Light
Mike Oram
x

First published by O-Books, 2007
O-Books is an imprint of John Hunt Publishing Ltd., Laurel House, Station Approach,
Alresford, Hants, SO24 9JH, UK
office1@o-books.net
www.o-books.com

For distributor details and how to order please visit the 'Ordering' section on our website.

Text copyright: Mike Oram 2007

ISBN: 978 1 84694 054 5

A CIP catalogue record for this book is available from the British Library.

Design: Stuart Davies

Printed and bound by CPI Group (UK) Ltd, Croydon, CR0 4YY
Printed in the USA by Offset Paperback Mfrs, Inc

We operate a distinctive and ethical publishing philosophy in all
areas of our business, from our global network of authors to
production and worldwide distribution.

DOES IT RAIN IN OTHER DIMENSIONS?

Mike Oram

BOOKS

Winchester, UK
Washington, USA

DEDICATION

To Tellos, my dear Space Brother, who always seemed to appear at the right times. You gave me hope as a child and vision as a man. Although we are separated by worlds, we are joined in the heart and mind. You told me once that I had to stop sticking my nose where it does not belong! Well, I hope your constant protection has not been too much of a burden to bear.

I would also like to thank Fran, my partner, for her tireless editing of this book, her textual contributions and for the writing of the final chapter. Without her help, this book may never have happened. She, like me, is a searcher for truth and has a mind that looks to the stars rather than to the mundane. This, I feel sure, is why she has helped to retain the sensitivity of this book when discussing experiences of a very personal nature.

My Love to you both.

CONTENTS

Never utter these words: 'I do not know this – therefore it is false.' One must study to know, know to understand, understand to judge.

APOTHEGM OF NARADA

The Bible mentions Jesus and Peter walking on water; it is claimed that the Buddha walked on water and these claims are believed worldwide by many thousands of people - none of whom have any evidence to back up their belief, which is based on second-hand testimony from many years ago. Why then, when claims such as these are accepted without evidence, do people clamor for 'evidence' when more cogent, recent and tangible personal testimonies to unusual experiences, such as contact with off-worlders, are presented? Why can reason extend to encompass possibilities in the one case and not in the other?

"UFOs are as real as the airplanes that fly over your head.... The classification was, from the outset, Above Top Secret, so the vast majority of US officials and politicians, let alone a mere Allied Minister of Defence, were never in the loop.....The time has come to lift the veil of secrecy and let the truth emerge so there can be a real and informed debate about one of the most important problems facing our planet today."

Paul Hellyer, Canadian Minister of Defence from 1963-1967, in a speech at the University of Toronto, 25 September 2005.

On 6 January 2005, *India Daily* reported on its country's internal debate on whether or not the populace should be told what the government knows about UFOs:

"New Delhi is in the middle of a big secret internal debate. On one side the largest democracy of the world is eager to explain to its citizens and to the world about the ongoing contacts with the UFOs and extra-terrestrials. On the other hand there are invisible untold international protocols that prohibit doing anything that may cause worldwide fear and panic."

From *India Daily* online at http://www.indiadaily.com

"We have, indeed, been contacted – perhaps even visited – by extraterrestrial beings, and the US government, in collusion with the other national powers of the Earth, is determined to keep this information from the general public."

Victor Marchetti, former Special Assistant to the Executive Director of the CIA in *How the CIA Views the UFO Phenomenon, Second Look, Vol 1, NO 7*, 1979.

"The phenomenon of UFOs does exist, and it must be treated seriously."

Mikhail Gorbachev, *Soviet Youth,* 4 May 1990.

11 August 2006 issue of the *Daily Mail,* an article entitled 'UFOs: Can

They *All* Be Hoaxes?' stated:

"Rear Admiral Hillenkoetter, a former CIA director, noted in 1960 that 'behind the scenes, high-ranking Air Force officers are soberly concerned about UFOs. But through official secrecy and ridicule, many citizens are led to believe the unknown flying objects are nonsense'.

Were the authorities imposing a 'world blanket of secrecy', in the words of the eminent Greek physicist Professor Paul Santorini...... who investigated UFOs for the Greek military? He suggested that there might be a cover-up because the authorities were unwilling to admit the existence of a force against which they had no possibility of defence. "

"I believe that these extraterrestrial vehicles and their crews are visiting this planet from other planets which obviously are a little more . . . advanced than we are. . ."

Astronaut L. Gordon Cooper, Mercury 7, letter to the United Nations, 1978.

And in 1997 he said: "I know other astronauts share my feelings... And we know the government is sitting on hard evidence of UFOs."

On 19 November 2002, *Pravda* published an article about Stalin's deep interest in flying saucers, and the many military and scientific bodies set up by the Soviets to secretly investigate the phenomenon.

"The US government might have spent more than half a century trying to convince suspicious conspiracy theorists that no UFO ever crashed at Roswell, New Mexico, but one man never believed the story. That man, according to Pravda (Nov 19), was Joseph Stalin. The Soviet dictator apparently thought the US was covering up with its story of a weather balloon crashing, so he ordered senior scientists to investigate. As a result, a number of programmes to study UFOs were launched in the USSR...Until the end of the 90s, there were seven research institutes and about 10 secret military departments of the [former] Soviet Defence Ministry that studied UFO phenomena."

The Editor, published by *The Guardian,* 23 November 2002.

"...I've been asked about UFOs and I've said publicly I thought they were somebody else, some other civilization."

Commander Eugene Cernan, Commanded the Apollo 17 Mission. The quote is from a 1973 article in the Los Angeles Times.

"We all know UFOs are real. All we need to ask is where do they come from."

Dr Edgar Mitchell, 1971, after his Apollo 14 Moon flight.

"Of course the flying saucers are real and they are interplanetary.... The cumulative evidence for the existence of UFOs is quite overwhelming and I accept the fact of their existence."

Air Chief Marshal Lord Dowding, RAF, in the *Sunday Dispatch,* 1954.

"I've been convinced for a long time that flying saucers are real and interplanetary. In other words, we are being watched by beings from outer space."

Albert M. Chop, Deputy Public Relations Director at NASA, in *True Magazine,* Jan, 1965.

"If I become President, I'll make every piece of information this country has about UFO sightings available to the public and the scientists."

President Jimmy Carter.

"At no time when the astronauts were in space were they alone."

Astronaut Scott Carpenter – who photographed a UFO while in orbit on 24 May, 1962. NASA has not released this photograph.

"This 'flying saucer' situation is not at all imaginary or seeing too much in some natural phenomena. Something is really flying around. The

phenomenon is something real and not visionary or fictitious."
Admiral Roscoe H. Hillenkoetter, Director of the CIA, 1947 -1950.

"I believe that UFOs are spaceships or extraterrestrial craft... The nations of the world are currently working together in the investigation of the UFO PHENOMENON. There is an international exchange of data. Maybe when this group acquires more precise and definite information, it will be possible to release the news to the world."
General Carlos Castro Cavero, Commander of Spain's Third Aerial Region, Spanish Air Force, in an interview with J.J.Benitez for *La Gaceta del Norte*, 1979.

PREFACE

If you are a dyed-in-the-wool skeptic on things classed as 'paranormal' and about the UFO /alien contact scenario in particular, then I guess you would not have picked this book up. So – even if you think you are skeptical – you must have a chink of your mind open to other possibilities. Keep that door open and read my story. If you are the sort of person who needs evidence, then read Fran's chapter at the end of the book and the *Suggested Reading* section and follow up the links to books with more 'nuts and bolts' information and web sites where you can see videos of craft and Beings. Although Fran and I have attempted to place my experiences within the global context of off-world visitors, this book is simply my story of an ordinary life that has included extraordinary episodes.

I have lost count down the years as to how many friends and acquaintances have suggested I write a book about my contacts. It would be a lie to say that it has not crossed my mind and it would be absolutely honest to say that I was scared to write such a book. I did not want to draw the sort of attention to myself that this book might create. So why am I writing it now?

One of those reasons is because of what happened to Fran and myself in Nevada in February 2004 and the culmination of that experience, when Tellos, my Space Brother, created before my eyes an etheric pink rose, which he placed into the centre of my heart.

Soon after that experience, Light Beings helped me remember symbols they had placed into my mind years before. They told me that these symbols work on a deep level to enable consciousness change and that I was to disseminate these. Apart from speaking at conferences, the easiest way to let as many people as possible see these symbols is to put them in a book.

Another reason is that it is the time to write such a book. Tens of thousands of people from all cultures are having very similar experiences to my own and this is, I am sure, part of the Great Awakening of our global consciousness. I am now 55 years of age and if I do not do it now, then it may never be done. This book, I hope, will go towards playing a small part in helping others to understand what is going on within their own lives. The 'Visitors' are already here! We do not need to look through giant telescopes or listen to signals from deep space in the hope that we can put to one side, once and for all, that we are not alone in the universe. Our neighbors are already here and have been here for a very long time. It is just that certain governments around the world have made a decision not to tell us[1]. In a 2006 interview with Italian investigative journalist Paola Harris, Paul Hellyer, Canadian ex-Minister of Defence, said: "I am convinced there has been a mysterious and systematic and very thorough cover up for half a century, if not more."

One of the reasons for that decision is said to be fear of panic. Public reaction would depend largely on how we were told. As one looks out into the night sky and sees the myriad of stars and deduces the number of planets this implies, it is perfectly reasonable to assume that life exists on some of those other planets and to presume that some of those life forms will have developed ways of traveling in the Universe. It should be a short step from that assumption to an expectation that some, at least, of our neighbors will visit us. Natural curiosity alone would surely prompt this, in the same way that we, on Earth, love to travel to other countries on our planet and see for ourselves what exists elsewhere. As our knowledge has grown and our physicists have introduced concepts of parallel dimensions, it is also not unreasonable to assume that there will be life forms that have the ability to move dimensionally and who will also make appearances in our dimension.

They could have told us back in the late 1940s and early 1950s, when they were sending goodness-knows-how-many planes up into the heavens, loaded with gun cameras, in the vain attempt to capture images of what they thought must be extraterrestrial vehicles. 1952 was one of two main early "watershed" years of the modern UFO era and it was in this year there was a huge UFO flap worldwide, starting in Washington DC. It began on 19 July 1952, when Washington National Airport and Andrews Air Force Base picked up a number of UFOs on their radar screens. These objects were traveling at about 100 mph but with the ability to accelerate to the, then unbelievable, speed of 7,200 mph. The Washington sightings featured multiple simultaneous radar and coincident ground and airborne visual sightings of UFOs over the White House and the Washington DC restricted airspace. As Albert M. Chop[2], former press chief for USAF and former information officer for NASA, said to Major Donald E. Keyhoe in 1952, after two Chicago engineers theorized that UFO sightings by pilots were pockets of ionized air caused by the recent A-bomb tests in Nevada, "I wish to heaven it were right. We could stop scrambling all those jets, tell the public this was it, and close the project. However, Air Technical Intelligence Centre had scientists look into that long ago, though they knew it was not the answer. We had sightings before the first A-bomb blast. No, it is just another wild idea by people who do not know the evidence. If they'd seen intelligence reports like these, they'd know better." (Above quote taken from Donald E. Keyhoe's book *Flying Saucers from Outer Space,* Hutchinson, 1954).

Wilbert Smith was a Canadian radio engineer during the 1950s and a world expert in electromagnetism and telecommunications. Working with the Canadian government, he founded Project Magnet, the start of UFO research in Canada, and was in charge of Canadian UFO studies between 1950 and 1962. Lt. Col. Bremner, a military attaché at the Canadian embassy in Washington, arranged an interview for Smith with Dr Robert Sarbacher on 15 September, 1950. Sarbacher was a very experienced electrical engineer and guided missile scientist and a consultant to the US Research and Development Board. In the interview Sarbacher revealed that UFOs existed, they didn't originate on Earth, they were being secretly studied by both the US and Canadian governments and the subject was the most highly classified in the US government, at a level higher than the H-bomb. This is all recorded in Wilbert Smith's handwritten notes of the meeting and a top secret memo Smith wrote to the Canadian Department of Transport on 21 November 1950.

Air Chief Marshall, Lord Dowding, was Commander-in-Chief of RAF Fighter Command during the Battle of Britain in 1940. In the early 1950s he stated that more than 10,000 sightings of UFOs had been logged. He went on to say: "I am convinced that these objects do exist and that they are not manufactured by any nation on earth. I can therefore see no alternative to accepting the theory that they come from some extraterrestrial source." In 1954, he said: "Of course the flying saucers are real and they are interplanetary. . . . The cumulative evidence for the existence of UFOs is quite overwhelming and I accept the fact of their existence."

Therefore, we know that back in the 50s, at least, they knew craft were interplanetary or interdimensional and kept quiet about that. When documents were released in the US under the Freedom of Information Act, it was revealed that the CIA, who claimed they had not investigated UFOs for twenty to thirty years, had thousands of documents, which showed they had never stopped investigating them[3]. Among the released documents on the CIA web site is one dated February 1993, reporting on the fact that the Japanese Government were to commence a study of 'supernatural powers, including psychic phenomena and even Unidentified Flying Objects.'

Along with panic it has also been suggested that releasing the truth about the alien presence would have a profound impact on some of our major religions as the belief structures set in place do not accommodate a populated universe view, much less populated dimensions or the fact that we are, in all likelihood, not a supreme example of Creation but a species still very backward in our development. Highly advanced beings from other planets and dimensions, flitting about our atmosphere and communicating with us 'lesser mortals' about regaining our personal power and changing the global consciousness of 'Gaia', may be too uncomfortable a meal for our controlling political and religious powers to swallow.

The third reason for secrecy could be financial. It has been speculated that the global economy would collapse as panic spread around the world following the announcement: "Aliens are here and have been for some time and for the past sixty years we have kept this from you for your own safety." The assumption has been made that many would be devastated at such an announcement and plunge into depression or panic and so be unable to work while others would treat the 'Visitors' as our saviors and would no longer see the point of going to work or paying the bills. Some would race to the hills in the hope of being picked-up in 'god-like' machines and whisked away to horizons new.

I can see the reasoning in all of the above scenarios but, as a human species, I believe we have to give ourselves more credit then that. Human Beings are very resilient and through thousands of years of evolution have proved that they can accept and adapt to great global changes, whether that be environmental, cultural or otherwise. If we had been told the truth back in the late 1940s, that strange machines were visiting our skies and that they may be extraterrestrial in nature, then we, as a race, would have slowly adapted to such a shift in worldview. There could have been discussions on radio, television and even in churches and schools and we would have found ourselves in a much healthier position then we currently are today.

Perhaps the major Governments[4] of the world now feel that they dare not tell us that they have known about this for sixty years or more, in fear that we may retaliate and feel angered that we have been sold a lie for so long. I strongly believe that would not be the case. An official announcement that we are not alone in the universe would give us great hope for the future. The chance to fraternize freely with the 'Visitors' from elsewhere, who are mostly here to help humanity evolve in consciousness, would eventually override any reactions of anger. We would look back to this time as a pivotal point in our evolution. A time when we were forced to awake to the existence of these other realities. A great shift in conscious awareness would take place as we realized, once and for all, that we are not just material beings living out a 3D existence on a geophysical planet, but are universal spiritual beings alive in a cosmos of limitless possibilities.

MIKE ORAM
www.inotherdimensions.com

1 See *Suggested Reading* 1/1
2 See *Suggested Reading* 1/A
3 See *Suggested Reading* 1/B
4 See chapter 7, where we cite governments that are more open with this information.

ACKNOWLEDGEMENTS

This book would not have reached completion without the brilliant artwork of John Pickering. He listened to my descriptions and seemed to have an uncanny knack of producing perfectly what I saw. Also, many thanks to David Coggins who spent five days at my home overseeing several regressions connected to the missing time at Area 51, in Nevada and the releasing of symbols from the Light Beings, given to me in 1994.

My warm thanks to Mary Rodwell, who kindly agreed to write the foreword to this book. Mary is a very special person who works tirelessly to help people who have contact with our Visitors. Using hypnotic regression therapy, Mary helps those who are traumatized or confused by their experiences, as well as contactees who wish to recover suppressed memories of their encounters. Mary helped me recover an emotionally-poignant memory of an amazing experience involving a crystal city and a Christ-like being but, because of the personal nature of this event, I have not included it in the book.

Many thanks also for the quotations in chapter 16, which are reproduced by kind permission of the White Eagle Publishing Trust, New Lands, Liss, Hampshire, GU33 7HY. Finally, to my many friends who shared with me the early days in Warminster, spending endless nights on the tops of Cradle Hill and Starr Hill - sometimes in the most appalling weather! You know who you are! My Love to you all.

THE EMERGENCE
© Mike Oram 2005

In the beginning was the word,
And the word was
Boy.
As I moved through fluidic blackness,
Reddened and wrinkled,
Safe and secure,
I emerged
From the womb of the Mother.

The cold, bright light threatened my very existence.
Alien hands pulled me from my homeland;
I was powerless against such strength.
My mind
In conflict to understand.

The emergence seemed too soon.
No!
I am not ready to leave!

Reassuring words were relayed to the Mother,
That all was well.
Why should such pleasure be aroused at my departure?
Why did the Mother have to push so hard to release me?
Had the Mother despaired from fullness of womb?

Perhaps the one who relayed to the Mother
That all was well
Had decided on such imminence?

Then,
Suddenly,
I caught a glimpse of reason.
My awareness expanded.
For one brief second time somehow stood still.
I became aware of something;
An experience even before conception,
And I saw
The decision was mine!

Then it was gone
And I found myself in the Mother's arms,
My head pressed against her breast,
The beat of her heart pumping me to sleep;
And I slept.

DOES IT RAIN IN OTHER DIMENSIONS

Foreword by Mary Rodwell, Principal of the Australian Close Encounter Resource Network.

"But my real parents are in space, and I come from somewhere out there."

Are we alone?

Logically, a thinking person cannot believe that, in a cosmos of unimaginable vastness, we are the only intelligent life. If we are not alone, the question has to be asked: are such intelligences already visiting planet Earth? And if so, how would we know?

Millions of individuals and groups of people around the globe have not only witnessed, photographed, and videotaped UFOs (Unidentified Flying Objects) and observed them doing maneuvers impossible with conventional aircraft, they have also experienced contact with these non-human intelligences. In 2005, a *Readers Digest* poll in Australia confirmed that 1 in 5 people had observed UFOs and believed they had interactions with them. A Roper poll in the US offered similar statistics, indicating this is a global phenomenon, affecting millions of people from every culture and belief. We have to conclude that either millions of people are hallucinating or we are, in fact, being visited by non-human extraterrestrial beings. Mike Oram is one such individual. His personal and intimate contact with these beings takes the reader through the gamut of the 'classic' close encounters to reveal remarkable understanding of our intimate connections with the Star Visitors. Such experiences, if true, as I believe they are, have profound implications for all mankind.

Contrary to popular belief, individuals with contact are not fantasy-prone *Star Trek* fanatics who believe anything. My research, as Principal of the Australian Close Encounter Network (ACERN.), covers over 1200 cases worldwide. My case studies include many professionals, such as lawyers, doctors and psychologists. Initially, many of them were very skeptical of their experiences, for it was preferable to believe the experience was not real; a mental aberration or worse. But they found it becomes increasingly difficult to deny the reality of these events when faced with on-going visual sightings, 'implanted' metallic objects in the body, unexplained marks, missing time episodes, emotional trauma, and especially when the event is a family affair. We also find this experience changes people in extraordinary ways, with heightened psychic, precognitive and healing abilities gained from their encounters. These facts alone show that something real and profound has occurred.

These encounter experiences create a conflict of paradigms because the experience challenges a person's understanding of reality and demonstrates that many of their previously held beliefs are invalid. For them to acknowledge contact is real, the experiencer is obliged to either expand his world view to include this reality, or continue to live in denial. Many will stay with denial through fear, but others will finally embrace or transcend this fear and accept the challenge to gain more understanding of their experiences of this broader reality. Contact becomes the catalyst for profound questions, such as: Who are these intelligences and why are they here? Who are we? What does it all mean?

Mike Oram did not struggle so much with his expanded reality, as struggle with limited minds that discriminated against such experiences. Mike's encounters covered the gamut of those mentioned, and much more. His encounters gave him insights into a multidimensional reality; one he sought to quantify in both traditional and esoteric sciences. Through this process he discovered even more tangible links to explain what he had been taught by his 'space brothers.' It is through these communications and the extraordinary information he received that Mike is able to take the reader into other realms of possibility to discover that what present science believes is impossible may well be possible. Mike knows this because he has seen and experienced it. He also received information on the 'true' hybrid nature of Homo sapiens and that some of the answers may be hidden within our DNA.

Many renowned scientists have come to believe the truth of our genetic origins may be found in human DNA. Dr Francis Crick, co-discoverer of the DNA molecule and author of *Life Itself*, wrote: "The seeds of life came in a space craft." It seems the very complexity of the DNA molecule confirms the possibility of intelligent design, and anomalies contained within human DNA cannot be explained through normal evolutionary channels. There are 223 genomes, which do not have the required processors in our genomic evolutionary tree and are unique to Homo sapiens. These genomes are two thirds the difference between us and the chimpanzee, and all relate to higher psychological functioning. The mystery is how they got there; a mysterious 'sideways insertion' of genetic material.

Is there evidence anthropologically and historically that we may have been genetically engineered by other intelligences visiting earth? The answer is yes, there certainly is, and it can be seen in primitive artwork, thousands of years old: drawings of space craft and strange humanoids with space helmets. Medieval and religious paintings clearly depict flying craft in the sky and strange beings. Notwithstanding many ancient writings, such as the Sumerian and Biblical texts, which speak of the 'Gods' who came in 'sky ships', visiting, interacting, and interbreeding with humans. Indigenous tribes of all cultures speak of such Gods; the Aborigines called them the 'Wandjina', 'Sky Gods' who came down from the sky and gave them laws to live by. The Dogon tribe in West Africa specifically comment on the genetic upgrading by such beings they call the 'Nummo'.

The evidence we have been visited by extraterrestrial intelligences suggests they could well have been responsible for our genetic upgrading. What is even more startling is that similar information can come from a small child! Mike was just four years old when he said to his mother, "You are not my parents, my real parents are in space, and I come from somewhere out there."

What would cause a young child to make such a profound statement?

It would be easy to dismiss because of its incredible nature, but what is astounding is that he is not the only child to vocalize such information. Hundreds of experiencers, many small children, comment that they "felt like they were adopted" and their human parents were 'not their real parents'. A five-years-old from Western Australia said to her mother: "You are not my real parents; my parents are in space and you are just here to look after me."

Bewildered parents question how their child could possibly know this? What is more astounding, many of them feel and sense a deep 'heart, soul' connection to the Star Visitors. We could choose to dismiss such information as a mere child's fantasy, except for the fact we know this is not something they will have learnt or seen in a child's story book or on television. The children give us one answer to this mystery, incredible as it may be! They speak about being taken onto space craft and being taught there. A five-year old boy told his mother: "I don't mind going through the walls and 'they' (the beings) teach me more on the ships than I learn at school." The parents could struggle to accept this, if it was not for the fact that they have experienced similar encounters. Contact is intergenerational, and this means it is a family affair, so that if parents are having contact then it is more than likely their children will experience it too. With the children, the beings can cloak or 'screen' their true form, to appear to them as clowns, owls, Santa Claus, or cats with big eyes. It is only later they will discover this was a screen memory for the extraterrestrial visiting them, which may turn out to be a small 'gray,' being or a humanoid, etc. In Mike's case, his screen memory as a child was a 'tiger' at the end of his bed.

Mike Oram was four years old when he said to his mother: "Something of incredible importance is going to happen on this Earth, not in your lifetime but in mine. It is to do with global consciousness and that is why I am here at this time, to experience this change." "My mother never forgot that conversation," Mike said.

For such a young child to make such an amazing statement is once again evidence that something incredible had happened to him. The reality of children's encounter experiences is often demonstrated by them articulating such profound information and one way this occurs is covered in my book. *Awakening*[1]. I explain how an eight-years-old girl called this process 'knowledge bombs', a kind of downloading of data in a form of universal language, through complex geometric forms, symbols, hieroglyphs and scripts. Mike Oram also received information this way. The information download is encoded so that it bypasses linear thinking and is understood on a deeper subconscious and super-conscious level. It was explained to Mike that the purpose of such scripts and symbols is that they are related to global awakening of consciousness. Hence, many, such as Mike, feel a sense of 'mission,' or purpose for being here. This sense of mission is a classic pattern of the phenomenon known as 'Star Kids', or the 'New Human'.

The New Human or Star Kids phenomenon is the hypotheses that we are evolving into a more multi-dimensionally-aware species. My research indicates this quantum leap in consciousness is being recognized all over the globe. Dr Roger Leir, well known for his pioneering work in Ufology (he has surgically removed 'implanted' objects from experiencers) also researched evidence that children born today are very different from just 40 years ago. He found that the developmental stages in children have accelerated, in some cases as much as 50-80 per cent, and these increases are all related to higher psychological functioning. Dr Leir states: "I have come to the conclusion that not only are star children amongst us, but the entire human race is being advanced forward at a rate that is unlikely to be due to slow evolutionary forces, it is far more likely that the rapid advancement of the human species is due to alien intervention in our bodies and minds."

I believe Mike Oram is one of the New Humans, which became more evident to me when I met him in person in Nevada, US, at the 2004 International UFO Congress. He has many of the classic traits of this phenomenon, such as, high intelligence, very spiritually aware, and passionate about the sacredness of all life. He also feels a deep bond with his space brothers, accompanied by a sense of mission, or purpose. It is also clear that Mike is important to the intelligences as they have protected him in several life-threatening situations. One such dangerous situation was when he had visited the notorious AREA 51 in Nevada, US. Mike experienced some very strange events whilst there, from missing time episodes to becoming extremely ill from the aftermath of the trip. The extraordinary details of what actually happened were later clarified in regression hypnosis. The reality of this experience, which left him very unwell for several days, was evidence that something significant had occurred. Mike discovered later what actually happened and it is both confronting and fascinating and leaves you in no doubt that Mike was very fortunate to be protected by his space brothers. I have heard many accounts where individuals were 'protected 'in a similar way via their encounters.

Mike is not fearful of the beings and has found no reason to be. His acceptance of them and this greater reality has allowed him to explore the Contact experience in far greater depth because of this. It means his book is one of a few that take the reader on a journey beyond this paradigm, to explore the more profound questions that the contact experience evokes. Non-human extraterrestrial contact for many can create huge fear. The fear limits understanding, as it challenges the core beliefs in ourselves, our origins and reality; the very fabric of everything we believe we are. But, as Mike discovered, if you can transcend such fears, trust and let go of outmoded beliefs, you expose yourself to a greater reality. Mike's heightened awareness and acceptance has allowed for deeper communication and the 'downloading' of complex information, sometimes in the form of scripts and symbols. These symbols are extremely important to awaken the 'sleepers', as Mike calls them. They act as a 'trigger' or catalyst to propel the individual into this transformative 'awakening' to a broader paradigm.

Mike's book assists the reader to explore the information that will help them release their own limiting beliefs, and gain insight into our deeper connections to the reality of extraterrestrial intelligences and their purpose for interacting with us. Through Mike's own journey we explore the spiritual and multidimensional nature of personal reality, understanding of our origins, our evolution as a species and how we can evolve and awaken into a higher consciousness.

Mike's book will be invaluable to the experiencer, the researcher, and spiritual seeker. It is a compelling account of extraordinary human experience with non-human intelligences, coupled with complex and thought-provoking information. It explores not only a human experiencing a multi-reality communication with extraterrestrial intelligences, but the very nature of human consciousness, and our evolution as a species. It also takes the reader on a journey within, to seek answers to the mystery of who and what we are, and will help dispel the fear that contact experiences evoke. Such profound experiences confirm the truth that 'we are not alone,' and have never been alone. That the acceptance of our extraterrestrial contacts can be a positive, 'multi-dimensional awakening.' The star kids say that they are here to help humanity evolve and Mike, through sharing his experience is fulfilling the 'mission' to assist us to grow, transcend our fears, heal and awaken. Mike's story supports millions of others who have similar encounters and encourages them to step out of the box; to speak their truth. We all owe a great debt to individuals such as Mike because as he courageously honors his truth, I am certain it will give others the courage to do the same, and through that we will all learn more of who and what we are, and why we are not alone.

MARY RODWELL
Counsellor/Therapist.
Principal ACERN (Australian Close Encounter Resource Network)
Vice President of the Star Kids Project.
Author of *Awakening*

Producer of *Expressions of ET Contact - a Visual Blueprint?*
& *Expressions of ET Contact - a Communication and Healing Blueprint?*
www.acern.com.au

1 Mary Rodwell: *Awakening: How Extraterrestrial Contact Can Transform Your Life.* Avatar Publications. June 2005. ISBN: 0973844205

WARMINSTER DAYS AND A LANDING AT STARR HILL

We met one evening
Down a dark and dusty track.
There was no time to be frightened;
There was no turning back.
I saw beyond his shoulders,
About sixty yards away,
A strange metallic disc
That seemed to turn and sway.

The sleepy little Town of Warminster, in Wiltshire, rose to global prominence after an incident on Christmas Eve in 1964. A high-pitched whine sounded around the area and people were struck to the ground by some unknown force. People ran out of their homes into the street, to look at their roofs, as it sounded like someone was tearing the slates from the tops of their houses, but when outside, there was nothing to be seen. I interviewed many of these people in the 1970s and these incidents were still very much in their minds. These were ordinary, sensible people, who experienced an extraordinary event, which would stay with them for the rest of their lives. In August of 1965, a meeting was set up in the Town Hall, for the sake of the public who were, at that time, screaming at the officials for an answer. The meeting was packed out and people spilled out onto the pavement. It was also stacked to the gunnels with reporters from various newspapers and television stations. It was coming up to the August Bank Holiday and it is reputed that well over 10,000 people arrived in the town over that coming weekend, from all around the world. It was said that even the pubs ran dry!

A few days after my article appeared in *Flying Saucer Review* (*FSR*) (see chapter 7), there came a knock at my door. A young man, the same age as me, had been knocking at houses along the road to try to find out where I lived, He had read the article in *FSR* and wanted to interview me for a small magazine, *Perception*, which he produced himself. I will call him Gerald and he lived at that time in Kent.

I invited him in and we had a long chat about my UFO experience while he made copious notes. Then he turned to me and said, "Have you been to Warminster?" I asked him why Warminster, and one hour later he was still telling me all the incredible things that were happening there. "You must go there," he said, and then continued, "Look, I'm going next weekend, why don't you come with me?" I readily agreed.

Going to Warminster was one of those experiences in life that changes you forever. One of those experiences that make you wonder how your life would have panned out if you had not done it.

At 18 years of age, this was the furthest I had ever been and just the thought of going all that way to Wiltshire was an adventure in itself. My parents never had much money and a trip to London for the day, or to Southend, was as good as it got. They would not have ventured too far, just in case they could not get back to their home in the evening. Once, when I purchased a house in Warminster in 1980, I drove 120 miles to their house, slept overnight and drove them 120 miles back to Warminster the following day, so they could see the house. We spent the rest of the day driving around looking at the beauty spots. After that, we drove the 120 miles back to Essex, to get them back to their safe haven, as they could not cope with the thought of sleeping elsewhere. I then drove the 120 miles back home to Warminster the following morning.

Back to the story. Gerald and I finally arrived at Warminster station, to bright sunshine, and went straight to the local café for something to eat. Then we made our way up to Cradle Hill (See Fig 1). A trip that I made thousands of times in the next few years. I cannot express to you well enough what another momentous moment this was. As we approached the top of the hill, we passed cars parked bumper to bumper, or tightly pulled into the verge to allow other cars to come back down. At the white gates at the top there must have been well over 100 people standing around in

Scratchbury Hill

Track Leading to Copse at
Cradle Hill
(now without a gate barring the way)

Barn at Starr Hill

Starr Hill

Fig 1

groups, talking about the latest sightings they, or someone else, had seen in the last couple of weeks. This was so incredibly exciting, especially as it was not that long ago that I believed I was the only person in the world who felt this way about our star visitors or who was having such visitations and now I was surrounded by people who were dedicated to looking into this enigma. These, mostly, were good, honest, decent people and fun to be with and this was, without doubt, one of the most magical times of my life.

Gerald and I were standing by one such group, listening to the conversation, when one lad started speaking about an article he had read in *FSR*, concerning a sighting in East Ham in London. He then went on to say that he had traveled to Rainham and tried to find where this person lived but failed to do so. Gerald looked at me and said that he was talking about me! "Go and tell him that you're here," he said. I felt too shy to butt in and say that the person he had been trying to find was right there behind him, on Cradle Hill, so Gerald tapped the lad on the shoulder and told him that the person he had been trying to find was right here and he turned and pointed to me. We all had a laugh about this coincidence and he introduced himself as Paul. We became great friends and over the next few years we made many trips to Warminster and had some quite amazing experiences.

One such experience happened in July 1970. Paul and I had arranged to spend a whole week in Warminster. Up to that point, I had just been going for long weekends; traveling down Friday evening and coming back home late Sunday night. Therefore, a whole week of sky watching was a great treat. The excitement was quite tangible. It was like tapping into the mains. Like putting your finger in a socket and receiving an almighty charge of electricity. This excitement stayed with me for years. We were on our way to Warminster, to spend seven days looking for craft from other planets, other dimensions, other times. This simply could not be bettered and the feelings of those days floods back into my mind as I sit and type these thoughts today. The energy of that time is still locked into the ether and once again I am turning the key that will unlock the doors of the mind, the windows to the soul, where these wondrous stories are concealed.

We arrived in Warminster late Friday evening and set up the tent on the campsite in semi-darkness. We were tired after our long drive and decided to get some sleep, ready for an early rise the next morning. I have found over the years that there are unusual amounts of synchronistic events in Ufology. This has been a constant thing and something that many other people have noticed also. In the morning, another one of those synchronistic events happened. Sometime in the night, after we had gone to sleep, in absolute darkness, a tent had been put up right next to ours, and when I opened our tent flap in the morning I was confronted by a lad standing on his head in a yoga posture. When he turned the right way up, I recognized that it was our dear friend, David. He had also, unbeknownst to us, decided to spend the week in Warminster. The three of us agreed to spend the time together and hope that this was some sort of omen to a fruitful week.

We had arranged to stay at the home of Mary, in Corton, a small, attractive village just a couple of miles outside Warminster. Having packed up the tent and dropped our stuff off at Mary's, we went out for the day. Our first stop was the large stone circle at Avebury, which covers an area of 28 acres. Next, we climbed to the top of Silbury Hill, the largest prehistoric, man-made mound in Europe; then took the track to West Kennet Longbarrow, which happens to be one of the finest chambered long barrows in the country. We were sitting on top of this ancient mound when we made a decision to go back to Mary's for something to eat, after which we would make our way back to the long barrow later in the evening to do a sky watch on top of the mound.

We made up a couple of flasks and sandwiches, grabbed our coats and binoculars, and piled into Paul's red Mini. Just as we were about to drive away, David suddenly said that we were not to go to West Kennet but that we were to go to Starr Hill instead. Starr Hill was on the opposite side of Warminster town to Cradle Hill and in those days, not many people went to Starr Hill. It was along a farm track off the Salisbury road, which eventually petered out at the end and faded onto the Salisbury Plain. There was a barn at the bottom of this track where we would turn the car so that we would then have an unrestricted view down the valley towards Imber. It was normally I that had the contact, or a feeling to be in a certain place at a certain time, but David was sometimes able to feel this also. Thus, there was no hesitation or questioning and we immediately changed our route and headed for Starr Hill.

We backed the car up by the barn and watched for a while but as it was still light, we decided to pass a bit of time and go back to the main road and head towards Heytesbury and then round towards Imber. We were on the back road near Imber, by a couple of old cottages, when we all noticed a red light in the sky. Paul screeched to a halt and we all jumped out of the Mini. In the garden of one of the cottages was an elderly man who spoke with a strong West Country accent. We pointed the red light out to him and he immediately ran indoors and brought out his wife and daughter who happened to be holding her young child in her arms. In his strong accent, he commented that he had heard such a lot about these things but that he had never seen one, until now. There was something very special about watching this whole family, including a small child, being excited as this 'Thing', as they were known in those days, gently moved across the sky over their cottage. When it was directly overhead, something strange happened. The one object split into three red balls, which zoomed off in different directions. There was not a cloud in the sky that evening and although the sun had gone down, the sky was still a lovely blue and these red balls were clearly seen against this.

Paul left the family a sighting report form and they said they would be happy to fill this in for us. In fact, it was quite plain to see that this experience had truly made their day. We got back in the car and decided now to go back to Starr Hill and stay there until dawn.

Back to Starr Hill we went, parked, sat, and scanned with eagle eyes both the valley and the sky. After about fifteen minutes, we noticed a very small light blink on down in the valley. Somewhere down there was a farmhouse and although we knew that we could not normally see this farmhouse from our position, we naturally assumed that it must be the bathroom light, perhaps at the top of the house, that had been switched on. We carried on talking and laughing when, all of a sudden, the light started to get brighter. It grew brighter and brighter, and then began to rise up from the ground. We shouted out in excitement and jumped out of the car. The light continued to rise and eventually two more lights appeared, so it took on the shape of a triangle of lights. The top light was revolving and as it did so, it lit up the area. We were beside ourselves with excitement and then I decided to turn the car headlights on full beam, as this was facing the object, and flick them on and off a few times. As I did this, it began to move towards us. The brilliant thing about Starr Hill was that there was total blackness; no street lights or lit buildings of any kind could be seen. So this object really did light up the area as the top light spun round. It drew closer and closer and we were jumping around with excitement and shouting out, "Contact! Contact! We are going to have contact!" Then it stopped. We watched and wondered what would happen next. After a couple of minutes, it started to descend. First, the bottom two lights disappeared and we were left with just the top light, low on the ground. Then, that too gradually dimmed and returned to its original brightness; then it just popped out and we were once again facing the darkness. I suggested that we run across the field, towards where it was last seen, and see if we could find it. We began to race through the crop in total blackness, when David shouted that there could well be adders in the grass and we might disturb them and be bitten. Without changing stride, we turned and ran back towards the car! I can see the funny side of that now. There we were, running towards some unknown machine, possibly not of human origin, without any fear and the next minute, running even faster back to the car in case we were bitten by adders!

We calmed ourselves down, and then continued our sky watch from outside the car. It was a beautiful, cloudless night and the stars were now out in their millions. Even if we saw nothing else that night, just to stand under this wonderful firmament and be amazed at such creation was enough to feed anyone's soul. However, this was not the end of the night; this was just the beginning.

About one hour later, another red light floated along. It could have been the same red light as it was coming back from the direction the other had headed towards earlier. As it approached, a few hundred yards above Scratchbury Hill, it did an odd thing. It followed the contour of the hill. If the hill rose, this object would rise; if the hill dipped, then the object would also dip. In fact, it seemed to keep an equal distance in altitude above the top of this hill. In the intervening years, as I have carried on my study of this intriguing subject, I have come across this behavior many times. All I can think is that the electromagnetic propulsion that this craft was possibly using was somehow in harmony with the Earth's own magnetic field!

The craft passed the end of Scratchbury Hill and the next in line was Starr Hill. We were at the bottom of Starr Hill, by the barn, (Fig 1) and Starr Hill was just on our right. On top of Starr Hill was an ancient round barrow and it was above there that it stopped. David flashed his torch three times and the red light, shining brightly above us, went on and off three times. David then flashed seven times and the light again responded. Once again, there we were, jumping around like three-year-olds in a sand pit. Then, a small red light came out of this object and landed in the field in front of us. When it touched down its luminescence went out. Another red light emerged, went in the field behind us, and did the same thing. A final red light emerged and landed further up the track, by the railway line, near the small humped bridge that we would have to drive over to return to civilization. The main red light continued on its way and we watched it until it disappeared from view.

We looked around, shone the torch, shouted out, and listened quietly to anything that might give us a clue as to what was happening. Nothing was happening, so we decided to get back in the car and drive back up the track, to the other side of town and then up onto Cradle Hill, just to see if anyone was up there and if there was, had they seen any of this happening from their vantage point.

We piled into the Mini and Paul started to drive back up the track. We drove over the small bridge, with the headlights on full beam and had just leveled out on the other side when, all of a sudden, there was an intensely bright flash. All three of us immediately put our arms up to shield our eyes from this intense white light. I was sitting in the front with Paul and we assumed it was the headlights, which, on reflection afterwards, we realized could not have been the case because such a huge burst of energy would have blown the filaments. David was sitting in the back and he was quite sure that this bright flash had come through the hedge on the left-hand side of the track. This is where the third red light had landed. It was suggested that I should get out of the car and look over that hedge in an attempt to see what had caused it. I stepped out onto the track, into the darkness and quiet of the night, and I can tell you now, there was electricity in the air, a static frisson. I looked over the hedge as best I could, as the hedge was rather high, but could see nothing. I got back in the car, Paul restarted it, and we resumed our journey to Cradle Hill.

As we approached the top of Cradle Hill, we quickly realized that no one was there. This was rather unusual, as you could almost guarantee that somebody would be at the top, even in the most severe of weathers. Paul and I have gone up there in the past in the most appalling weather, believing that no one would be as stupid as we were, to venture out on such a night, but sure enough, as we approached, there would be some lone figure huddled by the gate with his head down, clutching a hot flask. Not tonight. Tonight, for some reason, the hill kept its own company.

We waited a while and then decided it would be best to go back to Starr Hill, as that, for some reason, seemed to be where all the action was occurring. More importantly, we felt that we were now close to possibly having contact and we obviously did not want to miss a chance like that.

We drove back through the deserted town and onto the Salisbury road. As we approached the entrance to the track that we had to drive along, the red ignition light on the dashboard flicked on. This would normally mean a couple of things: the fan belt had broken and the dynamo had stopped charging, or some other problem with the dynamo, like the brushes worn down. Paul immediately stopped the car and we lifted the bonnet to see if the fan belt had broken. The belt was fine and without taking the dynamo to bits, we were not sure what to do. Paul got back in the car and turned the ignition; the engine fired up straight away and the red light no longer showed.

Quite excited by now, we sat and wondered what was going on. I suggested that it might not be beyond the realms of science that perhaps 'they', whoever 'they' were, were maybe trying to tell us something. Like, 'Don't come back down this lane tonight,' or were letting us know that 'they' knew we were coming back, or were even delaying us for some unknown reason! In the end, I suggested that we had to go back; in fact, we really did not have much choice, as this was too big a chance to miss. Luckily, everyone agreed and so we turned onto the dark track, which now seemed darker then ever. We drove over the small bridge and back to the barn. We parked up by the barn and waited. The silence was tangible as the three of us stared through the darkness down the valley towards Imber where, only a couple of hours before, we had experienced a thought-provoking spectacle. We opened our flasks, poured cups of tea and cradled the cups in our hands. The heat from the hot tea soon started to mist up the windows and in no time at all even the darkness itself disappeared. We were waiting for something but what that something was, we had no idea. Then, in the distance, we heard what we thought was someone walking. As though someone was walking along the track, on the gravel, and heading towards our car. Whatever it was approached the car, stopped, then continued to walk around the car. We wanted to wipe the mist away from the windows so that we could see more clearly, but were too unnerved to do so. You see, Paul had experienced this before, when he and three friends were sitting in his car at the top of Cradle Hill on a very cold and wintry night, and the exact same thing happened. Only then, the windows of the car were not misted up and they could see out into the darkness but could see no one. Paul said 'it' walked around the car three times before moving away. This was not the only time 'it' had been heard. In fact, 'It' had been experienced by many people over the past few years and was known as the 'Invisible Walker'! However, back to our invisible 'thing'. It came right up to the car, stopped, and must have been only the thickness of the window away but thank goodness, I thought, for that window. What was it doing? Was it trying to scare us? If so, then it had achieved its aim, so why did it not move on? Was it observing us and could it see through the window? If this was contact, then I think we could have done without it! I wondered what the police would have thought had we been discovered later that day. Three young men die of heart attack whilst sitting in their car at Starr Hill! After a few seconds, which I am sure at the time would have felt more like a couple of hours, the 'Walker' moved away and seemed to head in the direction of the field. The field that led down into Imber and from where the main craft had been seen earlier in the night. I suddenly felt a burst of courage flood through my veins and I shouted to Paul and David that we had to get out of the car and try to see what was happening. I opened the passenger door, jumped onto the path, and was quickly followed by the others. We stood in silence at the edge of the field, looking along the valley. Then, just as we thought it was all over and we could once again breath a sigh of relief, it was back! It now walked across the field in front of us and was no more then 15 feet (4.57 meters) away. The corn in the field was snapping and swaying as 'he' walked past. Right across our track he walked, then turned right and headed towards Imber and, we imagined, back to the strange craft that was somewhere down there in the valley. We stood in disbelief as the sounds of the footsteps gradually faded into the distance, until we were, once again, alone at Starr Hill.

This was the first time I had experienced the Invisible Walker and it was not to be my last. That night though, I was pleased indeed to have had Paul and David with me for company, as I was not ready to experience such things alone.

We drove back to Mary's at sunrise, grabbed a couple of hours sleep, had some breakfast and then went off on another jaunt to some ancient sites, returning to Starr Hill in the evening. This was a Sunday, and usually we would be driving home, but this time we still had another week to experience the delights of sky-watching and everything that sky-watching entailed.

We did not have to wait long when along flew the red light once more. Again, it followed the contours of Scratchbury Hill, again it answered our torch, and again it dropped its small cargo of red lights, whose luminescence faded once they touched ground. It then moved away, as before and disappeared in the distance.

Nothing else happened that night and as a new move into trying something different, the following day we went round to see Arthur Shuttlewood and Bob Strong. Arthur was something of a local celebrity at that time and was author of several books on UFOs around Warminster, and Bob was a close friend of Arthur's and shared many of the early years with him. We told them what we had been experiencing and they agreed to come with us on Tuesday night and see if they could throw any light on what had been happening.

We somehow got the five of us in Paul's Mini and made our way to Starr Hill. We parked by the barn and waited. We stayed there until 4 a.m. and then decided to call it a day, as we had seen nothing. This was the first night that the red light had failed to return and we seriously wondered if, whatever was happening, was perhaps just for us. After all, we were about to drive to West Kennet until David suddenly felt that we had to go to Starr Hill, so we could not be blamed for thinking such a thing.

On Wednesday, we decided that just the three of us would venture back down to the barn and see what happened. We did not have to wait long before the red light was back, following Scratchbury Hill and stopping over Starr Hill, answering our torch light and dropping its small cargo. The odd thing was, that whoever was in that light knew we were there or it would not have answered with equal flashes to our torch as it did. The frustrating part was that, as far as we knew, or were aware, this was all that was happening. What was going on here? This red light moved in absolute silence; it followed the contours of the hill, released three small lights that landed on the ground, answered the flashes to our torch, and then moved away. It moved in silence, hovered in silence, and released the other lights in silence. This was no ordinary craft. So, what was it?

On Thursday, once again, the same thing happened. Therefore, on Friday, we decided that if this object was not going to come and see us then we would go and see it! We knew that it would move over Scratchbury Hill, then stop over the top of Starr Hill to release the smaller lights. Therefore, we decided that if the mountain would not come to Mohammed, then Mohammed must go to the mountain – and that is exactly what we decided to do. We would, that night, climb up Starr Hill, stand on the ancient burial mound at the top, and wait for the light to arrive. We decided to put a red filter over the torch, to match the color of this unknown object and then, when the object was above us, flash the torch in the hope that it would see how close we were, and then we would see what happened!

We did not have to wait long. We arrived around 10 p.m. and within 15 minutes, along came the red light. This time, for some reason, it was not coming from the Salisbury direction and following the contour of Scratchbury; it was coming from open land in the direction of Longleat. This was the most wonderful sight ever. There in the fading blue of the evening light, suspended in the sky, in total silence and heading straight for us, was this red light. Only this time though it was ten times as big as before. It was huge! A huge red light, heading straight towards us as we were standing on top of Starr Hill, on the ancient burial mound. It was moving fast in total silence and in a few seconds it would be hovering right over the top of us. I quickly said to David, "Don't flash the torch until it is right overhead." I have no idea why I was saying this, but it seemed the right thing to do. Then, for some reason that was never sorted out, David flashed the torch while it was still in open sky and a few hundred yards from us. As soon as he flashed the torch it just simply vanished. There, in the clear blue of evening, this huge red light just simply disappeared, as quickly as you would turn off a light bulb. One second it was there, hurtling towards us, with our minds racing, then it was gone. As quick as a flash, it was gone!

I turned to David in the heat of the moment and asked why he had flashed the torch so soon but he really did not know, and anyway, it did not matter because it was gone. We felt deflated. All week we had been building up to this in the vain hope of conscious contact. Perhaps contact happened and we are simply not aware of the fact. Who knows? Perhaps we will find out one day. Anyway, it was not over just yet.

Ten minutes later, a car hurtled along the track, so fast that we thought it could only be some lads, drunk and looking for mischief. It screeched to a halt by the barn and backed up next to our car. We had a tape recorder and clothing in the car, so thought it best to get back down the hill and pray that there would be no trouble. As we approached the car, four incredibly excited lads met us. One of them was a dear friend of ours who was a male nurse, and he had three trainee male nurses with him. Kevin was shouting at us, to see if we had seen a large red object that just vanished in the sky. They had been up on Cradle Hill, on the other side of town, and saw it all from there. He just kept saying how huge this thing was and how it just vanished before their eyes. We agreed that we had seen it but we were trying to, rather selfishly, play it down, because we really had thought, and still did at that point think, that we would have open contact with whoever was controlling that light. The exciting thing about all of this was the fact that here were four individual witnesses from the other side of town, who had seen the same light and also saw it disappear. This was important, in case we were later accused of having imagined it all.

Kevin and his three friends returned to Cradle Hill; we decided to go back to the top of Starr Hill, and that is where we stayed for the rest of the night. No more happened that night and morning broke with the most stunning mist that covered the entire landscape below. We were soaked through, tired and hungry, but the scene that appeared in all its beauty and majesty quite simply took our breath away. It seemed as if we were high in the sky, standing on clouds of mist in some fairy tale land and looking below into what may have been the setting of an Arthurian legend.

Saturday night, we decided to do the same thing as the night before, made our way to the top of Starr Hill, and waited on top of the burial mound. We waited there the whole night, but saw nothing and when sun rose we went back to Mary's house to gain some sleep. We were disappointed but we did have one more day before we had to reluctantly make our way back home.

The three of us went to Stonehenge for the day; this was before any barrier barred you from entering the circle and touching the stones and really feeling the place. It was said that the barriers were erected because people were wearing away the stones. I must admit, I had not noticed them getting any thinner! In Victorian times, you could hire a small hammer and paper bag to take home a personal souvenir!

We were sitting on the grass, just talking, when I looked up into the sky. Directly overhead was a typically classic UFO. It was disc-shaped, with a dome on top and glittered brightly in the strong sunlight. The area was packed with people and we pointed this object out to a group of them but only one person seemed to be interested and she eventually stopped looking to catch up with her friends. We looked back up to the sky and watched this beautiful, silver disc hover and move over this wonderful, ancient monument and were amazed at how people were just not interested. This was a classic saucer, that many people would have given much to see, and there it was, in all its glory, with just the three of us for company.

Skeptics can be forgiven at times for putting sightings down to over-active imaginations for two reasons. The first is, as I intimated before, that some people get an inner sense to either look up at just the right moment, and so see what others miss, or to go to a specific place, where they have a sighting or contact experience, often alone. Thus no one can corroborate their claim. The other reason is that, sadly, by and large, people are just not interested. They are not curious about the possibility that we may not be alone. They don't question anomalies. People do not even look up at the sky. Therefore, often, in a crowd, it will only be the one or two people who were aware enough to see what was happening above their heads.

The government and media in the UK have done such a good job of obscuring and ridiculing this aspect of reality (because it really is happening!) that most folk just accept the lies and disinformation. They do not question explanations that are plainly ridiculous – often more ridiculous than the claimed sighting, for example: a classic stand-by official brush-off used to be that a metallic-looking object that, say, hovered, moved erratically and then shot off at great speed was really sunlight glancing off a weather balloon. Who is the more to be ridiculed: the person who says, 'Oh no, a weather balloon does not behave that way; I saw something quite different,' or the person who believes the explanation? Who is the more gullible: the person who observes and records craft, and sometimes lights in the sky, behaving in ways that do not fit accepted parameters of known flight machines and finds this raises questions and possibilities that (should) expand our consciousness, expand the possible parameters, or the person who just accepts the cheap and often juvenile and ignorant 'official' explanations without doing their own research into the phenomena? Scratch the surface of most keen Ufologists and you'll find a serious researcher underneath. Research that leads one to delve into areas of physics, quantum mechanics, space technology, astronomy, ancient history, ancient artifacts, the nature of consciousness and esoteric knowledge. Serious Ufologists are on a quest for Truth and that road leads to the asking of deep and hard questions. Einstein said that the reason he made the discoveries he did was because he went on asking questions after everyone else gave up. Those who accept the paltry palm-offs given by our 'officials' and media need to wake up and start asking questions.

That evening we returned to Starr Hill. We decided that, because this object did not seem to like us being too close to it, we would wait back down by the barn. As usual, we backed the car up to face down the valley towards Imber. After thirty minutes, we were not at all surprised to see the original light arrive and follow the contour of Scratchbury Hill, stop over Starr, release its cargo and then move on its way.

We were back where it all started and now we had to go home. I remember feeling so sad at the thought of leaving all this behind, as did David and Paul. We drove away with aching hearts and for a while said nothing. By the time we were approaching the outskirts of London we were already arranging our next trip to Warminster.

I really find it hard to put into words how incredibly exciting those days were. The frisson of expectancy was in the air; sightings were frequent and witnessed by many, including the media. People traveled from all over the world to the one place where they could be almost certain of seeing a craft from elsewhere. The camaraderie of a common interest was strong and lifelong friendships were formed during that time. Younger people today, who are interested in ufology, really have no idea of how exciting it was living at that time in Warminster. A lot of negative stuff has been said about Warminster, as well as the positive, but I would just like to say here, that if you were prepared to put the time and energy into going out to Starr Hill and Cradle Hill at that time in the 1960s and 1970s, and, of course, to other places around the area, you would have been rewarded with some remarkable sightings. I am absolutely sure of that.

Ufology has moved on a lot since those heady days, but Warminster has remained, for me, a very special place. It was a focal point at a certain time and you just had to be there to fully appreciate what was happening. After all these years, it still retains the brightest place in my heart, and will do so for the rest of my days.

However, life was to present me with many other adventures, both before and after my Warminster days, and this book recounts some of them, from my first childhood introduction to my Space Brother to recent visitations from Light Beings and the message they gave me to pass on to you all.

CHAPTER 1

YOU ARE NOT MY REAL PARENTS

We lost the meaning.
We lost the meaning to that pure and holy land,
That pure and holy land.

The iron railings at the front of our tiny concrete garden in the East
End of London were taken away during the Second World War as
the country was desperately short of metal. This left a 6-inch (15.24
centimeters) stone plinth with holes in the top where the railings would
have been secured. It was on the edge of this plinth that I landed after
trying to do a U-turn on my tricycle. I was two-and-a-half years old. I
remember climbing the stairs to the top part of the house where we lived,
calling for my mum and in a lot of pain. I was taken to the hospital and
was told by the doctor that I had a fracture and the arm would be put in
plaster. Six weeks later, the nurse was asking me to look for the scissors
to appear out the other end, near my wrist, as she attempted to cut my arm
free. I was once again ready to take on the world.

We lived upstairs in a tiny terraced house with no hot running water,
no bathroom and an outside toilet. There were large gaps at the top and
bottom of the toilet door and the corners near the ceiling were habitats for
spiders. In the winter months, I would sit on the wooden seat with my
hands cupped around a small oil lamp and hope that the spiders did not
move. If they moved, I was out of there with the speed of a bullet. Going
to the toilet in those days was a very dangerous and precarious thing to
do! We had no washing machine or refrigerator. Mum did all the washing
in the sink and the food was kept in the shade under the stairs. Friday was
bath night and was a major event. The small tin bath was carried up from
the garden and Mum would have two kettles continuously on the boil in
the attempt to fill up the bath. This created more steam than in a ship's

boiler-room and a heavy, moist atmosphere was the result. Everywhere was wet: the ceiling, the walls, the cupboards, the linoleum on the floor, the windows, and even Mum. I never quite knew the logistics of the order but my sister went first, then me, then Mum and last of all, Dad. By the time Dad got in the bath it must have been filthy but he never complained. I am sure there must have been much greater hardship in the war and this must have seemed like a little piece of heaven after that. My aunt and her family lived downstairs and it was all open-plan but we got on well – except for the time when I threw the potty out of our living room window and it hit my uncle on the head! It was a tin potty at that – and full!

At the age of four I had a conversation with my mother that stayed with her right up until she died in 1993, at 73 years of age. We were standing in the living room when I turned to my mother and said that there was no such thing as death. She looked down at me and said, "When you die, you die, Mike, that is it." "No!" I said firmly. "That is not it! Look, when you die a hole is dug in the ground and you are put in that hole and covered over with earth. The universe goes on for ever and for us to simply never take part in that universe again does not make sense. We will have other lives, other journeys[1], and our soul will continue to experience life." I did not know the word 'reincarnation' at the age of four but I believe that that is what I was trying to say. I was attempting to describe pictures that had come into my mind; images that were far clearer than any words could describe and that contained scenes beyond my experience. It was like watching a film and somehow, with the pictures I was seeing, came the words to use. Over fifty years later, above the Nevada desert, I was finally to learn where at least one of my other lives had been lived.

In the same conversation, I told my mother that she and my father were not my real parents. She was shocked, to say the least, and she retaliated: "Of course we are! You were born in this house!"

"Mum, you are my parents as far as bringing me onto this planet, but my REAL parents are in Space." Now, this was 1955. I was born in 1951 and we were a very ordinary, loving family. Poor, but content with our lot. I turned to look out of the window. I pointed to the sky and said to my mother: "I come from somewhere out there!"

Mum sat down in the armchair while I continued: "Also Mum, something of great importance is going to happen on this Earth. Not in your lifetime but in mine. It will affect all units of consciousness, whether they are Mineral, Vegetable, Animal or Man. It is to do with global consciousness; a vast change of consciousness and that is why I am here at this time, to experience this change."

This conversation was so bizarre for the era and for my age that both my mother and I remembered it clearly through the ensuing years. I can see myself now, a small figure in gray flannel shorts with crisply-ironed creases down the centre of the legs. Braces with brown straps held them up and I wore the braces over a light brown shirt. Gray woolen knee socks and brown sandals completed attire typical for that time.

The few people I have recounted this experience to have found it hard to believe that a child of this age would make such statements, especially considering the concepts and vocabulary involved. However it is precisely because it was startling that this incident etched itself into my mind and affected my mother so deeply that she referred to it again and again through her life. My partner, Fran, was more inclined to believe me because her own daughter used the phrase 'absolutely saturated' when 18 months old and by the age of five years was talking about concepts such as Beauty, Truth and Wisdom.

Mum looked at me thoughtfully from the armchair and told me that she was the seventh child of a seventh child and that her mother was Irish, and had seen the Little People. Once, her mother told my mother, she was walking along a country lane when she saw a strange little man sitting on the gate to a field. He had on brightly-colored clothes and a brown felt hat. He doffed his hat and said: "Good morning to you Maam; what a lovely day it is. I hope you are well!" My grandmother smiled and told the man that she was fine. She walked on but quickly turned back to look at him again and he was gone.

When I was five, my sister, Dad and I, built a snowman in the garden and put a scarf around its neck. We then went upstairs to look at it from the scullery (kitchen) window. As the three of us looked down at our creation, a fairy danced round from the other side. She was a whitish-silver color and had a traditional wand in her hand with a star on the top. Round and round she danced, as happy as could be, when, all of a sudden, she went round once more and failed to return and was gone. I asked Dad about this, years later, and he told me that he had lit a match and stuck it in the ground. This was absolute nonsense of course, because by the time we all got upstairs the match would have gone out. In addition, she danced around the snowman a number of times, lasting three or four minutes, before she disappeared. At the time it was happening we commented on how beautiful she looked and how she waved her wand and how bits of what looked like star-dust were left behind from the movement.

Like many children, I saw animals in my home. Oftentimes these creatures are imaginary and fade from existence as children mature. However, those who study Ufology and the associated anomalies concerning contact with our various off-world visitors will know that it is common for some of these beings to appear to children as an animal or bird, such as an owl. Presumably this is done to provide a less-frightening form for a child to see.

I never had an owl inside my home but I would regularly awake with the thought in my head: "Go to the window and see if the owl is there." Next to the house immediately opposite ours was a tall stand-pipe that came from the sewers below ground and reached to gutter level, to waft the noxious fumes above roof level. I would pad across to the window and there would be a very large owl, sitting on the top of this pipe. I would stand and stare at him for a few minutes then go back to bed. This happened a few times each month, sometimes two or three nights in a row, from the age of about four years until I was nine years old.

Sometimes when I looked for him he would appear as if through a faint, swirling mist but whether clearly seen or slightly covered by mist, he was always staring directly at my window and I was totally mesmerized by him.

Years later, in the early 1970s, four friends and I had gone south to look for crop circles. By early evening we were parked in a lane that led to Sutton Veny. We parked beneath a tree and had got out of the car and were standing by the field that contained the crop circle, discussing whether to go and see it in the dusk or wait until the next day, when a rustling in the tree attracted our attention. Torchlight revealed a huge eagle owl (we assumed) in the tree. It was enormous. Eagle owls are not native to the UK but we made this assumption because it was so large. The owl just sat and stared at us. Every so often we shone the torch into the tree to see if it was still there. It was – and the torchlight did not seem to bother it. It just gazed unblinkingly at us. For the two hours or so that we were in the lane, the owl stayed in the tree.

Another strange anomaly of those early years and for about the same time span, was a tiger that used to stand at the bottom of my bed with his

Fig.2

head turned towards me (Fig.2). I felt incredibly protected by this tiger and had no fear of him. He was there night after night, just looking at me with his large, brilliant eyes. I often called my mother to see him but she was never able to. Once I got out of the bed, knelt on top of the blanket and moved towards him. I called Mum in, lent forward with my arm, stretched out my fingers, and said, "Look Mum, I am one inch from his nose, if I moved another inch I could touch him" (yet I always knew I should *not* touch him). I looked round at her. "Surely you can see him now?" "No," she said. "I cannot see him."

I turned back to look at the tiger: his long stripy body, his enormous furry face, his beautiful eyes, all inches away from me. Serene and wise, protecting me from the foot of my bed. I smiled at him and told him that I was sorry Mum could not see him and I got back into bed. Mum tucked me in and left the room. I took one last look and went to sleep.

Little did I know that many, much stranger, experiences were ahead of me and that I would see the tiger in other guises throughout my life and eventually come to know his name.

1 See chapter 15. See also chapter 17.

CHAPTER 2

SPACE SUITS AND CALLING CARDS

"Welcome!" he said to me.
I heard it in my mind.
"It's been such a long, long while.
Yes, it seems a long, long time.
Come! Come follow me;
There are things that you must see."
And as we entered the craft,
A light surrounded me;
Surrounded me.

A ll I wanted to do in those early years was to meet a spaceman! I con-stantly looked to the sky and felt a strange belonging. Somewhere up there was my home! Do not get me wrong; I loved my parents deeply and my mother was always there for me. I never had to stay for school dinners, which I would have hated. I was a very sensitive and shy child and could not have eaten in the school canteen with all that mayhem.

In the early fifties, we played all our games in the street. It was safe and very few people had cars then. Our favorite game was Tin Can Tommy. An old tin can was placed in the middle of the road and we then decided who was 'It'. If you were 'It' you had to close your eyes and count to ten while everyone else ran and hid behind cars, walls, hedges, trees, dustbins. Neighbors were often banging on their windows and if lips could have been read – well! The person who was 'It' had to then try and find us and when he did, had to run back to the tin and bang it three times while saying: "One, two, three, I saw ..... (so and so)," and then that person was out of the game. If one of the kids who was hiding got back to the tin before 'It', then they would bang the tin three times and shout: "One, two, three, saved the lot!" Then everyone cheered and emerged from their hiding places as the momentary hero stood and proudly puffed up his chest. The person that was 'It' was 'It' again. If they found everybody before they could be stopped, then the next person to be 'It' was the last one to be found. It probably sounds very tame and silly now, to the children of today, but we found this game as exciting as anything. Other games were Hopscotch, What's The Time Mr Wolf? and Knock Down Ginger, where you would bang on a front door and run away (awful really). Another favorite of mine was to climb up the old gas-lamp post outside our house and swing on the horizontal bar near the top, (much to my mother's horror!)

There were few television sets in those days and we got our 'kicks' from comics such as *Dandy, Beano, Topper, Beezer* and the more serious *Eagle*, featuring Dan Dare, the intrepid Spaceman battling with the Treens and the Mekon. I had been following one particular episode for some weeks and the outcome was imminent. Would the great Dan Dare win or would the nasty, green-faced aliens finally take over the world? This was a battle of extreme proportions; an epic battle of Light over Dark for the sake of Humanity and all other Life on this Earth. Dan Dare, quite simply, had to win. I was upstairs sitting at the living room table with my comic opened out before me; my heart was racing as the story approached this significant moment in history. Then.......Yes! Dan Dare triumphed! This planet was safe once more! I shouted in exhilarated joy. "Mum!" I yelled at the top of my voice, "Mum! Come quickly! Come quickly!" What I did not realize, in my overwhelming thrill of Light winning over Dark, was that my mother was in the toilet at the bottom of the garden. She apparently thought that the house was burning down and raced up the garden and up the stairs and fell into the living room only partly dressed. I excitedly explained that Dan Dare had just won the most extreme battle and that we were safe once again! At this pivotal moment, I had not taken into account that MY life might now not be safe! Mum shouted angrily at me that she had just run through the garden, in front of her neighbors, only partly dressed and then up thirteen stairs, only to find out that all this panic was because of a comic-strip story! I looked down at my mother, who was in a heap on the floor with some of her clothing around her knees, and said, "You don't understand do you?" She looked up and said, "Oh, I do understand Mike, but you must never do this again."

I was six years old now and spacemen were on my mind as much as ever. The other boys and girls were into cowboys and Indians and the latest fads were cowboy suits for the boys and Indian Squaw outfits for the girls. The boys looked smart in their fancy chaps, guns, holsters and hats and the girls with bright feathers and Indian plaits. The cowboy thing was not for me though and I plagued my mum for a space suit that I had seen advertised in one of my comics. I did not expect her to buy it as money was in incredibly short supply. However, in a few days' time I was the proud owner of a space suit. My very own space suit! It was all silver, with a helmet that fitted right over the head and a plastic visor. On top of that, there was an aerial that came out from the back of the suit. I walked around the house feeling a million dollars and really felt that I had arrived. I looked out of the front bedroom window and saw all my friends outside, playing their game of cowboys and Indians. I opened the front door and stepped out, as if I was stepping onto a new planet for the first time. Everything came to a stop and they all stood and stared. They drew closer to inspect me. I stood proud and firm, waiting for the jealous comments, like, 'Bloody hell, I wish I had one!' or "You've got a great mum to buy you that!" Instead, they all just laughed and said that I looked absolutely stupid. I went back indoors and took off my beautiful spacesuit; never to wear it outside again.

Some weeks later, as I was nearing seven years of age, I awoke in the middle of the night and was aware of a presence in my room. I could see someone standing there and he seemed to be wearing a space suit, not unlike the one that my mother had bought me, only without the helmet. The silver was shimmering in the darkness and it reminded me of tin foil. He looked down and I heard his voice in my mind. He said that his name was 'Tellos'[1] and that he lived in the stars but was never far away. He then held his hand up in a peace gesture and said, "I am the tiger!" Then he was gone!

Eventually I went back to sleep. In the morning, I noticed on my bed, a card. I excitedly picked it up and saw that the spaceman on the front of the card was the same man that had appeared the night before. On the back of the card was a map on which were named the planets that he had visited, including the Earth. I ran and showed it to my mother and told her what had happened the night before. She did not quite know what to make of it but as she had had many weird conversations with me already, she did not seem to entirely dismiss it.

I cannot tell you in words what it felt like to hold this card in my hands – and I held it every day, night and morning. I would stare at his face and look at the planets on the reverse and the journeys he had made and tried to imagine what that would be like to go to other star systems and planets.

When I held the card in my hand, I felt a strong energy of love and connection. A bond; a bond that existed through Time and Space. As I was to find out much later in life, that is indeed the case and Tellos has been with me on more than one occasion and in more than one guise. More of that later.

The card had a strange feel; not like the cigarette cards that were popular in those days. It had a 'velvety' feel. I have felt nothing like that before or since. I had this card in my possession for over two years, but one day I arrived home from school and it was gone. I ran to find my mother and asked her if she had seen or moved it, but she said that she had not. I felt totally lost without this card, as it seemed to be my connection to the universe. The proof that Life *is* out there, and that there are people out there much more advanced and aware then we are. I am also sure that they would be prepared to help us, if only we would change. Perhaps they are helping us behind the scenes and we are simply not aware of this fact. We are, after all, Space People also. We are on a globe traveling through Space and are never in the same place longer then a second. Our spaceship Earth moves through space and around the sun at a phenomenal speed, yet we feel nothing. On top of that, the Galaxy is also moving through space at an even greater speed. What great mechanism is this? We have all come from the same Creative Source and, in that way, are one big family. It is just that some planets seem to be a bit backward, and poor old Earth is one of them.

Indeed, many hundreds of people, the world over, who report contact with off-world visitors, also report being told or shown that there exists beyond our world an alliance or federation of beings from different worlds and dimensions. Differing race members of this alliance visit Earth to observe and monitor our development (as do others not from the Galactic Federation and not necessarily well-intentioned towards us) and to help us, where they can, to raise our consciousness towards the Love vibration.

So, it seems that Tellos once appeared as a tiger and watched over me while I slept. He also came as a Space Man and left his calling card, which mysteriously disappeared two years later. It was all getting quite exciting and I wondered what would happen next! My poor mother could not keep up with all this and she must have been quite perplexed as to exactly what she had given birth to!

From the age of four to thirty-five years, I constantly asked my mother who I was and where did I come from. "You know what has gone on, don't you Mum?" She would say, when her guard was down, that she was not quite sure. Then she would change and say that nothing had gone on. I would question her again and then she would always get out of it by saying that she was a seventh child of a seventh child and everyone knows that odd things happened to the seventh child – and then we would leave it there.

1 Pronounced 'Tellosh'. I forgot about this experience until reminded many years later. See chapter 16.

CHAPTER 3

SEEING GOD

Angels in heaven,
Beyond the sky and sea;
Angels in heaven
Are looking down at me.
And in that moment,
When everything seems right,
I will tread the earth gently
Through the night.

G rowing up in London in the Fifties somehow seemed a lot safer than it is now in today's society. When I was a baby, Mum would leave me in my pram out on the pavement while she got on with her housework, as did most mothers at that time. Mum told me later in life that she was often stopped in the street to be told by her neighbors that whenever they passed by our house and looked in the pram I was always smiling. In fact they had nicknamed me 'Smiler'. Mum said that the first word I ever spoke was 'beer' and she could not understand where I had got it from because they never touched alcohol, except at Christmas, when Dad would be given a bottle of Dry Sack sherry from his employers. She said it was most embarrassing when I was pushed past a public house and there would be people sitting outside drinking and I would start shouting out, "Beer! Beer!" She told me that her face would go bright red and she would pick up speed to get away. It had been suggested to Mum that perhaps I had been a Publican or an Alcoholic in a past life!

Mum also told me that very soon after I had started talking, I would make up songs and sing them to her and Dad. She said that not only were they good songs but they were stories that had a beginning, a middle and an end. I still enjoy singing and composing songs today, at the age of 55.

Indeed, for some years, in the 1980s and 1990s, I had my own band, 'Storyteller'.

When I was a child I always wanted to see God. I would ask Mum how I could see him because I had a lot of questions that needed answering. Such as: "Why are we here?" "Where are we going?" "What is the purpose of Life?" "How many planets have Life on them?" The list was endless and Mum would say that I would see Him one day if I really needed to. I would sit in the garden and look up at the sky and try to find out where He was. I did not realize at that time that God, 'The Source', is everywhere. If you want to see God, you do not only have to look up to the sky, you can walk through a wood after it has rained and look at a dewdrop on a leaf and there you will find God. Look into the eyes of an animal or a child and there you will find God. Look at the beauty of a flower or the flowing river and there you will find God. God is in all these things because all these things are in God, The Source.

Later on in this book, I will tell you of experiences I have had where I have touched the Source and been in complete and utter Oneness. Where, quite simply, you are the Universe and the Universe is you.

One day, when I was seven years old, a friend of mine told me that his grandma had seen God. He said that she was walking along the road and she looked up and the clouds parted and she saw the face of God. Well, I was overwhelmed at this and ran home to tell my mother. "Do you think this could happen to me, Mum? Do you think that one day I could be walking home from school and the clouds will suddenly part and that I will see God?" Mum looked down and replied that she was sure that one day this would happen and I would also see God. I sat thinking about this for ages and wondered how I would react. Would I stay calm and pitch my questions at the right time? Would there be too many questions and would He get a bit annoyed at such a nosy little kid who wanted to know too much? Would I have to shout because He is so high up in the sky? As it was, it never happened that way, so I need not have worried after all! It happened in ways that I would have never dreamed of.

I spent many months contemplating what God was and how exactly I fitted into the scheme of things. What about the Spacemen; how did they view God or the Creator? If they were closer to God, did they have at least some of the answers? There was no one around that could answer my questions. There was no one in my family even that could explain my tiger and spaceman.

Later in my life, I was to question Tellos about God. He told me that on the frequency on which his being vibrated, it was possible to 'feel' God in a way that was beyond our experience in this 3D reality. He also said that there were beings that existed beyond his level, who were much closer to Source. As far as I understand what he told me, this apprehension of God went beyond intellectual knowledge. It was a 'knowing' at soul level. He commented that we might never truly and completely know God because we all *are* God; we are all part of Source.

One day, I was sitting on the wall outside our house, when the woman next door rushed out of her house in absolute terror. She had a huge, black beetle in her kitchen and was too scared to remove it. She asked me to do it for her. I was as scared of the beetle as she was but I did not like to say so. I mean, I was only eight years of age but you had to be brave in front of a woman, didn't you? I went into the kitchen and saw it on the floor. Large, black, and hard shelled. She told me that I could get it in the pan and brush and put it outside or I could tread on it. She did not mind as long as we got it out of the house. In my stupid fear, I decided to tread on it and stomped hard. It gave out a loud, crunching noise as I did so. As soon as I did this, the effect on me was profound. For a start, I felt a terrible loss as I took away this beetle's life because of my own fear. My own ignorant fear! What threat was that beetle to me? In fact, I posed more of a threat to it. A powerful loss and sense of wrongdoing swept through my body, which still lives with me today. One almighty lesson was learnt in one fell swoop as I swept away its life. That one action alone made it a worthwhile life here because I now respect life at a very profound level and I have truly paid for that in the remorse that I felt and still feel today as I type these words. Fear is one terrible feeling to carry around and holds us here on the earth plane. We have to learn to overcome fear to allow us to move on, and I will talk about this later.

Shortly after this incident, I was walking along my road and I saw two boys playing around with a worm in the gutter. I do not want to say that they were torturing it but it may have come to that if I had not stopped them. I gave them a real mouthful that what they were doing was very wrong, we must learn to live and let live, and I demanded that they walk away and allow me to put the worm in a safe place where it could continue its life in peace! They were so shocked that they gave in to an angry eight-year old!

When I was aged 27, I had an incredibly powerful dream. It was what I call a 'real dream' and I awoke in tears and very distressed. In the dream, I had befriended a sheep on a farm and for two years we were in telepathic conversation. We would talk about all sorts of things. I am talking here of 'mind level'. The mind is very different to what we are aware of in our everyday, conscious mind. One day, I was sitting crossed legged on the ground, talking to the sheep and we were deep in thought. Suddenly I saw the legs and wellington boots of a man who had come into the scene. He walked up to the sheep and stabbed it in the chest. Blood poured out and the sheep immediately fell down onto its front legs. It looked up at me and asked what had happened. I told it that this man had stabbed it and then walked off and I did not know why. I was in a state of shock and confusion. The sheep grew weaker and asked what it had done wrong. I replied that it had done nothing wrong and I did not understand. It got even frailer and fell onto its side. I could see its heart beating more and more slowly. There was blood everywhere. It asked me again what it had done wrong and again I had no reply. I simply did not know and I had no answer for it. Having no answer was as painful and distressing as watching it slowly bleed to death. Its eyes looked up to me and it asked one final time and again I did not know. I was riven with grief because I could not put its mind to rest, as it slowly passed away, as to why its life had been so callously taken away. I woke up in floods of tears and have never eaten an animal since that day twenty-eight years ago.

I have no wars to fight with meat eaters and I have always said that you cannot eat your way into Heaven. It is what is in your heart and soul that counts and how you treat humanity and other life forms around you. For people who eat meat, I only say: please be aware of where you buy your food. If animals are here for such a short time, as commodities, for financial gain, then please make sure that they live life as comfortably as we can possibly make them and that they at least die in dignity. I could state here the many things that are done to animals simply for the benefit of a quick buck, but it is not the purpose of this book.

CHAPTER 4

THREE BOYS IN A BOAT AND A SHINING STRANGER

I'm glad you came.
I can see the reason why you're back again.
Since you arrived
I feel inside my body that I'm more alive.
It has been so long
But now my heart and soul can sing a different song.

Not far from where I lived was Hackney Marshes and as children we found this place an absolute haven. There were ditches and streams, tall grass and mud, weeds of all shapes and sizes and even an old place where communal rubbish was once dumped. We played games there from morning until night. If we ventured to the far side of this alien landscape, we came upon the fast-flowing, dirty reaches of the River Lea, winding its way through the industrial heartland of Clarnico, the mint-sweet manufacturer, and Yardley, the perfume people. There was always a strange, unique, sickly, sticky smell pervading the atmosphere. A smell of mints and scented chemicals. Most of us could not swim and yet we would do the most stupid things, like trying to get across the bridge on the outside ledge of the railings. Slowly, inching forward in a sideways motion, hanging on to the rail and putting our feet between the uprights, with the raging, filthy river below.

One thing I did not realize, or connect with for years, was that the bombsites we played on were exactly that – bomb sites! We had six corners along our road and five of them were bombsites. It puzzles me still today, why were all the corners bombed? As kids, we would say: "Come on! Let's go and play on the bombsite!" (Or the 'bombie', as it was known). We would stand bottles and cans on what was left of walls and throw stones at them, which were in plentiful supply, and if we were really bored, we threw them at each other. Why no one was ever killed, I will never know!

Once, when we were playing hide and seek on the biggest site, one of my mates was lying on a nest of big, red ants. He was being eaten alive by them but because he did not want to be discovered and lose the game, he lay there until he could stay no longer, then jumped up, screaming in agony, covered in ants and looking like one giant red blister. Nevertheless, we were no more ill then the youngsters of today and although our parents loved us, we did seem to have a remarkably free rein. Things were different then; it was a very different place to today's society. Couples stayed in the same road once they got married and left home. Housewives would stand on their steps, with curlers and scarves, and shout conversations to each other, perhaps as much as ten houses away. They would be down on their hands and knees every week, putting Cardinal Red on the step, and they even washed and swept their part of the pavement! I think we have lost something here of great importance. We have lost not only community spirit, but pride in our surroundings and respect. We respected each other and it was perfectly safe to leave your front door open and, as I said earlier, to leave your baby in the pram outside on the pavement.

Next to the marshes was the Temple Mills shunting yards. A vast array of lines, goods trains, sheds, etc. It was out of bounds and private property, but for kids it was too much of a temptation to ignore. We would go down there in daylight or under darkness, cross the complexity of rails, looking out all the time for passing trains, and sneak into the sheds or climb onto the wagons. We would have a whale of a time and often get caught, like rabbits, in the bright beam of a torch wielded by a British Rail security guard. We would run for our lives, back across the rails, up the embankment and away to freedom.

Once, when we were playing down by the Clarnico factory, we saw, on the other side of the river, an old rowing boat, just resting on the mud and calling out to be played with. We found a bridge a short way upstream, crossed over the Lea and made our way back to where the boat was resting. It was full of water, so we started to empty it. When this was completed, we decided to get in the boat and take it for a short journey downstream. There were four of us: Harry, Peter, Colin and myself and this was not like something out of *Swallows and Amazons* on the delightful Coniston Water in the Lake District; this was a dangerous piece of water, filthy and muddy and running fast. I was the last to step into the boat and I decided, right at the last minute, that I would not go. I do not know where this feeling came from but it was so strong that I felt I had no alternative but to obey. So the others asked me to push them out into the river and as I did so I felt inside that all was not well.

It was now quite dark and we had lost any reference to time of day. I watched them quickly disappear into the darkness, as the current took them downstream. I stood and listened as their voices gradually faded away in the distance and then I quickly realized that here I was, in the deep dusk, on my own, and had to somehow find a way back across the marshes to get on the road that would take me home. I have a blank memory as to how I got back to the road as there were so many obstacles like ditches, holes, streams – some of which were in very deep clefts – and really tall weeds, etc. I do not know how this was managed. I remember climbing up the steep bank and stinging my hands on the ferocious stinging nettles that littered the place, then looking over this vast wasteland, barely visible in the dimming light, and wondering which direction I should run. I realized now that it was late, very late, and my only objective was to get back to the main road and home. I felt panic, tightness in my chest, and I was frightened.

Then, I felt an energy of peace and calm run through my body. Instinctively I turned my head and found myself facing a man. This was no ordinary man. He had long, flowing, silver hair and a shiny one-piece suit that was somehow glowing through the dark. I felt emotional and I feel emotional typing these words now, 45 years on. I later learned that this man was, once again, Tellos, my Space Brother. I told him I was lost and I needed to get home. He looked at me with eyes so blue I felt I could see the backdrop of the universe reflected in them. He smiled and held his hands out towards me in a gesture of peace and his Love tore through the darkness and into my being. I now felt safe. The words: "You will never be lost" filtered into my mind. He then drew closer, looked down at me and put his hands on my shoulders, I looked up, unafraid and melted into the dark night. "I am the stars and you are in my journey. You have seen me before and you will see me again."

I really do not know what that man was doing on the marshes at that time of night. We hardly ever saw anyone there, except other kids, as it really was a god-forsaken place. Somehow, I found myself on the road and from there I ran, non-stop all the way to my home. As I turned the corner of our road, I could see all the mothers out on the pavement, in a state of near panic, wondering what had happened to their children. I had no idea that it was, apparently, 11.30 p.m, far too late for ten-years-old children to be out.

The gathered throng saw me come round the corner. My mother ran to me. "Where have you been? Do you realize the time? We were just about to call the police!" The other mothers crowded around as I told them the story. I told them that the last I saw of my friends was when they were disappearing downstream in the old rowing boat. Colin, like me, could not swim, and his mother was in a dreadful state. My mother took me indoors and I thought I was going to get the biggest beating of my life. Instead, she looked at me and said, "I am so proud of you!" I thought, "What?" Then she continued: "When I saw you turn the corner and you told the story and that you had decided not to get into the boat, I thought, 'that's my son; the sensible one!' and sighed with relief." Well, they do say that God acts in very mysterious ways, and that is about as mysterious as you can get!

The next morning Mum came in to tell me the boys were safe, but when Colin arrived home he got the most awful beating and my mother said she felt very sorry for him. Later that day I found Harry and he told me that as soon as they left and started to drift down stream – they had no oars – the boat started to leak and Colin was trying to scoop the water out with the tin can that they had used earlier. The trouble was, the water was coming in quicker then he could scoop it out. Colin, as I said, could not swim and the boat was sinking ever lower into the water and he was sobbing. Harry and Peter were trying to guide the boat into the side but it was picking up speed and soon they knew why. They heard a roar and saw in the distance, white foam. They were fast approaching a weir and if they were sucked into that then it would have probably been the end for them all. He told me that if I had been in the boat as well, then the extra weight would have caused it to sink long before it even got to the weir, because it was taking in water so fast. Just as it looked like all was lost, they saw approaching them an overhanging tree and Harry grabbed hold of it and hung on for dear life while Peter held on to him to stop the boat continuing on its merry way. Colin, sobbing loudly now, carried on scooping out the water. They were all screaming out for help but it was midnight. Luckily, a man on night work nearby, heard them, ran, got a rope, and dropped it over the bridge and they were all able to scramble to safety.

That morning I told my mother about the strange man I met on the marshes and how he must have got me safely over the wasteland and onto the main road. I asked her who she thought he was, but as usual in these circumstances, she just replied, "Seventh child of a seventh child!"

After that incident I spent many days intensifying my search for the Space People and scanned the skies for hundreds of hours, looking for any movement that might suggest that they came from somewhere out there. Then I smiled at the thought that they were probably working overtime just trying to keep me alive on this planet. Indeed, over forty years later, I was admonished by Tellos for my propensity to 'stick your nose into places you should not go!' and told that, 'We cannot always be around to save you!" More of this in a later chapter.

CHAPTER 5

THE GREEN STONE

We're on a mission.
We're heading for the stars –
To the future.
Dimensions disturbed.
Press the button.
Start the engine.
We're leaving planet Earth.
Out into Space;
That is the destiny of Man.

If you followed Temple Mills Lane and bypassed going over the marshes, you eventually came to a vast area of green field. On Sunday mornings, football matches were played there and they were very well attended. There must have been ten matches going on at any one time and where the white line marked the boundary of one field, that same white line marked the boundary for the match being played next door and so on. If you happened to stand on the by-line to watch the games then, as far as the eye could see, there were separate matches being played at the same time. In fact, you were witness to at least 110 footballers running around after balls that were all the time intruding onto the game next door and it was not unusual to see three or four balls on any one pitch at any one time. It seemed to be complete chaos!

I loved to play football with my mates and we played as often as we could. We would go to West Ham and Leyton Orient, to watch a proper match. How they managed to play as they did on that field was a total mystery. I often wondered what some Star Traveler might make of it if he suddenly landed nearby, stepped outside his craft and was confronted by over 100 men in shorts chasing at least ten balls, shouting aggressively at each other, with the crowd shouting abuses to at least ten referees. Balls going in the wrong nets, balls going in the right nets and half a dozen dogs, on Sunday morning walks, running and barking after any stray balls that happened to be rolling around or, for that matter, balls that were actually in play. What report would he record in his cosmic journal to share with his own kind when he returned home!

It was one day in June 1962, when I was walking across these vast playing fields with my friend Chris. This was not a Sunday and it was very quiet. We were about two-thirds of the way across when I happened to look down. If I had not looked down at that precise moment then I would have stepped on or over it. It was, quite simply, an out-of-place object. It should not have been there at all and out of this vast area, it happened to be right at my feet! It looked like a piece of coke. I say coke, because it was like a large lump of coal but looked porous. Now the interesting thing was that in the middle of this piece of coke was a large green stone, like an emerald. It was cube-shaped and was embedded in the coke for possibly a depth of one inch (2.54 centimeters) and stood out from the coke another one and half inches (3.81 centimeters). It was a beautiful, clear, emerald green. I bent down and picked it up. Immediately I felt a resonance inside my body and mind. As if I had made a connection to something far greater then I could ever be. At the same time, I felt very emotional and showed the stone to my friend. He did not seem to share the same enthusiasm, so we just carried on walking, and I occasionally looked down at it in my hand.

I arrived home and immediately took it to my room, sat on the edge of the bed and watched it closely as I held it in my hand. In my mind I could see the stars; I could see the tiger, the silver-suited Spaceman and beings as yet unknown, but later to appear in my future. I could see more, much more. I could see how the universe was connected and that we were all One. I could see a different homeland; not the one here on Earth, but a homeland somewhere else. I do not know how I saw all these things but they were just there in my mind every time I held the green stone and looked into its heart; its own inner self.

I hid the stone in my bedroom; on a shelf where I kept my treasures. Every day, as soon as I was home from school, I would rush into my bedroom and hold the stone. As soon as I held this beautiful thing I was immediately at peace with the entire world. Interestingly, emerald (if emerald it was) is traditionally supposed to promote clairvoyance and all types of seeing because it opens up the psychic eye. It is also a truth-promoting stone, inspiring deep knowing from within. Who knows what similar properties my stone may have had?

A few days later, I was in bed asleep. It was the middle of the night when I suddenly awoke and was aware that somebody was in my room. Immediately, I sat up in bed, and could see in the darkness a glowing man standing at the foot of the bed. I asked him what he wanted but he did not answer. He then started to walk towards me and I pressed my back up against the wall, because there simply was nowhere else to go. I asked again what he wanted and then told him to leave. He walked up to my bed and took hold of the sheet. The next memory I have is of running out of the room and shouting for Mum and Dad; calling that there was someone in my room. Dad picked up the poker and rushed in there, quickly followed by Mum. They emerged a couple of minutes later and told me that there was no one there and I must have been dreaming. For the next six weeks I slept in their bed-settee in the small living room and they slept in my bed.

About a week later, I was with my parents in the living room. It was around 9 p.m. when my sister came rushing in through the door in floods of tears and in a very distressed state. She said that she had been in West Ham Park with four of her friends when four flying saucers appeared and hovered over them. Then, as they were watching them, she said that the craft shot down out of the sky and they all started running and screaming and were chased along the road. That is all she remembered until she burst through the front door. I was aged 11 then and my sister was 14. She never spoke about this again and for some reason I never questioned her.

The term *'flying saucer'* was originated by mistake. In 1947, Oregon journalist Bill Bequette, when writing up a report on unidentified aerial craft seen by pilot Kenneth Arnold near Mount Rainier in Washington State on 24 June of that year, mentioned the word 'saucer'. Arnold never claimed to have seen saucer-shaped objects but craft that looked more like a flying wing or the B-2 bomber that appeared much later in our history. He did, however, describe the motion of the objects as erratic, "like a saucer if you skip it across the water." The term *'flying saucer'* appeared in print two weeks later in the UK *The Times* newspaper. Recorded sightings and close encounters of unidentified craft show that they vary tremendously in type[1], design and method of travel, from nuts and bolts disc-shaped vehicles to plasma-like craft and craft that appear to be sentient. They all seem to be capable of enormous speeds and maneuvers that go beyond our current technology, such as instantaneous right-angle turns and 'morphing' from one shape to another. Some just 'appear' in our dimension and 'disappear' instantly or 'fade out'; some that have been examined on the ground appear to be piloted via a 'thought-link' from pilot to craft. The craft my sister and her friends saw were classic disc-shaped, metallic vehicles.

Two weeks after this, I had gone to the Hollow Ponds in Epping Forest, near Whipps Cross Hospital, with my friend Mark. We had walked across a large, open space and then into some woods. We emerged into a circular clearing where, in front of us, was the small, round pond. It was dark and the sky was clear, with a full moon, which was casting a beautiful silver light across the whole area. We could see the pond in this light very clearly and were commenting on how the moon was shining on its surface. Suddenly, another shadow appeared, near the left-hand corner of the pond, and was reflecting in the water. It was clearly a figure of human shape and we wondered who could be casting this shadow because no one could be seen standing anywhere near the pond. Then, the shadow started to move around the pond on the far side. The right corner of the pond was not quite visible because it was where the trees started. The trees formed a large semicircle and we were standing in the clearing in the middle. When this shadow got to the far, right-hand side of the pond, we could no longer see it and we waited for it to reappear as it moved round towards us.

This did not happen but instead, a loud stamping, crunching sound echoed from the woods and seemed to be heading in our direction. We looked at each other and wondered what on earth was happening. The noise grew louder and louder; the ground shook and branches could be heard cracking and breaking in two. Whoever this was, it sounded like they were as tall as the trees. It was imminent now that this colossus would be coming out into the clearing where Mark and I were standing. I turned to Mark to say, "Let's get out of here!" but to my shock and horror, he was already gone! I could see him in the moonlight, racing across the open field for the quarter-mile run back to humanity. I looked back at the trees and the noise was now overwhelming. I could see branches moving and trees shaking and at any second, whoever this 'monster' was would be coming out into the clearing where I was standing. If I hung around any longer I feared that I would meet my Maker and the time was not right for that. I turned once more to see Mark even further away and kicking up dust clouds as he motored along. There was nothing left to do but run – and run I did. Now, I was an incredible runner and would have run for England, if I had not ruptured a disc in my spine, saving someone at work who was trying to commit suicide by jumping out of the top floor of the office where I worked. That was eight storeys up in the place where I was a trainee tea taster, in the City of London. Anyway, I ran like I had never run before and in no time at all I had passed Mark and we both eventually made it to the main road.

By some stroke of luck, or divine intervention, I am not sure which, a bus came along almost immediately and as it was approaching, an old woman shuffled out of the darkness from where we had just emerged. This was no ordinary old woman. This woman looked like she had just come out of the ground; like something out of a horror film! I shouted to

Mark, "Bloody hell Mark! Look at that! What the hell is it?" She caught my eye and contact was made. It was the weirdest feeling. She pointed at me and said, "Come here! I want to talk to you!" She sounded like an old, wizened witch. I turned to Mark and shouted, "Where's the bloody bus?" Mark screamed back, "It's almost here!" and he shoved his hand out into the road, to make sure that the driver saw us, and waved it frantically. The old woman came even closer and she was no more then six feet (1.83 meters) away when the bus stopped and we jumped on and ran upstairs. We looked out of the window as the bus pulled away. She was still there standing and pointing at me. It scared the pants off me, I can tell you.

The bus drew to my stop. Mark stayed on board to go all the way to Stratford. I raced along my road and burst through the front door. My sister was in, with my future brother-in-law, along with my mum and dad. I blurted out what had happened and my brother-in-law jumped up, grabbed a knife and said, "Come on! Let's go back and look for her!" Mum said very firmly that no one was leaving the house that night and she did not want me going back there after dark.

Two weeks after this episode, I was at my mate's house. We had been out all evening, messing about on the marshes. We tumbled out onto the pavement, as I was about to go home. It was around 9.30 p.m. We were just chatting when, all of a sudden, we heard a soft, humming sound. Then it became much louder and we looked up, to see a huge flying saucer. It was round with a dome on top and windows around the edges, which were lit up with a powerful, yellow light flooding out of them. It practically touched the roofs of the houses as it glided right over the street and over the top of us. It was a typical flying saucer, like those which have now been seen tens of thousands of times around the world. We were both in a state of shocked excitement and I immediately ran home and to tell what I had seen. I felt sick and I was. My mother told me that it was imagination. I do not believe she believed that herself, for one minute, and I certainly did not.

That night when I went to bed, the tiger was back. I had not seen him for quite a while and was surprised at his return. I crawled out of bed and lay with my head near the foot of the bed, to get as close as possible to this beautiful creature. "I know who you are," I said. "You don't fool me anymore!" He looked at me, as he always did, with those wonderful eyes and if tigers could smile, then that is what he appeared to do. I talked to him a while more, then got back into bed and, quite contented, went straight to sleep.

In the morning, I grabbed my green stone and looked at its emerald-green surface. I felt its 'ancientness'. I saw the stars and connected with my other homeland. The land I told Mum I came from when I was four years old. I then put it back on the shelf and went off to school. My teachers in primary school, and in secondary modern, had all said to my parents that if only I stopped looking out of the window and dreaming I would get very good marks. 'The hardest thing we have to do is trying to get his attention.' The trouble was, I was not interested in the Battle of Hastings, Joseph's coat of many colors or cavemen grunting and pulling their women along by the hair! I wanted to know about the Universe, about the Space People, the flying saucers, where we have really come from, how many planets out there have life on them. The things that really matter. The TRUTH. A lot of what we were being taught was quite boring and pointless.

One year later, I arrived home from school and my sister was at home. She was now married and living in a flat in Leyton. She told me the following story.

She and her husband had entertained a couple of friends two nights previously and they had all rather stupidly messed around with an Ouija board. The next day my sister was in the flat alone when there came a knock at the door. She opened the door and there stood an old woman. In my sister's words: "She looked like she had just come up out of the ground. She was like the walking dead and she had an awful, musty smell!" At the back of their house, beyond the garden wall, was a large graveyard and my sister believed this old woman had come from there –

out of the ground! This woman then tried to force her way into the house and said she had come because my sister had been messing around with things with which she should not. My sister, in absolute fear, managed to eventually push the door shut and hid in the corner of the room for ages before plucking up the courage to leave the house and run round to our family home.

My mum was tough. She would not let any harm come to her children if she could help it. Therefore, she went back with my sister and waited in the front room in case the woman returned. She did return and knocked on the door. My mother rushed to open the door, grabbed hold of the woman standing outside, and really gave her a mouthful. "How dare you come round here, scaring my daughter like this! Go back into the hole that you crawled out of and stay there!" She pushed her down the stairs and shouted, "Don't ever come round here again or you'll really be for it!" She then slammed the door shut and went inside. My sister was sitting out the back, in the kitchen, and Mum told her what she had said and told my sister that she would not be troubled again. Only partly convinced, my sister went to look outside the front door, to make sure that the woman had gone. Sitting on the stairs was a woman in floods of tears. She lived in the flat upstairs, had forgotten her key and had knocked in the hope that my sister would be in and let her in. My sister brought her indoors and made her a cup of tea. My mother apologized and explained what had happened and luckily, they all saw the funny side of things. My sister, fortunately, never saw the dreadful old woman again and from that time on never used an Ouija board.

Shortly after this episode, I arrived home from school and, as always, I ran to hold my green stone. I always did this before I did anything else. It was gone! It was no longer on my shelf. I ran to find my mother and asked her where it was. She calmly told me that she had thrown it away. "What!" I shouted. "You haven't thrown away my green stone?" She looked at me and said that all this strange stuff had started ever since 'that stone' came into the house. "Where is it?" I screamed at her again,

"Where have you thrown it?" She replied that it was somewhere where I would never find it. I was devastated. I did not know what to do. I loved my Mum dearly, but to throw away my green stone was beyond redemption. I ran into my room and collapsed onto the bed. Just like the calling card, the green stone was my contact to the universe, and now they were both gone. Had Mum thrown away the calling card as well? I do not believe she did and I did not want to even go to that place anyway.

Now, at the age of 55, I still miss the green stone and the calling card. If only I could just hold them once again to see what it feels like today. To see what images I could pick up. What wonderful things may have been possible over the intervening forty-odd years if they had still been in my possession? I will never know, but I am sure other things will take their place and perhaps my experiences will happen in other ways.

1 See http://www.nuforc.org - follow the 'Report Database' link for files on the shape of UFOs.

CHAPTER 6

DID HE ALSO SEE THE STARS?

Please take my hopes and wishes
At such a time as this is,
For we all dream of better days.
We are of one creation;
One country and one nation.
And this is where my spirit lays.

I can honestly say I do not hate anything, with one exception, and that was my secondary modern school, 'Stratford Green'. My few years in primary school seem like a stay in heaven compared to that terrible place. The violence and general mayhem scarred me for years. If I had to make any comparison, then I would, quite simply, have to compare it to Roman times when innocent Christians were thrown to the lions. The thing about bullies is that they can only act in a group and they can only pick on the weakest. In fact, they are sad little cretins who make vulnerable children's lives a misery. A time that, supposedly, should have been the greatest days of one's life was, for me, the absolute pits of hell. I was stabbed twice in school, for the simple reason that I refused to fight. I hate violence (OK! I admit it! I have two hates and this is the second one!). I was once stabbed in the leg with a Stanley knife that was stolen from the woodwork class simply for that purpose. I cycled the two miles home and every time I pushed my right leg down on the pedal, it caused the blood to spurt out. By the time I had arrived home, my blue jeans had turned a bright red and my mother went into a state of shock when she saw me.

Mum insisted on treating my leg, but at 13 years of age I was not taking my trousers down in front of my mum, or my dad for that matter. I insisted on doing it myself. Mum got out the Acroflavin. It was a bright yellow cream and was used in the war to help wounds heal and prevent infection. Effective, but it stained yellow everything it touched and Mum was sure that I would get it on the bed sheets. I assured her that I would not and insisted on doing it myself. As soon as I opened the jar I somehow got it all over the bedding, as well as my underpants and jeans, and on top of that, I had a bright yellow leg. Mum was not at all happy about the stained fabrics, but there was some sympathy because I had, after all, just been stabbed.

The second time, I was stabbed in the corner of my left eye and the knife just hung there. Home I went again, this time with blood pouring down my face. My sister gave out an almighty scream and nearly went into cardiac arrest. Then she just broke down and cried, so she was not much help. My mum, God rest her soul, managed to stay calm and deal with the situation. How it never damaged my eye, I will never know. I presume that 'they' must have been looking after me again.

Luckily, I was the fastest runner in the school, and I lost count of the days when one of the bullies would say in class, "You're getting done tonight, Oram!" For the rest of the day I just concentrated on the final bell sounding and I had to make sure that I was out of the classroom first or I would be dead meat. Survival always made sure that I was out ahead of everyone else and once I started running they could never catch me. Although, once they gave up the chase, I would hear the dreaded words in the distance, "We'll get you tomorrow, Oram!" For the rest of the evening, that threat would plague my mind and just eat into me and, of course, at night it was very difficult to rest in bed.

Some of these kids must have had a death wish. I mean, in the lunch break they would go to the traffic lights on the main road and jump onto the back of lorries as they pulled away. It was called 'lorry jumping' for obvious reasons. This was a highly dangerous thing to do and you would often see them hanging on for dear life as their feet were dangling beneath the lorry and bouncing on the road, because they had not got a proper grip. How some of them were not killed, I will never know.

You always knew when there was going to be a fight because

tools would go missing from the woodwork class. Hammers, chisels, screwdrivers and, of course, Stanley knives. Once, there was a fight between two kids; one of them took off his belt that contained well over one hundred metal studs, and the other pulled a hammer from inside his coat. At one point, the boy with the hammer had the other lad in a headlock and was hitting him on the head with the hammer but what he seemed oblivious to, was that every time he brought the hammer back up to rain it down again, the claw part of the hammer was digging into his own forehead. There was blood everywhere but as soon the police arrived some older boys hid the offensive weapons while the culprits were taken away in an ambulance.

This sort of thing made me feel sick to the pit of my stomach and I felt that I had been dropped off at the wrong planet. Why did I need to witness this, and sometimes be on the tail end of it? What was the point, to come here and experience such depravity? How does that help you evolve?

One of their favorite pastimes was a game by the name of 'Yiddles'. I never understood the connection to this name but it seemed to refer to the cheeks on a face. There would be about thirty kids in the 'Yiddle' gang and in break time, when we were all standing around in the playground, they would group together. You knew what was about to happen and you hoped and prayed that it would not be you. You did not want to look too much just in case they caught your eye – that would be the deciding factor. Then, the chanting would start. Slowly and quietly at first: "Yid, yid, yid, yid!" Then, it would build up into an incredible crescendo: "Yid, yid, yid, yid!"

Then they would charge – and some poor, unsuspecting boy would get the full works. They clenched their fists and used the middle knuckles of the fingers like pincers and they would push them into the facial cheeks with incredible force and then pincer them so that the cheeks were squashed in the knuckles. Every one of the thirty or so wanted their turn and as the "yid, yid, yid, yid!" continued it drove them on and on until the job was done. The face of the person, who would be lying on the floor in agony, was bright red, blue, and purple.

The classroom for Religious Instruction was like an amphitheatre. The seats were in a semi-circle, rising in tiers towards the back. All the bullyboys raced in to get in the back row, not so visible and in immediate control of the situation.

The teacher who was in charge was nicknamed, 'Beaky', because he had a large nose. I am not sure now if I ever knew his proper name. For most of the lesson, he simply went through the motions. Nothing could be heard, because of the continuous chanting of: "Beaky! Beaky! Beaky! Beaky!" On top of that, he was bombarded with pennies, halfpennies, eggs, and milk cartons full of milk. How he ignored all this and carried on, I will never know. At the end of each month he would spread on his desktop all the money that had been thrown, count it up and tell us how much he had collected.

Once, when it had been particularly bad, he locked the door and kept us all in. The situation was getting dangerous so he sent a boy to go and get the headmaster. The headmaster arrived and stood in front of the class with his cane in his hand. He looked up at the class and demanded to know whom the culprits were. Suddenly, quietly at first, they started chanting his Christian name: "Charles! Charles! Charles! Charles!" Like the 'Yiddles', it built up into an incredible crescendo and the poor man just left the room and left 'Beaky' to deal with it. He finally let us out, but when he went to his car to drive home, it was on its roof. It was impossible to learn anything at that school, for the simple reason, you could not hear anything and violence was rife. I once saw a teacher hit so hard that he flew over three rows of desks.

Once I had my dinner money stolen. I had no chance; I was pinned up against the wall and if I had not handed it over I would have had a severe beating. I had to go home for lunch, instead of buying the large chip butty I had promised myself. Mum asked me why I was home and I told her, but what I did not expect was what happened next. In the afternoon, I was called out of class and told to report to the headmaster's office. I knocked on the door and went in and, to my horror, standing in the room was my mother with an Inspector and two other policemen. In addition, there was the headmaster and the boy that had stolen my money. Now, this was the hardest boy in the whole school and you just did not mess with him! The Inspector told me that they had been after this lad for a long time and finally they had something concrete on him. With my evidence, they could send him to Borstal. I still had eighteen months to live in that hell hole and there was no way I was going to say anything. I turned to the Inspector and told him that nothing had happened. He was really annoyed, so was the headmaster and so was my mother. I was told to go back to class. In the playground at break time, the word had obviously gone round the whole school. There was I at one end of the playground and the entire school was at the other. They had extra teachers on duty and I thought that if they decided to charge, then I would be dead. Luckily, they did not and I am alive to tell the tale.

There were kids there much worse off then me and I felt so very sorry for them. I would take them under my wing, talk to them, and try to convince them that it would be all right and that one day it would all be over and we would leave that dreadful place for ever (the school I mean). People talk about the youth of today, but it was pretty bad then as well, and if we had had such things as mobiles, I am sure they would have been stolen, much like today. In those days no one had any money and so there was not much to steal in the first place. Parents were very poor and still recovering from the war. When I think of what children get today for Christmas it makes me wonder what would have been the best times to have lived in. Then or now!

It all changed for the better when they burnt down the school. The last of my school days were spent in another school. A brand new one, as the hooligans had burnt part of the previous building by setting light to the curtains on the stage area. The headmaster at my new school was tough and he came with a reputation. His whole appearance and demeanor were imposing. He was tall, almost bald, dressed in black and wore John Lennon-style spectacles with wire frames and very black lenses; so black that you could not see his eyes through them. You just did not mess around with this guy. Not through fear but because of the strong vibrations of peace and power that he exuded. We were all lined up in Assembly one day, and he was walking the ranks, line by line along the rows. When he got to me, he stopped and whispered in my ear, "You do not have to dress like this, do you? You are worth much more than this. You know things that none of these other children do. You deserve to look smarter then this." He then carried on and never spoke to another boy. Out of five hundred or more boys, he only spoke to me. You see, to escape the beatings I was told that if I dressed like them they would leave me alone. Therefore, I got my mother to buy me jeans, combat jacket and steel-toe-capped commando boots. It worked most of the time.

His remark shook me slightly, especially as I had been singled out, and I asked Mum if I could buy a suit to go to school in. As I said before, we did not have much money but my parents seemed really pleased that I wanted to smarten up and my mother paid weekly for it. I helped her from my paper round money. Then a photographer came to the school and he wanted four boys to go on the front cover of a book by Edward Blishen, called, *The Roaring Boys*, and the headmaster picked me as one of the boys. It was great to see myself on the front cover of a book, but the irony was that on the back of the book it states: "They came from the back streets and slums of London's East End…They were the Roaring Boys…teenage delinquents living for kicks…young tearaways full of searing hate and fury." Anyway, I have my suit on in the photograph and it was, at the time, my claim to fame.

Towards my last few days at school, the headmaster came to me and said that some of the boys had gone on a holiday, on a barge at Abridge, and asked why had I not gone? I told him that I could not afford it. He said that he would pay for it and he could arrange for me to go there that day and meet up with them. He said he would arrange for a teacher to drive me down there. He looked me in the eyes and said, "Mike, I know more about you than you realize! I know what you have seen and how you feel! I know how you look to the stars for the answers to your dreams – and one day you will find the answers!"

There had always been something about that man. I could feel his energy. It was totally different to that of any other human I had met. I could have cried, as I was filled with such emotion. Who was this man? He had such an impact on me in such a short time. I had hardly known him, and yet he knew things about me that I had told to no one. Did he also see the stars? He gave me the confidence to believe in myself at such a crucial time in my life, as I was about to leave school and move out into the big world. At the tender age of 15, I knew that this man was different. Surely he was not the tiger; the man in the silver suit? Surely not!

CHAPTER 7

THE TRIP TO BROXBOURNE AND THE GIANT MOTHER SHIP

When all is done
The earth in silence will be.
Lost in time,
We move on superconsciously.
Fire from ashes,
The Phoenix will rise;
Fly away to some distant sky,
While shadows fall
In remembrance of all that went before.

I was really keen on freshwater fishing from a young age and some of my favorite haunts were along the River Lea, between Waltham Abbey and Ware, in Hertfordshire. It was lovely to get out into the countryside, sit by the river in peace and quiet, and listen to the sounds of nature. The trickling of the water as it ran between the tall grasses and bright colored water lilies. The fish, rising to the surface and taking the unsuspecting flies that dipped to rest on the liquid sheet as it traveled downstream. Watching the sun rise from the horizon, between distant church towers whose bells would, later in the day, peel across the countryside. This was the place of dreams; the place where body, mind and soul could take refuge from the onslaught of town living. A place of peace and tranquility that would help to heal the scars of school-day hell.

I made one such trip in 1968 with my dad, who was not a great angler at all but, as he was on holiday, he fancied a day out by the river. On the way to Stratford railway station, he purchased a copy of the *Daily Mirror* to read on the train. There we were, sitting next to each other and looking forward to a great day. My dad reading the newspaper while I sat gazing out of the window and thinking of nothing. Just observing the changing scene as we gradually left behind the humdrum of city life and entered the vast, green belt that stretched its way through the Hertfordshire countryside.

"Look at this!" my dad said, while holding the paper in my direction. I pulled away from my window view and looked at the double-page spread that Dad was holding in front of me. "Was God an Astronaut?" in large, bold letters was spread across the article at the top of the page.

"A new and exciting book by Erich Von Daniken, called, *Chariots of the Gods*. The author's theory that Earth, in its remote past, was visited by beings from other planets who perhaps fathered humanity!"

I took the paper from Dad and read it with tremendous excitement. This was the first time I had found some proof that all my childhood experiences may have had a footing in reality. All the thoughts that had risen in my mind at such a young and tender age, about beings from other star systems and dimensions, may have, after all, some check with the way things really are. That day I was reborn. I would reach out and move forward in my quest to understand what had been happening to me. I was not the sole experiencer (a word used in Ufology to describe a person who has experience of beings from places other than planet Earth) of other worldly beings visiting this planet! They had been here before! They have probably always been here. Therefore, it made absolute sense to accept that other humans have seen them also! I went fishing that day and had a very good time, but all the while I was rolling this over in my mind and I decided to start to look towards the sky for some answers.

In recent years a lot has been said of a negative nature about Von Daniken's books, and on some issues that may be a right judgment, but to be absolutely fair, Von Daniken opened a lot of minds at that time and put into the public domain many anomalies, such as: the Nazca Lines in Peru; the ancient terraced walls in Sacsayhuaman and other places, where giant stones weighing many tons are fitted with the most incredible precision; ancient drawings of suited beings with strange craft. You have no doubt read some of the books and know what I am talking about, but the thing is, it shifted my consciousness and gave me the impetus and belief to look deeper into what was happening to me and to see if there was a reason why this was happening.

Shortly after this, we were offered a council house in Rainham, Essex and so left the confines of the tiny top floor of our terraced maisonette home in Stratford for a more rural area. A quick walk to the end of the road and we were faced with fields. A far-flung location from the bombsites we played on as children. We had our own front door, our own front and back garden, a bathroom and an inside toilet. I was happy, Mum was happy and Dad was happy. In fact, we were all very pleased indeed!

Soon after moving to Rainham, I gained an interview with 'Wonderloaf', a local bakery. They wanted a driver to deliver bread to houses. The unfortunate thing was that you had to be aged eighteen and I was still only seventeen. I pleaded with the manager to take me on and promised that I would not disappoint him. He agreed and I started the following day. After the first three days of learning the round, I was left to my own devices and really enjoyed the freedom of being my own boss out on the open road. I got it into my head to try and see how fast I could complete the round and every day I tried to cut corners in the vain attempt to finish earlier then the day before. The customers seemed very pleased with this express delivery as they got the fresh bread to make sandwiches before their husbands went to work and also before the children went to school, but it did have its drawbacks. Cakes had to be pre-ordered by slapping a note in my hand, as I did not have time to take the basket to every front door to show them what was on offer. Once, when I was delivering to the skyscraper, one woman got a large sliced white lobbed at her from the lift doors as it opened. You see, I used to yell out, "Baker!" then throw the bread to the front door before the lift door closed. Only this time the customer wanted some fairy cakes and she said that the only way she could catch me was by waiting by the lift doors. The large sliced white had knocked her back a couple of steps, simply by the force and the sudden surprise of its emergence as the lift doors opened, but she did see the funny side of it.

One morning I had one of those 'inner feelings' that something was imminent and said to my mother that I was going to see a flying saucer soon. She calmly suggested that I take my camera along just in case! I did not do this because in my conscious mind I rationalized away the expectation. On the morning of 26 November 1969, at around 8.20 a.m. I did see an unworldly craft in East Ham, London, E6.

About half-way through my round, I would deliver to some houses in a cul-de-sac and would stop at the bottom, near the entrance to the park, to have a sandwich and drink from my flask. Beyond was the Beckton Gas Works and the day had dawned cold and clear. I suddenly saw, in the distance and coming towards me, a large cigar-shaped object that was a burning, bright-yellow color. It seemed to stop about a mile away, over the Beckton Gas Works, and turned so I could now see the full length of it. It was later estimated to be around one mile in length. I jumped out of the van and stood in the centre of the road, still holding my sandwich and cup of tea, with my head locked up towards the sky. I was transfixed and felt a part of my consciousness go into the craft and talk to the occupants. I was also still aware of standing in the road back at ground level. It was a most unusual experience. Regression sessions later in life have indicated that there may have been a lot more to this encounter.

Eventually, the milkman drove round the cul-de-sac and stopped just behind me. I knew, by experience, that he would go into the park to the public conveniences and would therefore pass by me standing in the road. As he passed, he said, "Good morning Baker!" and I simply could not answer him. Then, I thought, "When he comes back out I will tell him to look up at the sky and, if that fails, he is bound to wonder why am I standing there, not answering him and staring upwards!" Therefore, he would, at some point, know what was going on. On his return he emerged from the park gates and walked towards me. He walked straight by, got into his milk float, turned it around, drove to the end of the cul-de-sac, turned the corner, and disappeared! As soon as he had gone, I was told that this experience was just for me only.

I then came fully back into my own consciousness and was immediately excited and also confused. I needed to tell someone, anyone. I grabbed my *Daily Mirror* and found their number. I telephoned them and told them what I had seen. I explained that this thing was huge and took up a big part of the sky and that someone else must have seen it. They were not in the least bit interested and obviously considered me some sort of idiot. I slammed the phone down in frustration, pulled myself together, and attempted to carry on with my round.

I turned the van around, drove out of the cul-de-sac, and went to my first house. An elderly lady answered the door, took one look at me, and said, "What on earth is wrong with you Baker? You look like you've just seen a ghost!" I blurted out to her that I had just seen this flying saucer. I held out my arms, said that it was huge and took up a great part of the sky and that a part of my consciousness went into the craft, and conversed with the beings. She looked back and said, "There is no way you are driving that van in that state! Come inside and I will make you a nice cup of tea!" Again, I tried to tell what a momentous thing had just happened and again she replied, "Come in and sit down and I'll make you a nice cup of tea!" She eventually came back in with a sugary tea and again I attempted to tell her about what I had just seen and this time she replied by saying that she would telephone my boss and tell him that I was ill and could not carry on with my round.

By the time that my boss arrived with the relief driver I had come more to my senses and realized that there was no way I could tell them what really happened, so I decided, in the interest of staying in employment, I would just say that I felt ill and needed to go home for the remainder of the day and rest.

Some time earlier, I had read Robert Chapman's book *Unidentified Flying Objects* and remembered that it had been serialized in the *Daily Express*. I sent a letter to him via the newspaper. He wrote back that he

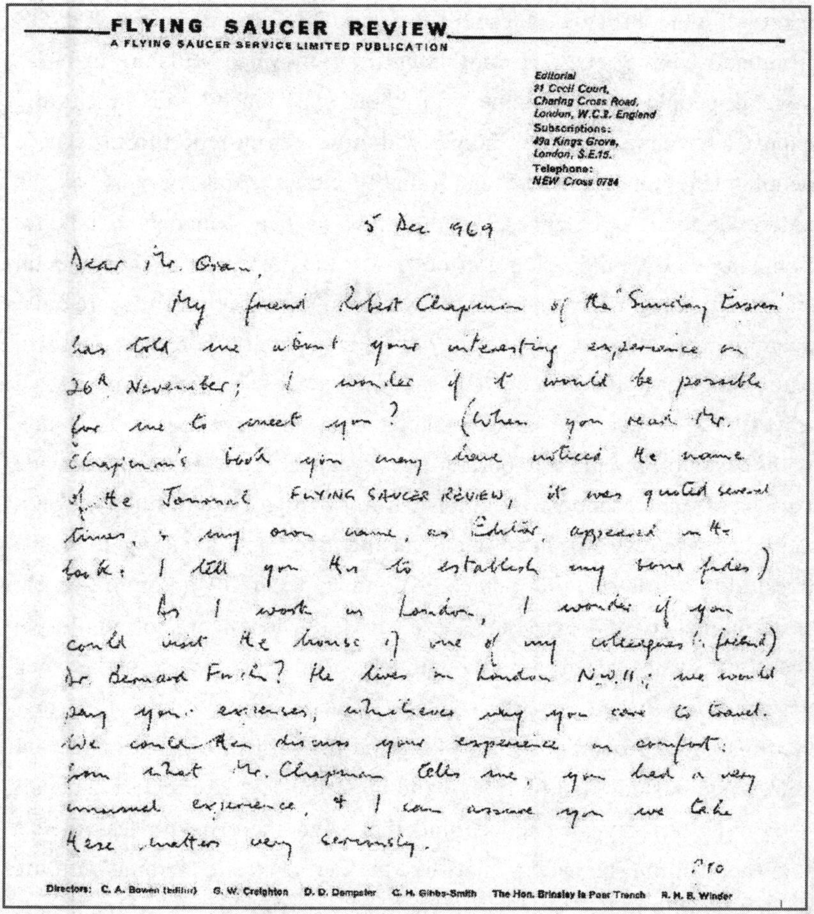

FLYING SAUCER REVIEW
A FLYING SAUCER SERVICE LIMITED PUBLICATION

Editorial
21 Cecil Court,
Charing Cross Road,
London, W.C.2. England
Subscriptions:
49a Kings Grove,
London, S.E.15.
Telephone:
NEW Cross 0784

5 Dec. 1969

Dear Mr. Oram,

My friend Robert Chapman of the 'Sunday Express' has told me about your interesting experience on 26th November; I wonder if it would be possible for me to meet you? (When you read Mr. Chapman's book you may have noticed the name of the Journal FLYING SAUCER REVIEW, it was quoted several times, & my own name, as Editor, appeared in the book: I tell you this to establish my bona fides)

As I work in London, I wonder if you could visit the house of one of my colleagues (& friend) Dr. Bernard Finch? He lives in London N.W.11; we would pay your expenses, whichever way you care to travel. We could then discuss your experience in comfort: from what Mr. Chapman tells me, you had a very unusual experience, & I can assure you we take these matters very seriously.

PTO

Directors: C. A. Bowen (editor) G. W. Creighton D. D. Dempster C. H. Gibbs-Smith The Hon. Brinsley le Poer Trench R. H. B. Winder

Fig 3

had sent it on to Charles Bowen, who was then editor of *Flying Saucer Review,* a magazine that started in 1955 and is still running today. I went to London to meet with Charles Bowen, and also Dr Bernard Finch, and the article about my sighting appeared in the issue of March/April 1970 Vol.16, No.2. (Fig 3)

There was a lot of UFO activity in Rainham and the surrounding area at this time and several articles appeared in the local papers. As a result of this, in 1970, I established a UFO Report Centre, RUFOS (Rainham UFO Society). I ran this until my move to Wiltshire in 1977. Several people contacted me with their experiences and were quite happy to have me go to their homes with my sighting-report forms. These people were totally honest and reliable citizens and, because of the nature of their experiences, quite simply needed someone to talk to. Someone who would listen and not make judgments as to their mental state. They knew themselves that they were of sound mind and were quite aware that what they had witnessed was not normal. There was, and still is, nothing set in place in our UK society to deal with such things. It is a travesty of justice that this has been allowed to happen. These are, without doubt, the most important events happening to mankind. A wide variety of craft occupied by other-worldly beings use our airspace on a daily basis and we still have scientists and astronomers talking about the possibility of life on other planets, who then, generally, go on to say that if intelligent life did exist 'out there', it would take them so long to get 'here' it would seem almost pointless. How dare they make such assumptions based on their own flawed systems and theories? Astrophysicist Robert Jastrow, talking on the subject of life outside our solar system, said, "If I hold my hand up to the sky, like that, it conceals a part of the universe, and behind that hand there lie no less then a thousand trillion stars and planets like the Earth. We are teeming with life in this world, and in that world of life, man and his entire planet are newcomers; are recent arrivals, not at the summit of creation, but somewhere near the bottom of the heap."

Scientists only seem able to see reality via the perspective of their own theories and research. They limit their minds, sometimes for years, and such tunnel vision and narrow thinking has held back progress throughout history. Below are just a few examples of past narrow vision and beliefs that were tenaciously adhered to, often to the point of persecuting those who dared to point to evidence that contradicted those beliefs:

We once believed that:

The Earth was flat.

We were the centre of the universe.

The atom was solid – but now we know that around 90% of it is space.

We could never travel faster then 20 miles an hour. (In fact, Desmond Leslie, who, in 1953, co-authored with George Adamski *Flying Saucers Have Landed*, remembered his grandfather saying that at one time it was believed that a human being would disintegrate if he went faster then the speed of a galloping horse).

Machines heavier than air would never fly.

No man could travel faster then the speed of sound.

No man could ever leave the pull of the earth.

Nothing can travel faster then the speed of light.

In *Space, Gravity and the Flying Saucer*, published in 1954, Leonard G. Cramp stated:

"By far the most baffling aspect of the Flying Saucer is the extraordinary rate of acceleration. Accurate readings by theodolite have indicated something in the order of 65 Gs."

I wonder what our scientists think of that!

Back to Rainham. The Report Centre was busy and most evenings, after work, I was off to someone's home to listen to yet another Saucer-sighting experience. I felt that I was doing something positive here for people. I could see the relief on the witnesses' faces when I told them they were not mad and that I understood what they were telling me. I would, once they had filled in the report form and told me all I needed to know, give them a potted history of UFOs. As I said earlier, they needed to get this thing off their chest and they needed to know that someone out there would listen to them. It is a total disgrace that still today, after sixty years, nothing has ever been put in place to help people understand these sightings of, and encounters with, our cosmic neighbors.

Below are just some of the front page reports of that time:

Rainham Echo, Tuesday, 18 August 1970

"A FLYING SAUCER SHOCK FOR YOUNG COUPLE

A Flying Saucer was seen at Rainham last week. In fact it almost landed. ..... Mr Jones told police they stopped about 10.50 p.m. on Wednesday, after they heard 'loud electrical noises.' He says the object, about 20 feet (6.10 meters) long and 10 feet (3.05 meters) wide, hovered only a little way above the ground for a few seconds before flying away towards Hornchurch. It was glowing red with four white lights along its underside. A spokesman for the Ministry of Defence said that he had absolutely no idea what this could have been .... "This one is a mystery to us."

Havering & Romford Express, 1 September 1971

"RESIDENTS SEE 'THING' IN SKY

Every night, families in Oldchurch Road, Romford, take part in a 'spot the blob' contest. And they're treating it seriously. The families are baffled by a mysterious pink object which has been spotted several times hovering over Dagenham. ......"It was as big as my house through the binoculars and moving about in a wriggling movement very fast," said Mrs. Saunders.........."It was reddish and twisting about ever so fast with a red light coming out of the side of it," she said."

The Advertiser, 14 February 1975

"PAM'S UFOs PUT HER IN A SPIN

The chances of spotting a UFO are many thousands to one, but the odds have been incredibly reduced for Dagenham housewife, Pamela Cliff, who now claims she has made four sightings........ "It was a roundish-shaped object with lights around its edge. It was very clear but I still had to get my husband Dave. He was a bit skeptical at first but had to admit he saw it too. It was there for about two hours until it slowly disappeared."…. It was also seen by other residents on the same nights in Dagenham and Ilford."

Rainham Echo, 24 March 1970

"BUS QUEUE SIGHTS A 'FLYING SAUCER'

Mysterious flying-saucer-like objects have been sighted over Upminster and Hornchurch, and police, the Ministry of Defence and the London Weather Centre can give no definite explanation for them. Two Echo reporters saw a mysterious glowing object on Wednesday, and a bus queue of 15 people sighted another disc on Thursday. Mrs. Joan Barry…. was standing with her neighbor waiting for a bus outside St. Lawrence's Church, Upminster, on Thursday. With them were a dozen or so other people. "We were waiting for a bus after bingo," said Mrs. Barry, "and we both saw a rainbow-colored disc in the sky over the Hall Lane area. As we watched, we saw it hover for a few seconds and then it glided away gently. As it glided it changed color and became bright orange."….. Said Barry Oliver: "We saw a bright oval-shaped disc hovering, then it shimmered and went into two images and disappeared."….. A spokesman for the Royal Air Force at the Defence Ministry building in London said there was no RAF activity in the area on either of the two nights."

A small selection from my sighting report forms:

22 October 1973. Two 14-years old lads were playing on the Rainham marshes near the railway lines when they heard a low humming sound which startled them. Looking over the track onto the marshes, they saw a large, glittering object landing. It was as big as a house (not exaggerating!). It was a metallic gray and the setting sun glistening on it made it look silver. It was round with a dome on top and looked like a classic Flying Saucer. They became very scared and ran away.

10 January 1973. "I was having my driving lesson when I saw the UFO in the sky. At first I thought it was an aeroplane but knew it was not because it had no wings and it was hovering. It then started to fall a little, then shot straight across the sky and disappeared." (This lady drew a triangle).

17 December 1972. "At about 10 p.m. I went to the bedroom. I could see the moon from my window so decided to have a closer look with the aid of binoculars. Just before I went to have a look at the moon, a flashing object caught my attention. At first I thought it was a star, but when I had a closer look with the binoculars I saw flashing lights of red, blue, green and silver. I called my wife to come and have a look and she said it was a plane. She had another look with the binoculars and said: 'If that's an aircraft, why has it not moved? It seems to be rotating and hovering!' We watched it for a further 20 minutes before it shot away. The next night I made it my business to look in the same spot but nothing was there. I went into the garden and there it was, hovering over Collier Row in Romford. It then shot off again."

17 July 1974. One man contacted me at this time, in quite a state of distress. I arranged to go to his home in Dagenham, the following evening. The family had been to visit friends in Abridge. They were driving back home around 8 p.m. His wife was sitting in the front and the two children were in the back. Driving along the quiet country lanes just out of Abridge, they noticed a light. It shot down out of the sky and was right behind their car. The children were very frightened and the mother tried to calm them down but was incredibly unnerved herself. The children actually thought they were going to be 'taken'! The husband tried to stay calm and carried on driving. The light followed them all the way home. He rushed to the house, opened the door and ushered the children and his frightened wife inside. In a panic he thought he would try and divert 'them' away from the house,

so he got back in the car and started driving around the streets and the light just followed. In the end he drove to the police station and ran inside, begging them to come and look. One police officer came out with him and they watched as the light just hovered in the sky above them on the other side of the road. After about 30 minutes the policeman said he had to go back inside and he left the man standing there alone. The man told me that he watched it for another two hours, after which it shot away and he made his way back home.

Using what knowledge I had of the subject, I did my best to help them understand something of what went on that night. I sincerely believed that, without the help of a good hypnotist, most of this experience remained hidden from public view. It was a different world then for Ufologists like me. The tools for this type of experience were not readily available then and even if I had made a few successful enquiries into that direction, the family, at that time, was not prepared to look into the matter any further. There was, of course, the inevitable missing time that seems to happen in cases of this sort. They were quite aware of that. They knew what time they left for their journey home and knew precisely how long the journey would take and almost two hours were unaccounted for.

They were lovely people and were so pleased to tell me their story and I probably helped them more than I realized. I did, in fact, keep in touch with them for a couple of years, in the hope that they would change their minds but, in the end, you have to understand that that is their journey and if that is the road they want to take then it must be respected.

Sightings in Rainham were not just reserved for the late 1960s and 70s. Once one of my neighbors found out about my interest in ufology, she was very keen to tell me of her experience back in 1954! She was walking home one fine summer's evening, after visiting a friend's house and took a short cut along a lane between two large fields. A strange whistling sound made her look towards the sky and high up, glinting from the late rays of the setting sun, was a flying disc with a dome on the top.

She started to feel fear, as this was a lonely lane, even in the daytime, and the nearest house, the farmhouse, was two fields away. The disc then shot down from the sky and leveled out just above the field in front of her. She was very afraid. The next thing she remembered was seeing the disc shoot back up into the sky with the same type of whistling sound and disappear into the night. It was now much later than it should have been and her mother questioned her about the lateness. She could not explain and never mentioned it to anyone until she revealed the experience to me in 1972. It had, she said, been on her mind all those years and she felt quite relieved to 'get it off her chest'.

On the 29 March 1972, I received a letter from the Branch Librarian of Rainham Library, saying that they were planning to have a lecture on UFOs as part of the winter program of activities. It was planned for Wednesday 8 November. They wanted me to provide photographs, press cuttings, etc., and also to advise on a suitable speaker. I was only too pleased to help and suggested I contact Charles Bowen, who was the editor of *Flying Saucer Review*. He agreed to come to Rainham and everything was set. One of the Librarians was also very keen on the subject of UFOs and she and another member of staff made a flying saucer from plastic and cardboard, painted it silver and fixed it onto a record deck so that it would revolve. We then set up various exhibition screens to display newspaper cuttings, letters and photographs. The event sold out and was a huge success. The local paper the following week had this to say:

Recorder/Review, 17 November 1972
"The Eyes In The Sky
Are spacemen really looking us over?
What does Rainham have that no part of Havering has? Answer: Flying Saucers...or Unidentified Flying Objects if you want to sound more technical.

More and more people in Rainham are becoming convinced that

they, or the area, are coming in for a close scrutiny by visitors from other planets.

Sightings of mysterious objects in the sky were reported from Hornchurch, Upminster and Rainham a year or two ago. They persisted for some time, but more recently they have come in mainly from Rainham.

And evidence of how many people are interested in things that fly past in the night came with a lecture on the subject at Rainham Library last week."

The article goes on to quote various local residents who had sightings of unusual aerial objects.

Sightings continued in and around this part of Essex and local papers still gave them front page space. Below is yet another example of what was being seen at that time:

Thurrock Gazette, 3 February 1978

"Two Purfleet women got the shock of their lives when they looked out over the Thames near the Kent Coast last week. Two balls of fire collided and revealed an unidentified flying object...stared in amazement as clouds parted and revealed a large object the shape of a child's spinning top...... "We could clearly see windows in the side, a light at one end and what seemed like flames along the bottom"...... "Suddenly we realized we were looking at something out-of-this-world and fell back in fright. June got her hand caught in the curtains in her excitement to get away. Then we rushed round to my brother's (house) to get him to look."......... "I was not able to see the details of windows and so on," he said, "But I did see a big, red, flashing light which was moving and stopping. It seemed to be too low for a plane. There was a strange white shadow too, but I can't describe it any more clearly than that."

I cannot leave this chapter without mentioning the well-documented, 'Aveley[1]' case of the 27 October 1974. The village of Aveley is three miles East of Rainham, on the opposite side of the A13 trunk road to Southend. John and Elaine Avis (pseudonym), together with their three children, were returning home in the evening when they noticed a blue light in the sky. The light struck them as being a bit odd and they did discuss it briefly but continued on their way. Further along their journey, and now just a couple of miles from their home, they drove into a strange green mist that enveloped the road. Unaware that their journey had taken an eventful twist, they arrived home and John immediately switched on the television to watch a film he had scheduled to see. To his great surprise, the TV had shut down for the night (as it did in those days) and he then noticed that it was 1 a.m. in the morning. They had two-and-a-half hours of missing time! They began to be plagued by unusual and disturbing dreams of small, strange-looking creatures. In the end they decided to have hypnotic regression and what was revealed to them has since become a classic abduction scenario:

Once they entered the green mist they were taken from their car into the UFO and a medical examination was carried out by four-foot-tall (1.22 meters) creatures dressed in white gowns. They had large eyes and pointed ears and were covered in fur. (*I have personally investigated two cases like this where four-feet-tall creatures with large eyes and covered in fur were seen. One was in Cumbria in 1930! Another on the Wiltshire/Somerset border in 1964.*) There were taller beings on the craft also and they were around six-and-a-half-feet (two meters) tall and appeared quite human in appearance. The smaller, furry creatures seemed to be under their control. (*This, I found, was also the case with the 1964 experience that I investigated.*) After the examination, the Avis family was shown around the craft and, amongst other things, was shown images of the destruction of the aliens' home planet. They were then put back into their car to continue the last two miles of their journey home, none the wiser as to what had happened.

My friend, who worked at Rainham Library and had an interest in UFOs, also lived in the village of Aveley and got to know the family. She told me, and it was also well documented at the time, that the family became more 'spiritual' and environmentally aware. John Avis developed more artistic skills and one of the boys, who was not doing well in school at the time, started to improve greatly. Again, this type of consciousness change is often reported around the world by the many thousands of people who have these experiences.

These sightings and experiences, I hope, will give you a flavor of what was happening in the Rainham area at that time. It was experiencing what we call a 'UFO Flap'. Why these flaps occur has never really been fully understood but occur they do. Warminster was just such a place in 1964 through to the 1980s. Bonnybridge in Scotland is ongoing[2]. South Wales experienced a flap in the late 1970s and the area concerned became known as the Welsh Triangle. Strange lights and tall white figures visited people; the most famous case being that of the Coombs family, whose isolated farm experienced all sorts of strange phenomena in 1977. Secured cattle found their way down into the village and when brought back and placed once more in the field, or barn, under padlock, within minutes or even seconds, another telephone call alerted the family that the cattle were back in the village! Clive Harold wrote a book about this case in 1979, entitled *The Uninvited*[3]. Gulf Breeze, in Florida[4,] experienced a flap in the 1980s. France, in the early 1950s, has been well documented. Mexico, in the last ten years, has had almost daily sightings and video footage of many thousands of craft has been captured on hundreds of camcorders[5]. Residents have been known to take their camcorders out in their lunch breaks to record strange alien craft! The authorities in Mexico and Brazil are much more open in their attitude to our visitors and so information is released via the media, not suppressed as it is in the UK.

In fact, the Brazilian Air Force work with National UFO investigation groups to pool information.[6] When I was in Mexico in 1997, I spoke to a local resident, who told me that 'ovnis' as they call UFOs, are featured almost daily on TV news bulletins. Mexican TV presenter, Jaime Maussan, has a weekly, prime-time program on a Sunday, showing the preceding week's UFO sightings and encounters.

There are many UFO sightings over Turkey and Turkish national television and newspapers cover these UFO incidents. Haktan Akdogan, a Turkish television presenter, UFO investigator and Founder and Chairman of Sirius UFO Space Sciences Research Centre in Istanbul and of the Turkish International UFO Museum and the world's first Traveling UFO Museum, has produced videos[7] of firsthand reports and testimonies by Turkish high-ranking military pilots and officers and the Turkish Intelligence Agency's involvements on UFOs. He says that the Turkish authorities are very open about the UFO phenomenon and he was invited to the Ankara headquarters of the Turkish Air Force for a special meeting with 3-star generals on the subject. Haktan Akdogan also publicized a 1 November 2002 incident, when many witnesses, including airline pilots and their crews, watched a UFO destroy a meteor that was on a collision course with Earth. Video footage of this was shown on Turkish TV and Haktan says he sent out twelve thousand emails about this to the world's media, but only six TV stations responded.

On 6 January 2005, *India Daily* reported on its country's internal debate on whether or not the populace should be told what the government knows about UFOs:

"New Delhi is in the middle of a big, secret, internal debate. On one side, the largest democracy of the world is eager to explain to its citizens and to the world about the ongoing contacts with the UFOs and extra-terrestrials. On the other hand, there are invisible, untold, international protocols that prohibit doing anything that may cause worldwide fear and panic."

From *India Daily* online at http://www.indiadaily.com/editorial/01-06a_1-05.asp

China treats the whole phenomenon with a serious scientific attitude. Members of many UFO research groups need a degree in a scientific discipline to qualify for membership: "If our conditions for membership weren't so strict, we'd have millions of members by now," said Mr Sun, a retired Foreign Ministry official, who is president of the Beijing U.F.O. Research Society. Even so, more than 40,000 Chinese are members of a UFO group. The Chinese Air Force attends important UFO meetings. Images captured on camcorders are published in newspapers and shown on TV. One national, bi–monthly, UFO magazine has a circulation of 400,000. UFO buffs in China are lobbying for a university degree program in UFOlogy.

The list of flaps and consistent appearances is endless and way beyond the scope of this book. Do some research on the Net or visit bookshops and second-hand bookshops and find out for yourselves about this constant activity around our globe[8].

1 See *Suggested Reading* 7/1

2 See *Suggested Reading* 7/A

3 See *Suggested Reading* 7/2

4 See *Suggested Reading* 7/3

5 See *Suggested Reading* 7/B

6 See *Suggested Reading* 7/C

7 See *Suggested Reading* 7/D

8 See *Suggested Reading* 7/E

CHAPTER 8

UFO BY PRIOR ARRANGEMENT

And as grey as rain
And calm as I am,
I shouted.
I shouted to shake the stars from their slumber:
"Look at me!
I am in the arms of angels!"

After my week in Warminster, mentioned at the start of this book, I finally arrived home in Essex around 1 a.m. and was surprised to find that Mum and Dad were still waiting up for me. They said they just wanted to make sure that I was safe.

I had burst through the front door and then immediately unloaded on my poor parents all that had happened in the past nine days. They sat there patiently and listened. Mum had a greater understanding of what was happening to me, as I had talked to her about it ever since I was a child, and, of course, she had never forgotten the conversation we had when I was four. In fact, she brought it up many times over the succeeding years.

Now Dad, well, he was a different kettle of fish! He was very down to earth and firmly locked in the here and now and I had never spoken about any of my experiences to him. I understood, in a way, where his attitudes were coming from. He was born in 1912 and in 1917 he clearly remembered his mother answering a knock at the door. He heard a heart-rending scream and ran through to the hallway to see his mother collapsed on the floor. A neighbor had already arrived and he was ushered into another room. His mother had received a telegram; notice that her husband was lost in battle and presumed dead. A senseless war that tore his family apart, as it did with millions of other unfortunate souls.

He then lived through the 1930s depression, where there was even less money. Times were hard and he eventually went to live with his elder sister, who was, by then, married and living in Grays, in Essex. He joined the Territorial Army and because of that, when the Second World War started in 1939, he was one of the first to be called up. He spent his time in Italy, North Africa, and other places. He told me some harrowing stories: one where his boat was torpedoed and by the time he managed to get off it was listing so badly that, soon after he jumped overboard, it sank beneath the waves.

Through the advice of his close friend's wife, my mother decided to write to him, as he received very few letters. He came home, married her, and then never saw her again until the end of the war. They eventually moved into the upstairs flat in the tiny terraced house that I mentioned earlier and my Aunt lived downstairs. There was little in the way of food or belongings and even less money. After losing his own father in battle and then fighting himself for his own country, they ended up with nothing. He became a welder and spent all his years in the same company, working for a low wage. When he retired at 65, he was presented with a cheap mantel clock for all his years of service.

It was a hard life and it took all that was possible just to keep his head above water. It was enough trying to survive down here on terra firma, without looking out into space to see what was happening out there!

I looked at Dad as I was retelling what had happened at Starr Hill and I could see, by that look in his eye, that he did not believe any of it and, on top of that, he was probably wondering what on earth he had helped to give birth to!

I turned towards him and promised that I would arrange for a UFO to come to our house so that he could see them. He looked up, but did not say a word. I then thanked them for staying up for me, went to the bathroom to clean my teeth, and retired to bed.

I knew that I was in contact with the 'visitors' because, on many occasions, I would get a telepathic message to either go to some location or to go and look out a certain window or open a door – and there they would be! So, I thought, 'If they are telling me where they are, then I do not see why I cannot ask them to come to see me!'

I sat in meditation the evening of the following day, and for the next two weeks, asking them to come so that my dad could see for himself that these things are real. I desperately wanted them to do this for me.

At the time, I was working at the Ford Motor Company, in Dagenham, and this particular week I was on the night shift. When on that shift I would go to bed at 3 p.m. in the afternoon and Mum would wake me at 9 p.m. I would then have a quick wash, have something to eat and leave home at around 9.40 p.m. to arrive at work at 9.55 p.m. This particular evening I was woken by a telepathic message at 7.50 p.m. I will always, in these particular scenarios, wake up on my back, be fully alert, with no drowsiness, and receive a clear message. I was told to go into my parents' bedroom and look out of the window. I did this immediately. I opened the curtain and looked out and into the sky. Directly above the house was a huge, silver sphere. This sphere looked alive. It looked like a giant, crystal ball and it seemed to be shedding bits of crystal as silver flashes; as if small stars were shooting from its edges. It was the most beautiful sight.

I ran downstairs and into the living room. Dad was sitting in his armchair and Mum was in the kitchen, preparing my evening meal. I calmly said to Dad, "Would you like to see one of those flying saucers, Dad?" To which he replied, "I wouldn't mind if I did, son." "Right!" I said, "Open the front door, and look up in the sky." My father never got excited about anything. He took it all in his stride in a calm and almost detached way. Not tonight! He opened the front door, stepped outside, and looked up into the sky as I had asked. "Bloody hell!" he exclaimed. "Quick! Go and get the binoculars!" I raced upstairs, came back down with the binoculars, and handed them to him. He looked through them, hardly believing what he was seeing. This beautiful thing just hovered above the house, in all its glory. I looked at Dad; he was so excited; this was really making my day. I looked back up to the craft and idly thought to myself, "You are waiting for quite a while in such a built up area." I got an instant reply in my mind as they said, "If we went away too quickly, your father would go back inside the house, sit down and try to find some way to explain it away. By waiting this amount of time, he will fully take into his consciousness what he is seeing and he will never forget it."

Then, it started to move and gracefully drifted across the road and over the top of the house opposite. We started to lose it over the rooftops and Dad, once again totally out of character, shouted, "Quick! Upstairs!" and in a flash, he was gone! The only time I ever saw my father move this fast was once, when we had gone to Southend-on-Sea for the day, we were walking along the promenade and he saw a ten-shilling note on the ground. He was down and up before I could say 'Jack Robinson!' Now, there he was running up the stairs, and I ran behind him.

I would like to mention at this point, something about my mother's net curtains. You never touched them! You could look and admire them but never, ever lay your hands on them! I never understood how she knew if they were touched. It was almost like some sixth sense. My father would never dare to touch them; it was more then his life was worth! I did, because I was always looking out of the window. Mum always knew but I somehow got away with it. I would even look at where all the pleats were, memorize them and replace them in that exact position after I had finished – but she still knew!

This was a noteworthy day for several reasons and one of them was the net curtains. Dad rushed across the floor, grabbed hold of the nets, and practically ripped them off the rail! For one minute there, I was more amazed at what damage he had done to the nets then the fact that outside the house was a huge silver sphere which had arrived by prior arrangement!

My father flung open the window and together we watched the craft slowly move away from the house. It seemed to stop over the River Thames, which was about a mile away. The river was just visible from the window and we could see the light of this silver sphere reflecting in the water below. It waited there for a few seconds, moved to the left for a short while, then suddenly shot away at a terrifically fast speed. It traversed the entire sky in under two seconds. Dad asked where it had gone, as it had moved too fast for him to follow, and I told him that it had vanished into the distance.

Mum had been busy getting my dinner ready in the kitchen and we had completely forgotten to call her to see this object. We told her about it afterwards and then I had my dinner and went to work early, before Mum found out about the net curtains. When I arrived home the next day, I noticed that Dad was still alive and so she could not have been too angry and I never brought it up in conversation for fear of reprisals.

Soon after my father's experience, my mother was changing the curtains in the spare bedroom when a disk-shaped craft swooped down from the sky and hovered outside the window. She said it was so close she felt she could have touched it, had the window been open. She described it as a metallic gray and the rim was at eye-level, with each end of the UFO out of sight either side of the window. It stayed for only a few seconds then shot straight upwards at an amazing speed.

Six years ago, my father passed away. He never recovered from my mother dying and had slowly gone down hill ever since. I do not think we realize at times how much we unconsciously rely on our partners. My Mum and Dad were together for fifty years, doing everything together. What an enormous chasm there must have been in his life when she was no longer there.

After a long struggle, Dad ended up in a Care Home and eventually in a Hospice. One day I had a strong feeling to make the long journey on the train to London, to visit him. When I arrived, I looked at him in bed. He was not the same man. His face was sunken, he was deathly white, and he did not look like my father at all. He had been senile for a long while but we were still at least able to talk about the war. That day, well, even that was impossible. I stayed for four hours and tried to make some conversation but it was impossible. In the end, I had to leave to get my train back home and I told my father that I had to go. As I was just about to leave the room, he turned and said to me, "Do you remember that light?" I asked, "What light, Dad?" He replied, "The light that came over our house." "Do you remember that, then, Dad?" I replied. "Yes," he said. I moved back into the room, stood by his bed, and asked him to tell me about it. He did. In fact, he told me every single, last detail of it. Isn't that what they said would happen? Did not they say that, by waiting for that length of time, he would fully take into his consciousness what he was seeing and that he would never forget?

I thanked him for telling me that. I gave him a kiss on his cheek and made my way home. In the morning, before I could return, he was dead. The experience that he had, a UFO by prior arrangement, was his last clear memory and the last conversation I ever had with him.

These beautiful cosmic travelers are helping us to change our consciousness and they certainly changed my father in some way that, until he passed away, I was not aware of. My father never showed his feelings. He was brought up in a world where men did not cry or express emotions. Why not, for goodness sake? Don't men have feelings as well? Why were men not allowed to show their feelings at the loss of a loved one? I remember when Mum suddenly died, it was a shock to us all, but Dad just sat in his chair and stared. He just stared into space. I would dance my mother around the room and always greeted her with a loving kiss on the cheek and I made a point of kissing my Dad on the cheek also. He would try to pull away; he was uncomfortable with that; it is not what men do. I always held him tightly so he could not get away and he put up with it. What he needed that day was a good cry; a way to release what he was feeling inside, but he could not do it. He just stared into empty space and it was a pitiful sight. He did tell me once though, when he was sleeping in the living room, that my mother came to see him and that she looked very well and was wearing her favorite lemon-color cardigan with her light gray skirt. She hovered in the air and said to Dad, "Don't worry about me now, I am fine. Look at me. I am in a lovely place now and I will wait for you." This vision helped my father a lot and it gave him something to hang onto. I am sure though, all he wanted was to be back with her.

CHAPTER 9

A CHANGE OF HEART

Down through the years,
Through hopes and fears,
We progressed on our way.
Life after life sprang from the strife
Until we were lost in the haze.

Ellen, my girlfriend at this time, had a deep hatred towards my love of Ufology and I never fully understood why. It did take up a lot of my spare time and it was always cropping up in conversation, but I always made sure it did not interfere with the five nights a week that we met. I often wondered if her attitude was caused by jealousy, as I was always talking to newspaper reporters, on radio shows and even TV. I also founded the Rainham UFO Report Centre and, through various contacts, was kept well informed of any local sightings. Most people were more than willing to be visited by me and to complete a sighting-report form. To be welcomed into their homes was, to me, a sure sign that these people had seen something, either in the sky or on the ground, that deeply puzzled them and all they wanted to do was to find someone who would understand, listen to their story and not tell them that they were crackpots. I may have been laughed at by a vast majority of people at that time, but to those few fortunate, or unfortunate, people who happened to experience flying saucers at close quarters, I was actually a godsend. It is not much to ask for, is it – somewhere to report a sighting? Alien craft have been coming here for thousands of years and in the last fifty years alone, millions of people around the world have sighted them. Doctors, astronomers, airline pilots, professors, milkmen, postmen, policemen, office workers, school children, teachers, politicians, tribes people in the giant rain forests, dogs, cats, and on and on, and yet, there was no genuine, official body that people could approach with an open mind and which could help them to come to terms with what they have seen. It was left to people like me to fill that role.

This is a huge subject, for goodness sake. On the one hand we have millions of people from around the world seeing and meeting Beings in craft from other planets, dimensions, time and space and yet we still have some scientists and mainstream media telling us that the chances of life appearing elsewhere is pretty remote. More bizarrely, they say that the distances are too far for them to reach us. How arrogant and ignorant that is – and out of date! On 5 January 2006, the *New Scientist* magazine published an article about a possible new hyper-drive motor which would propel a craft through another dimension at enormous speeds. It uses a new branch of physics that links quantum mechanics and Einstein's general theory of relativity. This new physics postulates a six-dimensional world in which the forces of gravity and electromagnetism work together. To quote from the article by Haiko Lietz:

"... the US military has begun to cast its eyes over the hyper drive concept, and a space propulsion researcher at the US Department of Energy's Sandia National Laboratories has said he would be interested in putting the idea to the test."

Such bodies don't put their money on pie in the sky.

One Sunday morning, a BBC crew was coming to my house to tape an interview for radio and they were running late. This did not help me, because I was supposed to be at Ellen's house at midday, to take her to her friends' home for dinner. These people were upper middle class, with new car, big house, big dog, and they possibly were not used to anyone being late for an invitation. I turned up at Ellen's home one hour late. She was furious. She verbally ripped my head off and told me, in no uncertain terms, that chasing flying saucers may interfere with my life but it certainly was not going to interfere with hers! She got in the car and nagged me all the way to Chelmsford.

We finally arrived; she leapt from the car and headed for the house, to quickly tell them that it was my entire fault, because I had been talking to reporters, for a radio show about flying saucers – a stupid topic in her mind. I sheepishly followed behind, to immediately be met with hugs from the hosts, both saying how exciting it was to have a dinner guest who was investigating UFOs and was about to be on TV and radio. The girl looked towards Ellen and said, "A celebrity, in our home! How brilliant is that?" Ellen was not pleased but I was very gratified.

Two weeks later, the *London Evening News* came to my home to do an interview, after hearing the radio show on the BBC. After the interview, they asked me if I was seeing anyone. I said, "Yes, I am," and I told them her name. They then asked me if it would be a good idea to interview her to get her side of the story. Now, because I believed that she hated this subject because of all the media attention I got, I naively thought that if she got herself in the paper as well, I may be able to solve this rather irritating little problem in one fell swoop. I happily gave them her address and they went round that same afternoon. I was so excited that I could not wait to see her that evening and hear what she had to say. When she opened the front door, I was faced with a look that I had seen so many times before. A look that meant that I was in big trouble! She screamed at me on the doorstep to never, ever, send reporters to her house again. She insisted that she wanted no part of this madness about flying saucers and Beings from Outer Space. "You may be more then happy to make yourself look a fool, but I am not!" she forcibly told me. We went to the pub for a drink but you could have cut the atmosphere with a knife and, quite frankly, I was glad when it was over and I got safely back to my own home.

Eight days later, I had gone to pick her up and take her to the pub. She was quiet, too quiet. Something was wrong, but I did not know what. I quickly ran through my mind all the things that it could possibly be, but all seemed relatively safe to me. As far as I was aware, I had not put my foot in it again, not since the last time, anyway, so I happily continued with the journey. We arrived in the car park and I parked the car. I waited and waited for her to get out but she just sat staring through the front windscreen. Had she sighted a UFO? I thought to myself, and glanced up into the sky. Had she fallen into a catatonic state and if she had, how long should I wait until I try to do something about it? Then, she moved. 'Thank goodness for that,' I thought; 'she seems okay.' Still staring at the front windscreen, she started to speak. "I was on the top of the bus this evening, coming home from work and there was a man sitting in the seat in front of me. He was reading the *London Evening News*. He turned the page and I saw the headlines. In big, thick letters, it said, 'UFO Search Puts Ellen Out of Focus'." She continued, "I jumped up, got off at the next stop, purchased a copy of the paper and here it is." With that, she slammed it into my lap so hard that I thought she had done me permanent internal damage. I sat and read the whole article and I must admit, from her point of view, it was not good. It started by saying that I had given up seeing my girlfriend two nights a week in order to track down my other love – flying saucers. It then ended with: "His girlfriend, Ellen, does not share his enthusiasm. She said: 'When I first met Michael, I thought he was mad. All he did was talk about flying saucers. He kept on about them. In the end, I told him to shut up. He did – and couldn't find anything else to talk about'. "

My days were now numbered, and I had the uneasy feeling that my name may have been given to a Mafia hit squad. Something had to be done fast, and I knew immediately what I had to do. It worked with my dad, so it should work for her. I sat in meditation, as before, and asked the Space Brothers for their help. I desperately needed her to see them. My life was hanging on this one event – and it had to be good.

After only two days, I received my first clue that something could be up. Every second Sunday I would take my parents to see my sister and her family. This was a journey of twenty-two miles, through mainly quiet country roads. My girlfriend never joined us on these outings but this particular weekend she asked to go. This was most unusual and I readily agreed. We had a pleasant day and left my sister's home around 10.15 p.m. We drove through Epping, then turned off along country lanes, heading for Abridge. We had been traveling along a lane for about three miles when my dad suddenly said that he had been watching a silver light in the sky, which appeared to be following our car. I looked up and to the left and suggested that it might be a star. "No," he said, "I have been watching it now for three or four miles and it is following the car. It is staying in the same spot and I do not know how it can do that. If we bear right or left it is always there in the same place." I had read of this happening several times before, so now I was starting to get quite interested. For some unknown reason, I still maintained that it was a star.

Then, Ellen, in a very quiet voice, said that she had seen it also and that she first noticed it as soon as we turned onto the dark lane. She said that it seemed to be waiting for us and when we turned down the lane, it started to follow. "Your dad is telling the truth, Mike," she continued, "and it is not a plane, helicopter or anything like that. It is very bright and an oval shape and now it is dropping altitude and is coming even closer. Mike, it is coming even closer! What is happening?" I tried to calm her down and as soon as I could, stopped in a small lay-by. The road was deserted but, just to be safe, I wanted to get the car off the lane and into the edge. We all stepped out into the darkness.

The sky was beautifully clear, with many stars shining, but this huge, brilliant oval light was outshining them all. I had turned off the ignition and we were in total silence, Ellen, Mum, Dad and me. The object had also come to a stop. It hovered above the field in all its glory, shining on the land below. I looked to Ellen. "Do you believe now?" I asked. She looked up, and I could see the light from the object reflecting on her forehead. The girl that once, so adamantly, did not believe, now had the light from a UFO reflecting on her forehead. I looked across at Mum and Dad and saw their faces so serene and Dad was, once again, witnessing a strange vehicle from another star system. "Look," my girlfriend said, "it's moving!" I glanced backwards, to see this beautiful, oval machine gaining even more brilliance as, in total silence, it moved across the field in our direction, gaining altitude as it did so. It went over our heads and momentarily lit up the tarmac of this tiny lane. We turned, to see it majestically zoom up into the night sky. In no time at all, it was lost to view in the starry firmament. That was another one of those moments. A moment to feed one's soul. The vast majority of people at this time did not believe and the government, as far as we were aware, believed even less. Look what they were all missing! This intelligence had, in recent weeks, twice answered my requests. I felt so connected to this intelligence. This is the family I told my mother about when I was a child. This was where my tiger came from. This is where Tellos resides and as the years pass I fraternize even more with these beautiful beings.

When I saw Ellen a couple of days later, another ground-breaking event happened. She asked for a sighting report so that she could fill it in. I took her one the following day and, very neatly, she answered all the questions, but was adamant that her name must never be mentioned. I still have this report and have not mentioned her real name here to retain her privacy.

About one year later we did go our separate ways, but not because of Ufology. People change, and that experience was not meant to hold us together; it was simply answering my request at that particular time. Did it change her in any way? Well, she never again laughed or belittled me about this subject and we did have some conversations after that about 'Life out there'. Therefore, I suppose it did change her at some level. This is the thing, you see, all you have to do is open that door a little. The gap can be imperceivable but that is all it takes to let in the Light. To show you that there is another way. Another way of looking. Another way of seeing. Another way of Being. Anyway, my life moved on and my experiences continued apace. I was to meet Tellos several times over the next few years and eventually, in Nevada in 2004, he finally revealed who he was. More of that later.

CHAPTER 10

THE TV SPACE MESSAGE OF 1977

We approached a planet
Circling their sun.
I felt inside my mind
That the journey's just begun.
I wondered about their science
And technology.
How could we have come so far?
Was this relativity?

In May 1977, I finally decided to leave Essex and make the move to Warminster. I had thought about it for a number of years but for one reason or another, it never seemed quite right. Now the opportunity arose again and Fate took its course.

I received a letter from Tom and Susan, who had moved to Warminster from Lincolnshire. They heard stories from some local Ufologists about my experiences at Starr Hill and Cradle Hill and asked me to go and stay for the weekend. There was no hesitation on my part and I was down there within a week. We all got on incredibly well and they asked me if I wanted to move down and live with them. This, I thought, really was the right time and again I had no hesitation in giving them a reply. I gave up my job as Assistant Export Manager at a large electronic components manufacturer, and made the move South. I was like a kid with a new toy. Cradle Hill was literally a short walk up the road and Starr Hill was just a short car journey. I could, if I so wished, now go out every night and sky-watch at the places where so much had happened to me in the past.

In those days, people were coming from all around the world in the hope of seeing our visitors from the skies, and they were often asked back for a late night cuppa and chat about the evening's events, or for stories that they could bring to the table from around the globe. We did meet some weird people who, unfortunately, have always gone with the subject, but also some very lovely, intelligent people who became our greatest friends and who would remain in touch for many years. In fact, some of them are still good friends and still keep in contact.

We were, at this time, running a small magazine on local UFO events, and were quite aware that our telephone was being tapped and that the mail was either tampered with or simply never arrived. This seemed to be a common procedure at the time, and although we found it rather irritating, we accepted the fact that the authorities (whoever they were) had to play their little games.

One such event happened on the 26 November 1977, when Space People interrupted the TV news broadcast that was being read by Ivor Mills on Southern ITV, at 5.12 p.m. They over-rode the TV signal to broadcast their message for five and a half minutes and TV controllers were powerless to turn it off! The engineers at Croydon, in Surrey, were initially not even aware that the break in transmission had taken place, as it did not register on their instruments. I had a friend at the time, who worked for the station, and he told me that they had special equipment laid into the system so that this very thing simply could not happen. It would register on dials and devices that were in place, which would shut that transmitter down, etc. He also had a copy of the tape and I wish now I had asked him for a copy, but at the time I just made a typed copy of the transcript. It was a calm, slow voice, but sounded like it was coming through static or, as someone once described, as if through water. It sounded very authoritative.

Two transmitters, at least, were used, but there was talk of at least five. The two that were mentioned were at Hannington, about six miles Northwest of Basingstoke in Hampshire, and at Rowridge, on the Isle of Wight, about four miles Southwest of Newport.

A large part of the South of England, including the Southern outskirts of London, picked up the message and it created some panic.

Switchboards were swamped for hours following the event, with people ringing up in terror, or simply wanting to know what was going on. Typically, some people thought that the world was about to end. This was a strange and intrusive event and was witnessed by hundreds of thousands of people and tens of thousands blocked the switchboards for hours.

For some reason, the South of England was then, and has been since, a focal point for UFO sightings. To this day, most of the UK crop circles appear in the South and many ancient monuments, sacred sites and a plethora of tumuli are in that area, for example: Stonehenge, Avebury, Silbury Hill, Glastonbury Tor, etc. Perhaps there is a connection here worth investigating?

Should not this have been front-page news? Should not the whole message have been printed for the rest of the nation to see? Was this not a message for humankind? What right have those in control got to stop us fraternizing with our friends out there in space, who have our well-being at heart? We had the opportunity here, of changing our ways and becoming more responsible planetary citizens. If we could ever become more responsible citizens, not only to each other but towards all sentient life on this planet and, of course, to dear Mother Earth, we would then have a greater opportunity of becoming part of a much wider universal family.

The following day, not one paper provided a full story of what had happened and not one paper put into print the message. Only the first paragraph was printed in some papers, and that did not go anywhere near what the message had to say.

News of the World, 27 November 1977:
"A Southern T.V. spokesman said later: 'We have been flooded with calls. Our engineers are trying to discover what happened. We are assuming it was a rather sick hoax. We cannot imagine how it was done, but it appears that someone must have managed to transmit a signal over ours. The equipment used would need to be fairly sophisticated and expensive'."

Sunday Express, 27 November 1977:
"A Post Office spokesman said: 'Either a transmitter, or some kind of link into land lines, was used by someone and they managed to get across to the transmitters at Rowridge and at Hannington'."

The Sun, 27 November 1977:
"Post Office experts tracked down the hoax transmission to Hannington in Hampshire. But they still do not know who was responsible or how it was done."

The Sunday Times stated:
"There exists a round-the-clock surveillance system to stop this sort of thing happening and the booster masts are equipped with safeguards, such as coded messages, known as insertion signals, as part of this monitoring system."

To put this matter to rest once and for all, the *Sunday Times*, on the 4 December 1977, put into print that the official answer was a student prank, using just £80-worth of equipment. However, the article failed to say why the TV company, with all its expensive, high-tech devices, which were in place at that time, failed to stop the five-and-a-half minute message, and why their station then decided to come back on-line only after the message was over!

It was difficult, listening to the tape, to actually capture the name of the messenger. It sounded a bit like 'Gramaha', but several other names were suggested. Here, for the purposes of this chapter, I will call him Gramaha.

The Space Message
"This is the voice of Gramaha, the representative of the Ashtar Galactic Command, speaking to you. For many years now you have seen us as lights in the skies. We speak to you now in peace and wisdom, as we have

done to your brothers and sisters all over this, your planet, Earth. We come to warn you of the destiny of your race and your worlds, so that you may communicate to your fellow beings the course you must take to avoid the disasters, which threaten your worlds, and the beings of our worlds around you. This is in order that you may share in the great awakening, as the planet passes into the New Age of Aquarius. The New Age can be a time of great peace and evolution for your race, but only if your rulers are made aware of the evil forces that can overshadow their judgments.

Be still now, and listen, for your chance may not come again. For many years, your scientists, governments, and generals have not heeded our warnings; they have continued to experiment with the evil forces of what you call nuclear energy. Atomic bombs can destroy the earth, and the beings of your sister worlds, in a moment. The wastes from atomic power stations will poison your planet for many thousands of your years to come. We, who have followed the path of evolution for far longer then you, have long since realized this – that atomic energy is always directed against life. It has no peaceful application. Its use, and research into its use, must be ceased at once, or you all risk destruction. All weapons of evil must be removed. The time of conflict is now past and the race of which you are a part may proceed to the highest planes of evolution if you show yourselves worthy to do this. You have but a short time to learn to live together, in peace and goodwill. Small groups all over the planet are learning this, and exist to pass on the light of the dawning New Age to you all. You are free to accept or reject their teachings, but only those who learn to live in peace will pass to the higher realms of spiritual evolution.

Hear now the voice of Gramaha, the representative of the Ashtar Galactic Command, speaking to you. Be aware also that there are many false prophets and guides operating on your world. They will suck your energy from you – the energy you call money – and will put it to evil ends, giving you worthless dross in return. Your inner, divine self will protect you from this. You must learn to be sensitive to the voice within, that can tell you what is truth and what is confusion, chaos, and untruth. Learn to listen to the voice of Truth which is within you, and you will lead yourselves on to the path of evolution.

This is our message to you, our dear friends. We have watched you growing for many years, as you, too, have watched our lights in your skies. You know now that we are here, and that there are more beings on, and around, your earth than your scientists admit. We are deeply concerned about you and your path towards the light, and we will do all we can to help you. Have no fears. Seek only to know yourselves and live in harmony with the ways of your planet, Earth. We, of the Ashtar Galactic Command, thank you for your attention. We are now leaving the planes of your existence. May you be blessed by the supreme love and truth of the cosmos."

End of message.

On the same day that this message broke onto the TV station, we had arranged to go to Chandler's Ford, in Hampshire, to stay with friends for the weekend. Chandler's Ford happens to be about halfway between Hannington and Rowridge, the two transmitters that broadcast the message. On Friday evening we telephoned Alan, the fourth member of our group, who lived in Trowbridge, ten miles North of Warminster. The important thing to mention here is that he was the only person who was told of our journey to Chandler's Ford.

We left about 10 a.m. and arrived, after a detour stop at Stonehenge, about 1 p.m. We went out for a couple of hours, walking in the country, and returned around 4 p.m. After tea and cakes, all the others went into the conservatory with their guitars and sang songs, joked and talked. I was just catching the tail end of the football results and then the news came on. Ivor Mills sprang into action, telling us the day's events. At that moment, there was lots of laughter coming from the conservatory and I decided to turn off the news and join the merry crew. If I had waited just a couple more minutes, I would have heard the broadcast message myself, but it obviously was not to be.

About thirty minutes later, we had a call from a friend, who told us what had happened. We telephoned a few more contacts and tried to get a bigger picture. At this point, I do not think we fully realized the impact of what had just happened, and we continued with our weekend of fun. Of course, we went out the following day to buy the papers. As I said earlier, the papers had already been 'got at' and not much information was available.

We arrived back in Warminster around midnight on the Sunday and waiting outside the house was a very annoyed Alan. He immediately approached our car and demanded to know what we had been doing in Hampshire. He said that Saturday evening two 'official-looking' men knocked at his door and asked him if he knew what had happened in Hampshire with the TV break-in. He answered that he was aware of the broadcast. They then told him that they knew we were at Chandler's Ford for the weekend, staying with friends, and they wanted to know how we had done it! Alan asked them how they knew we were at Chandler's Ford, to which they replied that they 'just knew' and that he was to leave it at that. He replied that we simply could not have done it and with that, they pushed past him, went straight upstairs, and into his UFO room. He said that they knew where his UFO room was. He was angry. He ran upstairs after them, and again they insisted that we had done the broadcast. They then left. Alan was now confused and he believed that we had been the cause of this 'break-in'. We were, after all, in the vicinity of the TV masts where it had all taken place, and that did seem to be a bit of a coincidence. Once again, we assured him that we were not responsible; it simply was not technically possible for us to do such a thing. He came in for a cup of tea and then went home, still angry that these men had pushed their way into his home.

The only way they could have known where we were that weekend was by listening in to our telephone conversations and the only way they could have known where Alan's UFO room was, was to have been in the house before, without his knowledge!

We never had any repercussions from all of this and the 'student prank' story obviously worked a treat. It is easy for them really, as it does not take much to pull the wool over people's eyes. A vast majority of people do not have the interest and energy to think about what is going on around them, and once an official body has spoken, it seems to be good enough. They need to heed the warning given by Gramaha: "Be still now, and listen, for your chance may not come again."

CHAPTER 11

DISCS, LIGHTS, AND THE STRANGE FIREBALL OF 1978

The river
Softly runs through ancient land,
Passing sunken standing stone
Set by antediluvian hand.
Here I sit,
To watch it glisten in the sun,
And shake the tall, sharp, knife-like blades
Whose roots along the bank do run.
What mighty reservoir
Could for an eternity contain
Unending fathoms flowing
Onto Man's domain?
May this be magic,
Or Nature's universal law,
How such a mass is charged
And moved forever more?

I traveled to Warminster, in Wiltshire, many times in the late 1960s/70s and in those eventful years experienced numerous sightings of UFOs, spending endless nights on top of Cradle Hill or down by the barn at Starr Hill, on the other side of town. Sometimes, for fun, we would flash our torch beam into the sky, wait a few seconds and back would come a flash equal to our own. Luminescent craft would hover nearby and again we would flash the torch a number of times and the craft would respond, equal to the number. We were so blasé in those days, due to the frequency of events, that these experiences were almost reduced to parlor games. I saw landed craft; aerial craft where smaller objects were ejected and landed in a field close by us; aerial craft that appeared in front of our eyes and disappeared in the same way; craft that affected our car and craft that would hover for one hour in front of our eyes and then continue their unknown journeys.

Many times the question has been thrown at me: 'Why have you seen so many UFOs?' The answer is simple: I receive a thought impression to be somewhere at a certain time, or to look out a window, or to open a door – and there in the sky will be a bright disc or luminous ball of light, hovering, waiting and a consciousness from it reaching into my mind. Back in 1983, on one of my *transitional experiences* (a word I prefer to use for when I am *'taken')*, I was told, telepathically, that I did not need to see them physically anymore. They said it would serve no future purpose and that now I was to use my mind to reach up to them. They said they were prepared to meet me half way, but that I also had to make some effort to raise my own frequency towards theirs. As soon as I started to do this I did, in fact, lose the need to see them in our skies and spent more time in meditation and raising my consciousness towards them. Since 1983, my *transitional experiences* have occurred with much greater frequency and in this higher presence I have touched the 'Source' and experienced truly the feeling of 'Oneness'. In that *state* there simply is no separation. You and the Universe are One. This, I am sure, is one of the gifts of fraternization with this higher source. We are being helped to re-connect with the 'Oneness' and, hopefully, through that contact, gain a greater understanding of who we really are.

However, one day in 1978 I had a sighting of the 'nuts-and-bolts' nature that left me speechless. I called it the night of the 'Fireball'.

We had a friend staying with us from America; his name is Marc Brinkerhoff [1] and apart from being a brilliant artist, he has also had many UFO experiences.

The day was 16 April, 1978, and Marc and myself, together with some friends, climbed to the top of Scratchbury Hill in Warminster to have a sky watch. At about 12.15 a.m. the others departed to another part of the town and Marc and I found ourselves alone.

We were lying on our backs on the grass, looking up at the millions of stars and talking about seeing a UFO, which, after all, was why we were there in the first place. After a while, Marc got up and went for a walk along the top of the hill. I stayed where I was, gazing skyward, wondering about life on other planets, and feeling, as I often did at times like these, an ability to communicate with the whole universe.

All of a sudden, I heard the sound of someone running towards me. I could feel the ground trembling (I was, after all, lying down and my ears were quite close to the ground!). Then, whoever it was ran right past me and I felt them brush past the right side of my head! I heard a voice in my mind, a telepathic message: "The Earth is dying! The Earth is in pain!" It was like a cry in the wilderness; a call from Mother Earth herself, as if desperately reaching out to someone! Anyone! I immediately sat up, thinking it was Marc playing around, but he was over in the distance in the opposite direction and I could just make him out in the darkness. I called to him and he walked over to me and said, "Who was that running past?" He, like me, had heard someone quite clearly but could not see who or what it was! We were excited but also a little bit unnerved, so we sat down on the grass and talked about the incident while scanning the sky above and the valley below.

A few seconds later I saw, in the distance, a small, star-like object coming towards us at great speed and I pointed it out to Marc. As we sat watching, it passed right over our heads and as it did so, expanded to about 50 times its size and brightness. It just 'exploded' into light. This explosion of light lasted just a few brief seconds, and then it went back to a tiny, star-like object and carried on its journey across the night sky. It was almost like it was saying 'hello' as it passed overhead! That expansion of light was an impressive thing to see. Marc grabbed his Super 8 cine camera and managed to capture a few frames. A still was taken from the film and is produced here. It was taken at 1.07 a.m. (Fig 4)

About an hour later we made our way back home and had hardly

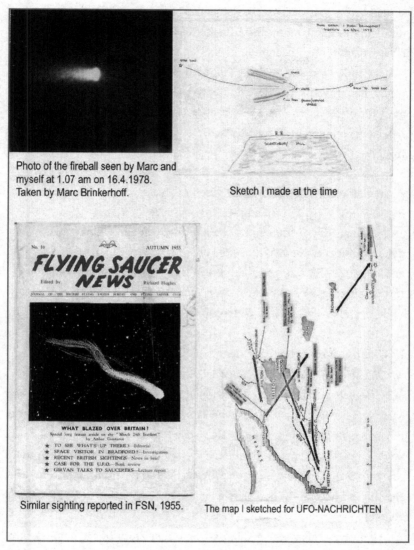

Photo of the fireball seen by Marc and myself at 1.07 am on 16.4.1978. Taken by Marc Brinkerhoff.

Sketch I made at the time

Similar sighting reported in FSN, 1955.

The map I sketched for UFO-NACHRICHTEN

Fig 4

stepped through the front door when the phone started ringing and we received calls for the next 24 hours from people who had seen the same object, or what seemed to be the same object! One man, a coach driver, skidded to a halt because the object he saw was so bright that it was reflecting in his wing mirrors! It was, in fact, behind the coach, but that is how bright it had become.

The following day I made a plan of the whole event, and the odd thing was, it had traveled in different directions within the same time frame and gave off different colors. Some people saw, as we had, what looked like red sparks coming out of the back. Below is just an example of sightings from the Bristol area alone:

a: Traveling S.W. @ 12.05 a.m. 'green and yellow'.
b: Traveling West @ 1.30 a.m. 'yellow with red tail'.
c: Traveling S.E. @ 1.05 a.m. 'green with green and yellow tail'.
d: Traveling N.E. @ 1.00 a.m. 'red and blue with red tail'.
e: Traveling S.W. @ 12.55 a.m. 'green and yellow with same tail'.
f: (our sighting) Traveling S.E. over Scratchbury Hill @ 1.07 a.m. 'white tip with streams of red and yellow sparks and yellow, white and red tail'.

I actually wrote this up for a German magazine called *UFO-NACHRICHTEN*. Issue 251, June 1978.

Given that many people telephoned in to report the object, it seems Marc and I were the only ones who saw it as a small star before and after it became an explosion of light. Everyone else, it seems, only saw it as a huge, comet-like thing. It definitely was no comet or meteorite, of that I can be sure, as it was seen for at least two hours flying all around the Bristol and Weston-Super-Mare area alone, and following a horizontal course!

There were many other reports from other areas of the country but I have mislaid them over the years.

It does not end there, so I will continue.

A few years ago I purchased a package of 1950s Flying Saucer magazines, and one of them, *Flying Saucer News* of autumn 1955, edited by Richard Hughes, carried an article of an incident almost identical to the one I have just described to you. It was titled, 'What Blazed Over Britain?' by Arthur Constance.

I really could not believe this article! The colors, timing, trajectory; could it really be the same object 23 years later, or something remarkably similar?

It happened on 24 March 1955 and the object was seen across the entire country. There is even a map produced in the article that looks incredibly similar to my own. A large fiery object with tail was seen for many hours moving in all sorts of directions! One man from Wales saw the object first of all as a dot, then it burst into a glowing red object, then it went back to being a small star and shot upwards! That is almost identical to what Marc and I saw!

In the article it mentions that Arthur Constance, the following morning, purchased 180 newspapers from all parts of the country and settled down to an investigation that lasted 8 weeks.

So, what were these widespread events of 1955 and 1978? A large, fiery object on a horizontal course and which, for several hours, was seen to move to all points of the compass. One man, like us, also saw it as a small star before it burst into life and then returned once again to a small star! Some people also saw this object as a disc-like shape, both in 1955 and 1978! The colors seen in 1978 were the same as the colors seen in 1955: red, green, yellow, blue and silver and with tails and sparks!

As always, the authorities tried on both occasions to explain the objects away as meteorites. An explanation that simply does not fit the facts!

Who was the 'Being' who ran past my head and gave me a warning concerning Mother Earth, just before this object approached? Who he was and what the object was, I have no idea, but for me it is another anomalous event that will stay with me for the rest of my life.

June 1974. After hearing about the experiences I had been having in Warminster, my work mate Tim asked if he could accompany me on my next visit. I was happy to say yes and was also quite excited at the thought of what may happen to this 'raw recruit' down in the depths of Wiltshire.

We left Essex around 7 p.m. on the Friday evening and arrived at Starr Hill about 10.30 p.m. I backed the car up to the barn, turned off the engine and stepped out. We were immediately met with the silence that only places like this can provide. A true sanctuary for the adventurous mind. The sky was clear, which was always a bonus, and we were alone. Tim was amazed to see how much brighter the stars looked when there was none of the light pollution that you get when living in towns and cities. It was great to be here again; the excitement was almost tangible as it ran through my body and pulsed up and down my spine like the tingling effects of electricity. These were the days of wonder and whatever some people have said about Warminster; if they had seen only a quarter of what I experienced there all those years ago then they may have thought a bit differently.

We stood for over one hour looking for any movement in the sky that may have told us that we were not alone. Occasionally we pointed to the numerous satellites that would cross the starry heavens throughout the night. I might add here that sometimes these innocent-looking 'night travelers' were not always what they seemed to be. Often I would see one suddenly stop, wait a while then go back in the direction it had come from or move off at ninety degrees and take another course, then stop again! Satellites do not behave in this way and it was often open to debate with other sky watchers as to what some of these things were.

I suddenly saw something bright in the corner of my right eye and turned my head to see, heading straight for our direction, a very large, bright light following the little lane along which we had driven, and only about 300 feet (91.44 meters) off the ground. I excitedly pointed it out to Tim who was a bit unnerved by this sudden appearance. "What the hell is that?" he shouted. As the light got even closer it moved slightly to our left and out into the field and when it was level with us it stopped. It was a yellowish/white color and big! There was no noise at all and the utter silence that you get at Starr Hill seemed to make this even more eerie then it was. It stayed in front of us for over twenty minutes then decided to continue its journey. It was now heading onto the plains and I suddenly ran as fast as I could towards it. I could hear Tim's agitated voice in the background: "Wait for me! Don't leave me on my own!" as he raced to catch up with me. The light had again stopped. Tim arrived and, out of breath, told me that he thought I was just going to keep on running and he feared he would be left there alone. We again looked up at the light. What was it doing? It seemed to know we were there and it seemed to know that I had raced after it. Was that why it stopped the second time? We watched in silence for a few more minutes and then it began to move once more. It went round in a big semi-circle and came back to the opposite side of us. It waited approximately two more minutes then started to move away and gain altitude. It was now picking up speed all the time and in a very short space of time it had joined the millions of stars that were just pin-pricks of light. Tim was scared but also over-the-moon at this experience. It certainly pleased me as I felt a bit responsible for bringing him here in the first place.

Around 3 a.m. I decided to take him over to Cradle Hill, on the other side of town. I mean, he had to visit Cradle Hill, didn't he? At one time the most famous hill in the world for keen Ufologists. I was very surprised to find no one there. One car drove up shortly after we arrived and we had a brief chat with the occupants. They had driven a long way to get to Warminster and were en route to pitch their tent in the camp site in town but could not resist just a quick glimpse of Cradle Hill to whet their appetite. I then decided to take Tim for a walk up to the first copse. There were many strange stories about this copse and a visit was always on the cards. We climbed over the gate and started to walk up the track. We were discussing the light we had witnessed earlier at Starr. About a third of the way along the track a glowing man literally appeared by my left-hand side. Tim was on my right, by the edge of the field. At this point, Tim had not seen him and was happily talking away to me about how he felt after the 'light' experience. Out of the corner of my eye I was watching this man as he continued along at our pace. I now started to feel that I knew this person and later on in life (i.e. the regression sessions) I recognized who he was. He was, of course, my Space Brother whom I had seen as a child. I tried to stay calm and sent him thoughts of love. Do I tell Tim? Will he freak out and ruin what is happening? At this point I felt inside my mind that I had to keep looking straight ahead and continue walking to the copse. "Who are you?" I asked in my mind. This was really surreal because on the right-hand side, Tim was happily chatting away about the 'light' while I was now talking telepathically to my Space Brother, who was on my left! "You know who I am. Did your friend enjoy his experience?" "So that was you in the Light? You knew we would be here and how much this would mean to him?" I turned towards Tim and told him not to be scared but he needed to turn his head in my direction and as he turned towards me I also turned back to now fully look at my Space Brother. Tim gave a loud yell and, before our eyes, this man from the stars simply dematerialized. Tim was now hyper and wanted to know what the hell was going on. This was, after all, his first visit to Warminster and to things of this nature. To Tim, it was like a baptism of fire. I explained what had been happening while he was chatting away to me and obviously oblivious to my visitor. "This was arranged for you," I told him. "This was all arranged for you. How does that make you feel?" Tim was in no fit state to know how he felt and so we continued up to the copse. We had only taken a few steps when something else happened. I suddenly felt a strong heat right in the position of my third eye in the middle of my forehead. It was so precise it felt like a type of laser beam. I said nothing, but shortly after, Tim said that something was happening to his head and it was getting very hot. "Is it right in the middle of your forehead?" I asked. "Yes," he said, "how do you know?" I explained to him that the same thing was happening to me. It lasted for around two minutes and simply switched off in both of us at the same time. What this was I didn't have a clue but it was an interesting start to our weekend.

We were expecting much of the next two nights but nothing else happened for the duration of the time we were there. Mind you, there was no way we could feel disappointed, after all the things that happened on that first night. I did not think Tim would ever set foot in the place again but he did venture down one more time. This time though he went with his new girlfriend. I think secretly he wanted to impress her or scare her into his arms! He never saw a thing the entire weekend but perhaps his motives were wrong!

Living in Warminster was brilliant! We were meeting people from all around the world; people with similar interests and experiences. Lovely, genuine people, who, like ourselves, were trying to find their place in the world and the truth of what was going on. Our beliefs and experiences did not quite fit into 'normal society' and many locals thought we were either mad or under some delusion. The sad thing here is that, in the thirty years since, and despite massive global evidence that we are being visited, it has changed very little and governments still suppress the truth and people are still too apathetic to seek it out for themselves.

However, in the summer of 1978, my friend Jane, who worked for 'Help the Aged', was meeting up with other members of the organization in Weymouth, Dorset. They were having a collection day. She was taking her sister, Anna, along for the ride and asked me if I would like to join them and keep her sister company. It was a glorious day and a trip to the seaside would be fun, so I agreed to go. The three of us got into the car and I sat in the back, next to a seat full of collecting tins.

In just over an hour we arrived at the sea front. The sun was high with not a cloud in the sky. The beach was packed with parents and their children. Excited children with buckets, spades and ice creams. There was a Punch and Judy show in full flow and everyone seemed to be having a jolly good time. Jane found a suitable place along the promenade to park the car and with around 14 tins on her arms, she clanged up the road to meet the other members. We arranged to meet back by the car in four hours time.

Anna and I started to walk along the promenade when Anna noticed some donkeys on the beach and said that she would love to have a ride on one. So, for that short moment in time, flying saucers were not on my mind as we were in the process of looking for the next set of stone steps that would lead us down onto the beach and the donkeys. Suddenly my head just jerked backwards and I found myself looking straight up into the sky – and directly overhead was a typical flying saucer. It was round, with a dome on top and what looked like portholes around the rim. It was a metallic silver color and very highly polished, reflecting the powerful rays of the midday sun.

I watched it for around ten seconds and then called out to Anna to look up to the sky also. She quickly looked up, "Oh my god!" she said. "It's a flying saucer! I've never seen one before and it's absolutely beautiful."

We must have gazed up at this unexpected sight for at least a further forty seconds when I suddenly remembered that I had my camera hung around my neck and it was ready to shoot. It could have taken no more then two seconds to look down and grab the camera and point it skywards. I waved the camera around in the air trying to focus onto the strange object. "Where is it?" I asked Anna. "Where has it gone?" In complete amazement Anna told me that as soon as I looked down to grab my camera, a small cloud formed in the sky and the flying saucer shot behind it. She was pointing up and to the right of where the UFO had been and sure enough, there in a cloudless sky was a tiny white cloud, about six times the size of the saucer. For a short while it stayed motionless in the sky, almost as though it was playing some game. I held the camera tightly and was ready to shoot if it decided to reappear from its cover. It was a strange feeling because the beach was heaving with people; kids screaming, parents shouting and laughing, the Punch and Judy show in full swing, ting-a-linging ice cream vans, donkey rides and people walking along the prom as we were doing. Everyone was having a great time but all were totally unaware of what was happening in the sky above them. The small cloud then started to move slowly across the sky. It kept the same shape and never dissolved. We watched it until it moved beyond our physical vision.

I turned towards Anna. "Do you realize," I said, "that hundreds of people are here today, having fun and enjoying themselves and hovering above them for a short while was a craft from another planet, time or dimension and they all missed it. Isn't life strange?" This is another example of what I was saying in a previous chapter, that people just do not see what is happening above or around them.

There was not a breath of wind that day, yet that little cloud moved along at a steady pace, protecting its valuable cargo. I wonder how many more clouds there are like that?

When Jane returned four hours later, with her array of collecting tins, we told her what had happened. She was, of course, upset to have missed it and I could easily sympathize with how she felt. We went and had something to eat then made our way back to Warminster. It had been a strange day for many reasons and on reflection, with the force with which my neck swung back to make me look skywards, I was obviously meant to see it. Perhaps it was meant for Anna, as she had been desperate to see one for years, and what a sighting she had. With this subject you are always left with more questions then answers and so this sighting was added to the expanding list with the rest of them.

1 See: http://www.brinkart.com/

CHAPTER 12

TRANSITIONAL EXPERIENCES: THE CHANGING NATURE OF CONTACT

And as dark as the night
And unsure as I am,
I opened up.
I opened to the Divine Light within us all.
Is 'This' Love?
Universal Presence to the tips of one's fingers.

I have had many types of experiences throughout my life and as time has passed the nature of contacts have changed to include many transitional encounters in which I am taken, usually from my home, either physically or astrally, to meet with a variety of types of beings.

I am including below just a small sample of these.

2 June 1981, Warminster.
I immediately awoke from sleep and sensed that something was imminent. I turned to look at the clock. It was 2 a.m. precisely. In these situations I simply prepare my mind and wait for whatever is going to happen. I never usually wait for very long. A human-type form appeared in my room and stood by the window looking at me. Very quickly, a buzzing started in my head and rushed through my body. My whole body, in these situations, vibrates at an amazing speed. When it reaches a certain frequency or pitch, I then lift off the bed and go either through the closed window or ceiling. I love reaching this frequency and I also love the lift-off from my bed. The weightlessness feels good for my body and I feel less restricted.

We both went up into the night sky and I saw, high above me but rapidly closing, a huge, bright light. In a few more seconds we entered the light and I became aware of what looked like a spiral staircase ahead of me. The stairs appeared to be made of a green substance that was almost liquid and as I moved from one tread to the next, the one I had just left lost its form and disappeared. Initially I was reluctant to attempt the staircase because it appeared so insubstantial but the being that was with me, whom I could not see but whose presence I was aware of, urged me to climb to the top and, in the end, I did. Once on the stairs, they felt solid and there were even handrails. At the top of the staircase was a ceiling that seemed to be made of energy. It was the texture of a white, fluffy cloud but opaque and pearlescent. The voice told me to put my head through the 'level' – or words to that effect. When I did, and clambered up the final steps, I found myself in a circular room. I felt at the time that the stairs were not real but were part of a test; that having the courage to climb them was part of a test.

In the room were several shiny, metal-looking beds, more like operating tables but with the top surface padded in a pale cream material, which seemed to come up out of the floor. There were also machines of some sort around the walls of the room. A young-looking woman (about 28 Earth years) walked over to me. She was dressed in a one-piece ski-suit-style uniform, grass green in color; a similar shade to the staircase. She had around her waist a distinctive belt. It was the buckle that made it look unusual because it was a square tablet with small lights glowing on and off. She welcomed me to the craft and noticed that I was looking at the belt. She read my mind, which they all seem to do. "You wish to ask about this belt?" she said, pointing to the buckle. Before I could respond, she continued, "If I was to remove this belt I would cease to exist!" Why do they sometimes talk in riddles? Was she saying that she is a hologram projected by the technology of the belt? Or was there some other reason? I actually felt inside my mind that the belt controlled the environmental condition within her space suit and if the belt was removed whilst in an alien environment, she would die!

I was then asked to lie down on one of the beds. I don't remember getting on it but do remember that it was surprisingly comfortable. Another bed abutted to the foot of mine and at one point I lifted my head up and saw her lying on the other bed. Our feet were almost touching. I saw that we were connected by a thin black cable that ran into golden-colored metallic 'bracelets' around our ankles. I was told, in a nice way, to lie back down and keep myself flat. I was aware of movement around the beds and also that something was being done to both of us but was not sure what. Three or four more human-looking beings were positioned around the two beds. After a while they seemed to be finished and we were allowed to get up.

The two of us left the room via an arched doorway and turned left onto a corridor with curved walls. On the left-hand side of this corridor were similar open doorways but the inner, right-hand wall was made of a diamond-shaped mesh surrounding a wide, vertical tube. The tube appeared to be made of cream plastic or opaque glass and through it I could see swirling, misty colors: pale pink, yellow and a light mauvey-blue. I wondered at the time if this was part of the propulsion system.

We turned into the third doorway along and entered another small room and sat down. We sat on two seats that were connected side-on to the wall, so that the occupants would face each other. They looked solid, like brushed chrome but moulded to one's body as one sat. She asked me telepathically if I wanted to know anything. Well, I had a million things I wanted to ask her and so I immediately started firing questions, about, as the saying goes, 'life, the universe and everything'. She seemed to have a vast amount of knowledge and recall and her replies were instant and concise. In my mind I just kept seeing the faces of my friends back in Warminster when I repeated all that she was telling me. Once again she read my mind and told me that it was not the time to be releasing this knowledge. I have been told this before and also by the Light Beings in 2005. I don't understand this at all and find it very frustrating. Anyway, I had a plan! When it was time for me to leave the ship and say my goodbyes I would try to continually run over and over in my mind the words 'I will remember, I will remember' and I felt sure that would do the trick. She knew what I was thinking; she gave me 'one of those smiles', but I had a plan and I was sticking to it.

Then she said: "It is time for you to leave!" Immediately a silver-suited male appeared in the doorway. He had the fair hair I was used to, but shorter, almost in a bob that ended more or less midway between the bottom of his ear and the nape of his neck. He took me another two or three rooms further along the corridor and into a small chamber with a large central circle marked on the floor. This circle had a fine copper edge to it and within that circle was a slightly smaller circle, also edged in copper. Between the two copper rings was just a gap, so I assume the inner circle must have been supported underneath in some way as it was not attached to the floor. I had to move forward and stand on the inner circle. The male held his hand up, palm facing me, and said in my head: "Until the next time, I bid you farewell." I knew that I was supposed to hold my own hand up and that, indeed, this was a familiar ritual to me, but I was so intent on breaking whatever blocks they put on my memory that I ignored the courtesy gesture and just began to repeat in my mind: 'I will remember, I will remember.' A tube of light came down around my body, the buzzing started and instantaneously, that's how it seems, I was back in my bedroom lying on top of the duvet. For one brief moment I seemed to retain in my conscious memory all that she had told me but one second later it somehow pulled to the back of my mind and was gone. I heard, above the house, a faint humming sound. It gradually picked-up frequency and started to move away. I knew this was a craft and jumped off the bed, flew down the stairs and out the front door, to see a small light moving at great speed up into the night sky and in the next second it was simply out of sight. I went back inside, put on the kettle and made a cup of Earl Grey. I looked at the clock and noticed that it was now 4.10 a.m.

I was taken to this craft twice in the space of the next seven days and I feel absolutely sure that they have some influence on or some connection with, the future of mankind. By that I mean not just these particular beings, but all those visitors from our space and dimension and those from other dimensions who have concern for, and sometimes a part in, our evolutionary development, especially in relation to consciousness. Something is going to happen on this earth that will affect all units of consciousness; something of incredible importance. Humans and all life upon Mother Earth may have an opportunity to move into a higher state of awareness. To move their conscious being into the fifth dimension and on to a new stage of development and evolution. If the human race does not change, then the destruction of the Earth by humanity will become inevitable. The wrong people are in charge of this planet and society seems to be breaking down. Mother Earth is hanging on by threads.

Morning of 16 May, 1986, at 2.05 a.m. Went to bed at 00.30 a.m. and I was strongly aware that something was about to happen. I was not too sure of the 'energy' so I said my prayer of protection. 'As long as you come in the Light and Love of the One and Only True Living God then you are welcome. If you are not of the Light then you are not welcome here and I will not allow you to enter my space.'

At 1.35 a.m. I found myself incredibly hot and could not get comfortable. The bed sheet was damp with my sweat so I decided to get up, pull back the duvet and have a walk around. I looked out of the window a couple of times and went back to bed at 2.05 a.m. I had no sooner got under the duvet when the buzzing started in my head and moved through my body. I was aware of someone standing by the bed as I lifted off. I now followed the familiar route of going through the ceiling and up into the sky and into the 'light'.

I will digress here slightly to say that this particular facet of encounters with beings and craft is very common across the world. Rarely is this journey witnessed though. In 1989, a variety of witnesses, including Javier Perez de Cuellar, then Secretary General of the United Nations, and his two bodyguards, later revealed to be CIA agents, saw Linda Napolitano[1], accompanied by two 'gray' aliens, being floated from the closed window of her Manhattan apartment into the air and into a hovering UFO. When telling investigator Budd Hopkins about her experience, Linda tells of the fear she felt as she passed through the window pane and up into the sky in a beam of brilliant, bluish-white light that shone down from the bottom of the craft.

The two CIA agents were disturbed by what they saw and one wrote to Hopkins, describing his guilt at not being able to help Linda and saying:

"She was floating in midair in a bright beam of whitish-blue light, looking like an angel (in her white nightgown). She was then brought up into the bottom of a very large oval (about three-quarters the size of the building)."

Fran's Notes (FN:).

Linda was definitely *not* in a hypnagogic state, which is how these experiences are explained away by skeptics, psychologists and others ignorant of the true nature of this aspect of reality! To be fair, it would appear that experiences during the hypnagogic state can often mirror those experienced by contactees. A definition of the hypnagogic state is:

"That state of drowsiness preceding sleep, in which images or hallucinations are sometimes perceived."

Sleep paralysis can also occur during the hypnagogic state. One cannot claim that *all* experiences that occur to UFO contactees during the night-time are *not* experiences perceived in the hypnagogic state but equally, one cannot claim that they are! Each experience needs to be looked at on its merits and taken in the context of that person's overall experience (many contactees have a lifetime of regular contact with a wide variety of types of contact) and then compared to the body of similar reports from around the world. It is not inconceivable that beings from elsewhere may take advantage of that state simply because we are more receptive once the chatter of the conscious mind dies down.

Temporal lobe epilepsy is another favorite way psychologists and skeptics 'write-off' the experiences of those who interact with other beings. The medical definition of temporal lobe epilepsy is:

"An epileptic seizure often associated with temporal lobe disease and characterized by complex sensory, motor, and psychic symptoms such as impaired consciousness with amnesia, emotional outbursts, automatic behavior, and abnormal acts. Also called *psychomotor seizure*."

Again, some aspects of the *transition* experiences can be compared to some experiences of sufferers from temporal lobe epilepsy but to repeat, these need to be kept within the context of everything else the person experiences during their contact time and within the context of the current vast global phenomenon in which thousands of people from all walks of life, from diverse cultural backgrounds and speaking many different languages are all claiming the same experiences and, more often than not, experiences that include other witnesses.

Another globally-common aspect of these night-time experiences that would rule out the hypnagogic state theory is that those taken are sometimes returned with cuts, scoop marks, bruises and other body marks. They may be returned and placed in bed the wrong way round or in the wrong clothes, or with their clothes rearranged, for example: nightgowns and pyjamas on back to front. Even more bizarre and disconcerting are those occasions when people are returned to the wrong place. In her book *Abducted*, Ann Andrews tells of the many occasions when, as a baby and small child, her son, who has had ongoing transitional experiences, was found outside his cot, outside his room, outside the house whose outer doors were locked from the inside, even inside a locked shed. Another UK contactee first started to enquire into his own transitional encounters after a contact experience when he was 16 years old and had been visiting a friend for an evening of TV-watching. He spent the night at his friend's house, but awoke in the morning, after the experience, nude, in a bedroom in a different house some three miles away, his clothes still in the bedroom in which he had gone to sleep and inside a house still locked from the inside. If you read up on the many personal encounters that have been recorded you will find more such tales of folk who have been taken from their beds and put back in the wrong place.

cont:

A particular 'gripe' of mine is that so many, many times, when encountering skeptics and 'debunkers', I find that they just have not done their homework. Oftentimes they know the merest fragment about the subject. Recently I was asked to appear on a TV documentary that purported to look with an unbiased view at the phenomenon. I had my doubts as to the unbiased nature of the program when I saw that two major participants, already signed up, were well-known professionals in the fields of psychology and parapsychology, one of whom I have worked with before and both of whom I feel fail in their ability to look beyond their own beliefs that these experiences fall into one of the above two   categories, and who do not seem to take into account the diverse body of evidence that accompanies the overall phenomena, of which night-time journeys are only a part. I was further confirmed in my suspicions of the efficacy of the proposed documentary to give a fair, extensive and unbiased view when talking to one of the producers, who had never heard of Area 51, the Roswell crash, Budd Hopkins and Dr John Mack. A cursory search of the Internet on the subject of UFOs will throw all those up, before doing any serious research. With those factors before me I did not feel I was in safe hands and declined to do the program.

This and the following four paragraphs were added after I had sent the completed manuscript to my publisher. On the afternoon of Tuesday 12 September 2006, I received an unexpected telephone call from a TV producer, inviting me to take part in a two-hour discussion program, in London on the 14 September. I was told that this was a serious discussion program on the topic of UFOs and the paranormal. I asked how he had got my contact number and was told that this was from another TV company. I refused, explaining that I had been invited to take part in similar programs by various TV companies but always declined because I did not trust TV personnel to take the subject seriously and that my belief was that most such programs were set up to ridicule the participants. Nor did I trust them not to have invited dyed-in-the-wool skeptics, such as psychiatrists and psychologists, who tirelessly explain away world-wide phenomena as 'frontal-lobe epilepsy' or 'the hypnagogic state'. He said: "We would dearly love you to take part... We really want you on this program." He then went on to say that the program would consist of a group of people who have had paranormal experiences on one side of the studio and a selected audience on the other. The experiencers would have time to talk of their experiences and discussion would then ensue. I asked what the program was and he said: "It's a Kilroy-type program and I can promise you it will be a serious discussion." After protracted conversation, during which I was repeatedly reassured that the program would be of a serious nature, and after conferring with Fran, I finally agreed to do it. We decided that because I had been assured so many times that this was to be a serious debate, it was a good opportunity to present to the public some of the facts of this worldwide, on-going contact phenomenon, which is part of our reality on this planet and which will, in time, affect us all.

Just prior to our departure, I received an email from the show's Production Secretary which revealed that the show was hosted by a well-known female presenter. Only when we had arrived home did we discover that we had been involved in a new 'provocative' chat show.

On arrival at the studio and after I had signed the consent forms, the producer explained that the one-hour (not two as I had been told) show was divided into three, twenty-minute segments, each dealing with a different topic. He informed me that I was the 'star' of the 'paranormal' section (I think 'patsy' would probably be a more honest appellation when explaining their role to future guests) and told me I would have two minutes to talk about my experiences. Not what I had been led to believe during our telephone conversations. When I protested he replied: "Be succinct!" No one in their right minds can expect a person to explain a lifetime of contact with beings from elsewhere, which must perforce also be put into the context of the historical, ongoing global contact reality, in two minutes! In the event, those two minutes were interspersed with flippant remarks and low-level questions from the female presenter and amounted to a complete waste of time. When I say that the introductory preamble compared me to Captain Kirk and one of her first questions was: "Do they look like the little beings on the Cadbury's Smash advertisements?" that clearly indicates the level of serious interest in the subject and the level of her intellectual acuity.

I was then taken to a dressing room to await a call to the studio and, whilst in there, got another clue to the fact that what was ahead was not what I had been led to believe when the folk from the previous show (three are recorded in one day) returned to the Green Room and some of them stopped in the corridor to conduct a very heated discussion regarding their treatment during the recording of the show. The 'F' word was used quite a few times and it was clear that the treatment of those particular guests and their subject matter had engendered much anger and distress. Had I not been concerned that my expenses would not be paid (for there was no way I could afford the trip), I would probably have left at that stage.

Once on the studio set, the treatment of the participants in the previous sections of the program was crude and often hostile. It was clear that the aim was cheap entertainment at the discomfiture of others. It is a comment in itself that one of the main participants walked out. The introductory links clearly set a flippant and base tone and I knew what I was in for – indeed that applied to all of the invited participants who had paranormal experiences and who, like me, had been assured of a chance for a serious discussion. After the show, Fran and I had a meal with two of the other guests and found they had raised the same doubts as I had and had been similarly assured prior to accepting the invitation and subsequently felt similarly let down and betrayed. If people want to make or watch trash TV that is their choice. I personally never watch low-level material and certainly did not ever want to be part of such a program. I question if this is the way reputable TV should operate.

I think the greatest disappointment arising from this whole distressing experience was the abuse of trust. I came to trust the producer and what he told me about the nature of the program and was pleased that, at last, someone was prepared to take this very real and very extensive aspect of reality seriously. The greatest phenomenon in the whole contact reality is why people feel the need to ridicule and belittle experience that goes beyond their own frame of reference. It is a mind set and level of conscious thought that I cannot relate to. So, I would seriously warn anyone involved in this whole UFO/ Visitor phenomenon, who might be contemplating taking part in any TV or radio show, to be prepared for ridicule and not to be afraid to leave if treated disrespectfully. Too many minds are, as yet, still closed.

To go back to my own experience: I vaguely remember standing in a room and, the next minute, well, that's how it seems with these experiences, I was leaving the craft and descending towards the ground. A man dressed in a silver suit was with me and in a future regression I later came to know that he was my Space Brother, Tellos. As I looked down I saw hundreds of closely-knit houses and I remember thinking that this must be a city or town, but as I got closer it seemed to look familiar. We landed in a small garden. I looked around and thought to myself, "Why have we landed here?" My Space Brother telepathically told me that this was the home where I lived as a child. "Yes," I said excitedly, "of course it is. I can see that now. It's just a bit different to the old photographs I have in the family album taken in the 1950s." I looked up at Tellos and asked again why we were here. He turned to look at the sky and pointed. "Look up there," he said. I looked towards the sky and saw what I thought was a hot air balloon and, for some strange reason, it triggered a memory of six days earlier when I had seen the same thing. I am talking here of when I was a child of six years of age in 1957. I have always had a memory of seeing what I thought was a hot air balloon land in next door's garden. This was ridiculous of course, but that is what I remember. However, going through this experience again had triggered an earlier memory of a similar sight but this time the balloon was landing further away and I remember being disappointed about that. Then it started to get misty; it was a light mist and I could still see the balloon through this. Then, it got a lot thicker, like a thick fog. A light gray color and not unlike the smog we got in London at that time. The balloon still shone through this thick fog. It was a yellowish/white light, almost like it had its own luminescence. Then it started to get even thicker and I felt at this point that something was wrong. I turned around to walk away from the balloon and there was a similar light near to the ground and I started to walk towards that. The fog was so thick now that it felt like I was walking through treacle and I found it very difficult to move. Everything seemed to be slowing up and becoming sluggish and, again, I felt that something was wrong. Then the familiar buzzing started in my head and I became very disorientated and felt faint. I lost consciousness and was aware of falling. I was actually back into the mind of the six-year-old and was experiencing this from that part of my life. Something of great significance happened at that point to me as a child, and I still feel that 'significance' quite clearly as I type these words now. What it was about I am not sure. Why it was shown to me almost 30 years later I do not know. We are dealing with different levels of consciousness here and sometimes we have to accept that it may have nothing to do with the consciousness in our 3D mind. It may be something going on somewhere else, in the greater part of our awareness. We are multi-dimensional beings and we have to trust in the fact that these experiences are working at 'all levels' of our being.

If I get the chance and if it is right to do so, I will look into this at a future time. I now have images to reflect on in meditation and maybe that is the way to go. The higher mind will only release to us what we can deal with at any one time. Once you open your mind to these other realities your sense of purpose will open to you. Not only are we all one family here, we are one family with all that is out there too, but before we take the next step 'out there' we have to get our own house in order. We have to become aware of how we treat other humans and the animal kingdom, which also has a right to be here and experience the expression of conscious life. How we treat the planet is important, not just for now but for the future families that will incarnate here as part of their journey and, of course, our responsibility of care includes halting the destruction of our forests, stopping the wholesale mining of our minerals and ending the pollution and damage to Mother Earth herself.

What if you were told that there were a group of assorted beings who were on a journey through deep space, aboard a large spaceship. Their journey would take thousands of lifetimes to complete. Generations would be born on the craft and all that was needed for this long voyage had to be taken with them. There was nowhere to stop and refuel or replenish supplies. Yet those aboard the spacecraft began to use up their supplies recklessly and with no thought for the future. They polluted the on-board atmosphere, introduced diseases that killed or incapacitated many of the crew and even deliberately damaged the ship itself. What would be your opinion of those on the craft? Surely they must be mad or bad, to behave so recklessly and with such little concern for themselves and the craft? What if I said that the crew were called humans and that the closed-system spacecraft was the planet Earth? Would you change your opinion – or your behavior?

We do not own this planet; we do not even rent it. It is a gift from the Source to allow us to grow and become ever greater beings of Light. One day we will leave this earth for good. Our time will come to escape the cycle of death and rebirth and when that time comes we need to be able to look back and see a wonderful healthy planet for others to come and enjoy.

27 July 1995.

I could not sleep so I went into the living room and sat in my recliner. It was 3 a.m. No more then one minute passed when a man appeared in my room. He sat in the armchair next to mine and began to talk. I somehow recognized this man but he seemed to be in a different body. He seemed to be in a more earth-human form. He then nodded his head to indicate that my thinking was correct. Suddenly he changed and he now appeared in a white cloak and hood and he lowered his head. The action of him lowering his head seemed to be a trigger and I knew that it was imminent that I would be going with him. The buzzing started in my head and I slowly lifted off the recliner and maneuvered round so that my head faced the window. I then went straight through the closed window and immediately felt the change of air outside. The buzzing increased and I shot up into the night sky. I went very fast and had a tight feeling in my head due to the acceleration. I went into a light and found myself in a small room, which was square but had metallic-looking walls with rounded corners. There were no furnishings in the room. I was told to watch the wall and a flat screen with curved edges appeared as part of the wall itself, showing scenes of exploding bombs, with the words 'First World War' and 'Second World War' underneath the images. I thought I was then going to be shown a vision of the future but I suddenly heard a 'click' and the next thing I was coming back down and into my living room. For some reason I felt very drained and I sat in the recliner for about twenty minutes and noticed that it was now 3.34 a.m.

The following night the man returned and I was taken back into the light in the sky and the small room. Once again I was told to look at the wall and this time I was shown a vision of a flooded area, which I have seen on two earlier occasions. It is an image of Loch Ness but both roads East and West of the Loch have disappeared under water and it makes the Loch look totally different to how it is today. The man turned to me and said: "It's difficult to recognize, isn't it?" Once again I heard a 'click' and felt the buzzing in my head and body and I was returned to the living room.

24 October 1995.
I went to bed at 10.35 p.m. but awoke abruptly at 12.45 a.m. I sensed quite strongly that something was about to happen and prepared myself. A man appeared in my room, dressed in the classic one-piece uniform. This is made from what appears to be a very fine, silvery material with no obvious fastenings. It seems to be one-piece but could be a jacket and trousers with neat and concealed fastenings. In the early days of my experiences I used to wonder how they got these clothes on; did they use thought? Now I wonder if the fastenings are Velcro. I have read a few accounts from experiencers and military intelligence personnel, claiming that Velcro was one of the technologies passed on to us by our visitors. The man wore shoes that looked like they were made of a similar material to the suit but perhaps I thought that because they were also silver. While the suit had the usual folds and wrinkles of clothing material, the shoes were smooth, and narrowed at the toes with a rounded tip. They may have been boots, as they appeared to go under the trousers, which were fastened tightly around the ankles. He had no headgear but wore his fair hair to just above shoulder length, with a centre parting. As with most of the visitors of this type that I have encountered, he looked to be between 25 and 30 years old, by our standards, but was, I am sure, much older.

The buzzing started in my head and ran through my body. It reached a certain pitch and I lifted off. For some reason we went to the end of my drive and along the lane, traveling in an upright position but a few feet in the air. We turned the corner and then – 'Whoosh'. It took my breath away and my head shot back with the sheer speed that we were now traveling. It was like someone had grabbed hold of me at 100 mph as they shot past! We crossed over the small stream and started to gain altitude as we sped over the field. We were heading straight for the telegraph wires and I thought I would be decapitated! It was apparently all under control and we moved upwards, towards a bright, white light high in the sky. As we drew nearer and the light was immediately above us it appeared to me to be about the size of the front of a two-storey house. We arrived on the craft and I was coughing with a very dry throat, from the air I had inhaled as we traveled at speed. This would imply that we traveled physically, but it is not always easy to know if one goes in the physical or astral body.

There were five helpers that were waiting for 'arrivals' and as I arrived others were arriving also. The helpers were also in the silver suits and behind me two were guiding a new arrival through a doorway, one on each side, holding an arm. I sensed that they met the arrivals in a chamber elsewhere and brought them to this room. In front of me, around 27 feet away (8.23 meters) was the back wall of the room, a long wall and I cannot remember seeing the edges of the room. Along this wall ran a backless bench, which may have been part of the wall somehow, and on this sat a collection of adults. To my right, in front of this bench and nearer to me by about ten feet (3.05 meters) stood another group of about ten or so adults. I got the impression that these were newer arrivals than those on the bench. Most of the people were in day clothes but three women were in their nightgowns and two men were in pyjamas. All were subdued and looked confused but not alarmed. No one spoke but they stood or sat as if slightly sedated.

I have no more recollection of what went on until it was time to come back. I made my way into the kitchen to get a glass of water, as my throat was still very dry and my head felt odd and warm, like the after effects I sometimes get with the buzzing. I could still feel it twenty minutes later and eventually went back to bed to try and get some sleep.

15 April 1999.
I was in the kitchen making a drink. It was 10.15 p.m. All of a sudden there was a very loud noise in the hallway, immediately outside the kitchen door. For some reason I felt very uneasy. I sensed a presence and felt that all was not well. However, I shrugged off the feeling of disquiet and went to bed to read a book until I fell asleep.

At 1.44 a.m. I awoke suddenly and sensed someone in the room and the familiar frequency change began in my body. I struggled to pull out of it, as I was not happy with what was going on. I forced my eyes open but was immediately told to close them and, for some reason, I did. I then heard voices speaking: "Have we got him yet? Has he arrived?" There was other talk but I could not catch the words. What happened after that I do not know and was only aware of the situation after the buzzing returned and I floated back down and into the kitchen! This sometimes happens, that a person is returned to a room or place other than that from which they are taken.

Sunday Night, 25 August 2002.
It was 11 p.m. in the evening and I was reading a book and listening to some quiet background music. I had been feeling that something was going to happen for the past two hours. The energy felt fine and I was content to allow the evening to unfold. Then, quite suddenly, the energy gained momentum. It was now quite tangible and I put the book down and glanced around the room. Tellos materialized right in front of me and smiled that smile that eats into you and touches every fiber of your being with the depth of love that knows no boundaries. "It's time," he said, and in the next moment the familiar buzzing shot through my body and I lifted off. I just love this frequency so much. Everything is expanded and you feel so much more alive then you do in normal 3D form. I now found myself looking for the light of the craft and very soon it appeared in front

of me. I entered the 'light' and for a while lost my conscious mind, which seems to be common practice for most people having this type of experience. My next memory was of Tellos appearing once more and again we lifted off in the same manner as we left the 'craft' and shot down to the earth below. It was unrecognizable from such an altitude and it was not until I was to land that I realized where I was. We were standing in Portway, in Warminster, and outside the house I lived in back in the late 1970s. I was so excited! I was like a kid with a new toy. There did not appear to be anyone in and I peered through the window of the old, 18th-century terraced cottage. I cupped my hands around my eyes to get a better view. "Oh what great days we had when we all lived together!" I said to Tellos. "Come on," he said. "I am taking you somewhere else." We lifted off and went past the Nags Head public house, on past Cop Heap and up to Cradle Hill. 'Can you believe it,' I thought to myself, 'me and Tellos standing together on Cradle Hill!' I took a deep breath, then gave out a long sigh as I slowly turned around and scanned the view. "Do you remember all the experiences you had up here?" he asked, as he also looked around. "Yes," I replied, "they were the most amazing days of my life." I now felt very emotional as years of experiences, friends and car journeys from Essex, came flooding into my mind. Such richness and treasure. The mind can embrace so much if we only 'dare' to take the chance to look into other realities and possibilities. It is simply to do with the way we 'think' about ourselves and our surroundings. It truly is as simple as that. If we could just move away from the conditioning as to how we believe and accept what is 'real' and what is 'not real' and if we can be bothered to do this, then our mind would show us things that at the moment are beyond our comprehension. A man once said to me that even if a flying saucer landed in his garden he would not believe it! I do not know how to assure someone like that as to the realities of other worlds, but just think of how much he will miss along the way.

"It's time to go back," Tellos said, and we lifted off once more and in no time at all we were high in the sky and heading towards the 'light'. The next thing I remember is arriving back over my house and coming back into my sitting room. I entered the living room and, after a couple of minutes of getting over what had just occurred, I went to the kitchen and drank a large glass of water and then went to bed. In the morning I was sitting up in bed working over in my mind all that had happened the night before when, at 9.10 a.m, the telephone rang. It was the girl from the flat below. She was ringing from work and sounded terribly excited. "I was going to bang on your door this morning but I didn't like to," she said, "so as soon as I got in to work I just had to ring to tell you what happened last night!"

About three weeks earlier I had bumped into my new neighbor and we were talking in the car park. For some reason, I happened to mention that I was interested in UFOs. This caught her imagination and I was invited in for a cup of tea to continue the conversation. I have to gauge with people as to how much I tell them, as too much information can become uncomfortable and it can then have an adverse effect and also, some people have such closed, fear-based thought processes that they cannot handle deviations from what they consider 'normal'. However, she was asking all the right questions and I found myself telling her about my contacts and how I had arranged a UFO for my dad back in 1970 and also for my girlfriend a couple of years later. "I would love to have an experience like that," she said, "could you arrange it for me?" I told her that it does not work for everyone and it will only happen if she is 'ready' in her mind to have such an experience. Once, when Fran was away for six weeks, I asked Tellos to visit her. She awoke with a start in the night, to find three space people standing by her bed and her immediate reaction was terror. Instantly they went. "How do you think you will react?" I asked my neighbor. "Because if you show any fear then the experience may not happen at all or it will be cut short." Her response surprised me because she said that she would be absolutely excited but that she would stay calm and allow the experience to happen. "I will have no fear," she said, "and I want this to happen." I then told her that it would take about two to three weeks but I could not promise anything.

Now, during this excited phone call, she went on to tell me that the previous night she had an experience that changed her life. She was sitting up in bed reading when a light appeared outside her bedroom window. She started to get a buzzing in her ears and also a humming. A tingling went through her body and she slowly lifted off the bed and up to the ceiling. She then went through the ceiling with a fast whooshing sound and up into the sky. She saw a bright light way above her and went into that 'light'. She remembered no more until it was time for her to come back and she was lowered back onto the bed. She telephoned me a further four times that morning because she could not believe what had happened to her and she was just so excited. She said that she wanted to tell everybody about the experience but I warned her not to tell anyone who lacked an open mind because she just might regret it.

Whether this had been arranged by Tellos, I could not say, but it was, after all, an interesting coincidence. On the same night that Tellos came to take me to Warminster, my new neighbor downstairs was also visited by a light and had an experience that has 'changed her life'.

1 See *Suggested Reading* 12/1

CHAPTER 13

FACING THE FEAR

So now, looking back, I had nothing to fear.
Fate, its course through life is certain
To lift the veil and part the curtain;
To mend the soul through all it's hurting
Towards the Light with love and nurturing.

As implied in my account of the April 1999 experience, in the previous chapter, not all experiences are pleasant or positive. In fact, many are quite the opposite and even those encounters that are for our good can be frightening in the extreme when viewed through our 3D consciousness and mind set. It would be very naïve indeed to assume that 'out there' is all goodness and light; opposites and polarities exist on many planes and we need look no further than our own planet to see just how extreme these polarities can become, resolving themselves into good and evil. However, I feel it is quite safe to say that it is a relatively small percentage of Visitors that do not seem to have our well being at heart and some of these could very well reside in, on and around our own planet!

Many people who have experiences with other beings, especially where they are taken from their homes and beds, live with fear of these events. They experience or interpret what is happening to them as negative, unpleasant or even terrifying. The key word here is fear. We fear the unknown. We also fear through lack of understanding – and maybe, lack of total conscious memory of what actually transpired. Too little knowledge can be a dangerous thing and will cause us to react, through the conditioning of our minds, in a very predictable way. Watching too many horror films is not only bad for us but instills in our minds negative images of the basest kind. These images will lay undisturbed, filed away in their little boxes until a time comes when we need an explanation for what may be happening to us, such as having 'Alien Contact'. The only data we then have available is what is inside those files! Films and bad press generally create a belief pattern that horrible things are 'out there' waiting to eat us alive. I can assure you that there are certain 'patterns of energy' on our own world wanting to suffocate and consume us on a daily basis and we would probably find it much more beneficial to fraternize with some of these beings from other dimensions!

It is vitally important for us, as human beings, to remember who we are. We are, by right, very powerful spiritual units of consciousness. We are ancient in terms of our cosmic journey. Old souls playing out evolution on a grand scale. Nobody can take away our power unless we decide to give it away – which we do, regularly and in many ways.

Meditation is important. Going into the stillness of the mind and into the core of your being will enable you to have a greater understanding and knowledge of other fields of awareness. At this energetic level you can connect with the Source. The Prime Energy of 'All That Is'. From this magnificent place you can then draw your own power and light. And in times of need you can draw on that power and light for protection and reassurance. In this place there is no fear and through this understanding you will have much greater awareness of what is being experienced and, ultimately, you will be more fulfilled. There is no need to feel inferior or fear that you will not be able to cope. We are spiritual beings of great potential and at that level we can meet with other beings from the standpoint of spiritual love.

A very small percentage of my experiences have created fear and left me feeling concerned and I will explain here how I dealt with such things and how working through the fear and coming out the other side made me a much stronger person. This leads me to wonder whether even these experiences have in them some intrinsic value.

Here is one such experience that happened on 1 October 1996 at 2.50 a.m.:

Around midnight, whilst sitting in bed reading, I became aware of a strong feeling inside my body that something was about to happen. I was picking up an energy that I did not recognize. Eventually, around 1 a.m. I surrounded myself with Light, turned off the lamp and went to sleep.

I awoke at 2.20 a.m. to go to the toilet. I went back to bed and turned onto my right-hand side to go back to sleep, still with the impression that 'something' was around! About two minutes later I knew it was imminent and then the buzzing started in my head. Something was happening to the energy in the room; a disturbance that felt different to the usual anticipatory change. I lay there, keeping calm as I always do, and tried to become aware of what was happening. All of a sudden something leapt onto my back. The pillow behind me sank down and what felt like a knee dug painfully into my spine. I tried to move but could not. There was a sort of purring sound, not unlike a large cat, in my left ear. This was quite loud and I had the feeling of someone, or some thing, leaning over me. I could feel warm, sweaty breath going inside my ear. There was something seriously wrong here and I began to feel vulnerable. It was dark and I couldn't move. I wanted out and desperately tried to move. I discovered from earlier, similar experiences that if you break this paralysis and turn to confront the perpetrators they will leave.

After an enormous struggle of will and muscle, both of which seemed paralyzed as if by an outside force, I eventually managed to move my right arm, albeit very slowly and then I started to gradually turn over. The knee or limb pressed into my back was quite severe and was causing a considerable amount of pain and I desperately wanted to confront who or what was doing this. My head was now three quarters of the way round and I could see the darkened outline of a figure appearing above me. This was scary stuff but I needed to reclaim my power. Nobody could take away my spiritual light and I knew this. As I turned my head a fraction further and started to see a more definite shape, there was a whooshing sound, a loud sucking noise, like the last dregs of water disappearing down the sink hole, and this strange being, or whatever it was, shot straight back through the wall. Back the way it had come, I presumed! I turned the light on and got out of bed. I went to the bathroom and looked in the mirror and saw a red mark in the small of my back, where this creature had been pressing. I washed my face and ears, where it had breathed on me, made a cup of tea and sat down in the living room to think about what had happened. I felt this was no spaceman or entity capable of building a spacecraft and moving through space! No, I sensed that this was something primeval, something perhaps connected to this earth but in another time and space. Perhaps there is a kind of dimensional doorway in my bedroom? There are many questions that need answers. Anyway, I finished my cup of tea, went back to bed, turned off the light and eventually went to sleep.

Two days later this unpleasant creature was back and was once again pressing its knee into the small of my back. What made matters worse was that now it was gripping my shoulders tightly with its hands. The sweaty breathing in my ear was most disturbing and my mind now went into overdrive as it tried to make sense of what was happening. It had returned with a vengeance, a renewed vigor, and I feared that I may not have the strength this time to turn and confront it. What would happen if I could not muster this strength? What grisly fate would befall me? No, I had to summon the strength from my spiritual self; the energy I experience when in meditation, when I touch the Source. I am a powerful spiritual being and no creature of 'the night' was going to intimidate me! Did it not realize who I am? How dare it come into my space without an invitation! I once again moved my arm and then started to move my head. I again slowly turned to confront this misguided thing. Again I started to see the outline of what it was. The breathing into my ear seemed to quicken, as though it was trying also to increase its power over me. 'Over your dead body!' I thought to myself and continued to turn. I was just starting to see what I thought were its eyes when, whoosh, back it went. Sucked into wherever it came from.

This time I found it more difficult to sleep in the dark and decided to plug a small, 10-watt night light into the socket by my bed. Just enough light to take away the dark. The biggest thing to deal with here is the dark. That is the main obstacle to overcome. I also lit a candle every night for three months, as that is how long it took before I felt confident to return to normality. I find the candle to be a very powerful symbol for this sort of issue. I am not religious and have no need, personally, for the church or other denominations. My body is my temple and in that temple I feel I can commune with the Source. The doctrine of 'Original Sin' fills me with horrors and is nothing more than a cancerous growth that people have imposed on them and then carry around their neck throughout their lives. Having said that, for some people, leaving a Bible beside their pillow would be a good thing to do, or even the burning of incense. Some people may gain courage leaving a crystal beside or under their pillow. You should do whatever feels comfortable for you and what will give you the strength and courage to slowly work through your fear. There is nothing wrong with admitting you are scared or uneasy; it is how you deal with the issue that is what is important here.

After three months of lighting a candle, something quite remarkable happened. I woke-up one morning and found that all the fear was gone! Not only that, but I now seemed to be working on a totally different level. I felt I had moved up a few gears. It was most tangible and this 'change' allowed me to be in much greater control for any future events.

Working through fear can be a very esoteric experience and is a requirement in many mystery schools. The more I read about Shamanic Initiation the more I wondered about my own experience. Was this just an experience where a strange being emerged through a type of energy portal or were other factors at play here, that in the end took me to 'another place' in myself as part of a growth pattern? Turning it all, therefore, into a positive experience, because I am now working from a totally different part of my being, where fear is not such an issue.

Sometimes, through our fear, we may miss opportunities to explore deeper parts of ourselves. Opportunities for growth in a changing world. If there is going to be any sort of radical change in our collective perception of reality then we need to be ready, 2012 or otherwise. (Indeed, the ending of the current Creation Cycle and all that entails for our spiritual future, both individually and collectively (there being in reality no difference – just Oneness) may take place as early as 28 October 2011 and thus 2012 would be the first year of the New Age[1]). We need to let go of fear, look to the Light, seek Source, and embrace the opportunities for growth that may take place.

Someone told me over 30 years ago that we see what we want, fear or expect to see. Well, when the time comes, let us look for the Light that resides in us all.

1. See *Suggested Reading* 13/1

CHAPTER 14

THE LIGHT BEINGS ARRIVE

Never in all my life have I felt such heat burn through my body;
At that moment my heart gave birth to a million suns.
The power of that moment was so strong I feared for my existence!
Could my body of fragile flesh truly accept and feel such Love?
My soul caught fire today.

Saturday, 18 June 1994, at 2.50 a.m, something remarkable happened. An experience that left me deeply emotional and also excited for the future. I had, for some weeks, been sleeping in the living room, with a mattress on the floor, due to problems caused by an old back injury. It was warmer in there than in the bedroom and this had helped my recovery. However, for some weeks after I had fully recovered I still slept in this room. I wanted to go back to my bedroom but found it very difficult to do so. One night I made myself go back to my proper bed and, in a very short space of time, I began to feel highly uncomfortable and returned to the living room. I could not understand why I was feeling this way but reluctantly gave in. On that night of the 17 June, I had a strong feeling that something was about to happen. This was nothing new; it was something I had experienced many times before. I was perfectly okay with this feeling and would start to relax my mind and slowly become more sensitive to my surroundings. I would say, 99 per cent of the time this feeling ends with contact, either with my Space Brothers or another ET race.

I live in the top of a large country house and my living room has two walls of windows, six in each, making twelve in all, which give plenty of light and visibility. This is a beautiful room and one that is easy to relax in. A room that allows you to be creative. I have had many experiences in this room.

I awoke suddenly, instantly alert and aware that something was about
to happen. I looked at the clock; it was 2.50 a.m. I scanned the room, just
to see if I had company! When I am purposely woken at times like this I
will always wake totally alert. There is no drowsiness, as when you come
out of normal sleep. No slowly coming to your senses. How this happens
I do not know, but it is a feature of these experiences.

Then, something quite wonderful happened. A golden funnel[1] came
through the window. (Fig 5) It reminded me a little of a trombone. The
larger opening was inside the room and the outside part looked smaller.
While I was wondering what was going on, hundreds of colored lights,
like fireflies, darted out of the funnel and into the room. They danced
around near the ceiling. Then, numbers came out of the funnel, quickly
followed by letters and symbols. They all proceeded to dance around the

Fig 5

top of the room. Years later I saw illustrations in a book of ancient Hebrew writing, and some of those letters looked pretty similar.

Fran's Note (FN:). The ancient Egyptian Right Eye of Horus Mystery School teachings involved a mixture of Sacred Geometry and meditation. Once he had reached a certain level, the initiate might experience the 'vision' of a golden tube, from which came numbers and symbols. In his book *Nothing In This Book Is True, But It Is Exactly How Things Are*, Bob Frissell explains the geometric patterns and shapes that are formed during the first six stages of Creation. As the Creative energy moves within these shapes, three-dimensional objects begin to appear and the first to emerge is a tube torus. Next to form is the tetrahedron, the first of the Platonic Solids. Bob Frissell reports that Stan Tenen, of the Meru Foundation, "removed the minimum amount of matter to delineate the tube torus (giving the 3D Phi-Spiral[2]) and placed it inside a three-dimensional tetrahedron. He found that by shining light through it so that the shadow of that shape was projected out onto a two-dimensional surface, he could generate all the letters of the Hebrew alphabet, exactly as they are written." By moving the position of the Phi-spiral all the other main languages appear: Greek, Arabic, Sanskrit, and English. Language from Light.

cont:

Watching all these lights, symbols and numbers dancing around the ceiling was incredible enough but then something even more remarkable happened: two beings of pure, golden light emerged from the funnel. The one slightly in front, I sensed, was masculine and the other that was just a little further back, was feminine. The odd thing was that when they were coming through the funnel they looked about one foot (31cm) high, but as soon as they were out of the funnel they were around six feet two inches (1 meter 88 centimeters). This was a strange effect because I never saw how it happened. It was so fast, it was instant. The moment they emerged into the room, their size changed.

They came and hovered over me as I lay on the mattress and their faces were no more then one foot (31 centimeters) away. Their finely chiseled faces were beautiful to behold. Human in form but perfect. The golden brilliance shone down on me. Their eyes had seen all there was to see and Love was the answer.

At this point I somehow knew that they were going to merge with my body and I felt a sudden great pull towards these 'Light Beings'. (I do not know who these Beings are or where they come from so, for want of a better description, I have always referred to them as 'Light Beings', for that is how they appeared to me – beings of light, or energy in a much less dense form than our own). My heart felt heavy and my heartbeat increased. I started to breathe more heavily when, 'Whoosh', a phenomenal energy rush raced through my body. This was the energy of the Light Beings and I pulsated from my head to my feet. There was a wonderful feeling of love, purity and peace.

Then, above me was the most brilliant and pure 'White Light' that I have ever encountered and I knew that my immersion into that Light was imminent. I suddenly became aware of all my failures in this life and felt that I was not worthy to enter such a place of Divine Presence. And yet, I knew that this emergence was going to happen and I really had no say in the matter. Once again I felt a strong pull through my being and I found myself in 'The Light'. Once in this Light, all my failures in this life just melted away. It simply did not matter. It was such a small aspect of what I really am that it is just 'another experience'! I felt much more evolved in spirit than I do in my body. I was in complete and utter Oneness, and in this state there simply was no separation. It was like I was the Universe and the Universe was me. Nothing could exist outside of this Oneness because this Oneness was all there was. There was no 'outside'. This was complete in itself but – there was something else. There was something else even beyond this. There was some other 'Force' that surrounded all this and, quite simply, it was 'Love'. A universal, unconditional Love. At the back of all that exists is 'Love'!

Then, all the symbols went into my head and the masculine being told me that these symbols contained all the knowledge of the universe and at some point in the future they would release the understanding of these symbols. Or, if the time were right, my higher self would activate the understanding.

I then felt myself drawing back out of the Light and the Light Beings withdrew from my body. They went back through the funnel, followed by the numbers, symbols, letters and finally the stars. The funnel disappeared and I found myself alone.

My whole body was tingling and my head was buzzing. I lay still for about 30 minutes until the effects died down somewhat. I looked at the clock; it was 3.40 a.m. I sat up and made some notes. Throughout the whole of the following day I could still feel this energy in my body, along with the tingling, electrical effect.

The minute my consciousness shifted to this higher plane I saw quite clearly that the higher self of 'Mike' was much more highly evolved then this personality here on earth. It was shown to me as a necklace of pearls. The higher self was the complete necklace and the many pearls strung along the thread were parts of this 'Self'. 'Mike' was just one small aspect of the whole. I am sure this is the case for most people on this planet. 'Mike' has a commitment to this higher self. How he lives and leads his life on earth will, without doubt, have some effect on the whole. Much the same as we, as a species and a planetary body, have a responsibility to 'The Source'.

I have merged with the Light Beings several times since 1994 and I would like to point out here that it is a much different place to where my Space Brothers reside. When I merge with the Light Beings I go into a state of complete Oneness and in that place I feel I am at one with the Source. With my Space Brothers I have a totally different feeling. I do not merge as I do with the Light Beings but there is a love and bonding way beyond what we feel here on earth. There are no 'labels' or 'attachments' to this love; it is just a pureness of being together. An absolute trust and connection, where one feels extremely safe. Although my consciousness does not merge as it does with the Light Beings, there is a connection in the mind that would make you think that is so, because here on earth the personality gets in the way for such a connection to take place. This type of connection with my Space Brothers is something that humankind is working towards and a shift in consciousness would help take us to this next level.

An Interesting Coincidence

Just two months later I received in the post the September/October 1994 edition of *UFO Magazine*, edited by the late Graham Birdsall. On page 22 (Tony Dodd's page of latest UFO reports in UK), there was a small article about two fishermen who were traveling to the Lake District and as they approached one of the lakes they sighted a huge UFO. Below is the report:

"Two men were driving in the Lake District..... on Saturday June 18th 1994. They were attending a fishing trip and were not far from their destination.

At 2.30 a.m. one of the men suddenly shouted, "What the hell was that?" They observed a large, dull orange-colored, rotating sphere. They stopped the car to get a better look at the strange sight and noticed that the object was hovering silently about 100 feet (30.48 meters) above the ground against the backdrop of the valley sides.

They described the sphere as having a diameter of 300 feet (91.44 meters). Dark spots were visible over its surface. The phenomena moved slowly down the valley rotating as it moved out of sight before suddenly vanishing."

Credit: Bill Eatock.

I was fascinated by this sighting as it was the same night that I had my Light Beings experience and around the same time. I wrote to Tony Dodd and asked him if it would be possible to speak to the two fishermen so that

I could find out exactly where they were on the road to the lake, as it was the lake near where I live.

I received a letter saying that one of the fishermen was prepared to talk to me but the other man was too unnerved by the experience and wanted to forget the whole thing. I contacted the man that was willing to talk and asked him if he could remember exactly where he was on the road. He replied that they often went to the Lake District to fish and knew the road very well and he could tell me exactly where he was at the time. "Just before you come to 'the lake' (he named it)," he said, "there is a small lane on the right. It was over the junction of that lane that this craft was hovering. We stopped the car and got out and looked up at this thing. It was huge, about 300 feet (91.44 meters) in diameter. It was slowly turning and making a very low humming sound; almost silent. There were what looked like round windows around the edge and bright light was flooding out of them. It looked like a typical flying saucer. We watched it for several minutes and there was no other traffic on the road. Then it started to spin a bit faster, the humming increased and it headed off up the valley."

This little lane goes directly past my house and this craft would have practically gone by my living room window, which was no more than half a mile from where the fishermen stopped their car! Whether this was connected to the Light Beings, I do not know. If not, then it was certainly a busy night for a quiet rural area!

However, recently I have had a series of regressions, one of which was to look more closely at this experience. David Coggins arrived at my home on 3 July 2005, and spent five days looking into some of my UFO experiences. He has been working with 'Experiencers' for twenty years. During the regression, we got to the point where I remembered the Light Beings arriving and I became aware that they were again present in the room while the regression was taking place. With my eyes closed I told Fran and David where they were, but before that, David had already silently pointed out to Fran how the flame on the candle that was in that part of the room was flaring and changing shape.

At this point, still under hypnosis, I asked for a notebook and pen. Here, in Fran's (my partner) words, is what happened next:

We gave Mike an A4, spiral-bound notepad and a biro. The biro was a mistake; we had intended to give him a felt pen. He was lying almost flat in a recliner chair and propped the book on his stomach, holding it upright with his left hand with the biro in his right hand. The biro was thus almost perpendicular and we were worried it would run dry, held at that angle.

He began to draw neat rows of symbols, slowly and carefully, feeling along each line with his fingertips, still under hypnosis with his eyes closed, and then moving down to the next line. As you will see from the images reproduced in this book, no line overlapped or was very crooked. Where they curved it seemed to be deliberate. When he drew the globe and symbols on Fig 9, he drew the globe first, felt with his fingers and went back to the top of the page and drew the symbols, then he went back and drew the bent arrow, then the lines radiating out around the globe and lastly the symbol on the circumference of the globe. All with eyes closed.

He drew for over an hour; at times commenting on what he was drawing, at times very moved by the meaning of the symbols. It was very apparent to both of us watching that other presences were in the room and that he was being guided; that the symbols previously given to his deep subconscious were being released.

I would like to say that I understand the suspicions and skepticism regarding hypnotic regression and had more than a few doubts and fears myself until I sat through a few sessions and saw how it worked. I also felt the presence of the Light Beings - quite beyond my own frame of reference and again, no evidence for this, but it certainly was not imagination. I did not see them (I gather that if something is vibrating at a different frequency we cannot see it - this applies to many things we accept, such as radio waves, microwaves, etc. We don't see them but we see, hear or feel their effects) but I did feel the energy change in the room, quite dramatically, saw the candle flame suddenly widen and shoot up in the air and heard and saw the change in Mike once they arrived. His voice became more authoritative and it was obvious he was 'listening' and then relaying answers to our questions, rather than 'looking internally' and describing what he saw, as when talking about events he was exploring under regression. I think David and I were both glad the other was there during those sessions (originally it was just intended to be David and Mike) because we could each corroborate what the other saw and felt. The police use regression to help people remember things like number plates, etc[3]. Remote viewing requires a brain-wave state akin to that achieved during hypnotic regression and remote viewing was, and is, a highly prized tool developed by the military for long-distance spying. It was discovered through this that the mind is not limited by either space or time, even eons of time, so, for me, that gives added weight to the possibility that in the relaxed, regressed mind-state, it is possible to see clearly experiences buried in the subconscious mind or, maybe, to actually go back to the time and look again.

During this time we asked questions and following are some verbatim excerpts from the regression:

Mike has just been given the pad and pen:

Transcript of Mike Oram's Taped Regression Session, Tuesday 5, July 05
© Mike Oram 2005
N.B Transcript starts after D's initial process to relax Mike into the deeper level of consciousness.

Hypnotist = D
Subject = M
Questioner = F

D: When I talk to you, I am going to ask you questions about yourself and about your life. You will answer them very, very clearly. Can you tell us a little bit about yourself? Tell us how long have you lived in this house?

M: *16 years.*

D: 16 years you've lived in this house. Can you remember the first day you moved into the house? Because what I am going to do, I am going to put my hand on your forehead and when I put my hand on your forehead I am going to enhance your memory and I am going to bring back memories that are locked away in your subconscious and you are going to remember very, very clearly, in lots of details. You are going to go back to the time when you first moved into this house and tell us what attracted you to the house and what happened the first day that you moved in.

M: *It's the 16 June.*

D: How did you move in, how did your furniture come?

M: *Pickfords.*

D: Pickfords. Where did it come from?

M: *From Holme Mills.*

D: From Holme Mills. Did you come in your own car?

M: *We came in our own car. They'd been told it was a bungalow, so they were a bit pissed off about that.*

D: You remember all the details. Can you tell me what your first job was when you left school?

M: *It was some sort of money transaction place – but I was only there for two days.*

D: You were only there for two days? What happened after two days?

M: *I got a job as a .. in a tea brokers - in Ewart, Carr and Hope.*

D: Did you like that job?

M: *I liked it at first, I was a messenger boy, then I got ... I wanted to be a trainee tea taster so I managed to get a job at Lipton's.*

D: Did you like the job at Lipton's?

M: *I did.*

D: Yes... and you are remembering everything about the job and the things that you liked at Lipton's. Whereabouts was that?

M: *Bethnal Green Road. Top end, near Liverpool Street.*

D: You're doing very, very well and you are remembering in very much detail, very, very graphic details about your past, about your past life. In particular, I want you to go back and I want you to tell me about any unusual or interesting experiences that you've had during your life. I want you to tell us about them........any interesting or unusual experiences that you've had during your life.... and I want you to tell us about them. Mike, are you listening to my voice?

M: *Yes, I am.*

D: I want you to go back to the time when you had the experience with the Light Beings in June of 1994. Do you remember that experience with the Light Beings?

M: *Absolutely.*

D: Can you describe the Light Beings? Can you describe where you are at the time?

M: *I was lying down on the floor, on the mattress. I woke up instantly. I knew something was going to happen. It was dark and so I watched and waited. Then this golden funnel came through the window and all these stars came out and danced round the room.*

D: The stars came into the room and danced around?

M: *Mmm.*

D: You can see those very, very clearly now can you?

M: *Yes. They danced around at the top of the room in a circle motion, in a large circle.*

D: How many stars were there? Lots?

M: *Over a hundred.*

D: Over a hundred. What happens next?

M: *Then these numbers came out ....*

D: .... Are you in the room at the time?

M: *Yes, I'm lying on the mattress.*

D: You're lying on the mattress.

M: *These numbers came out.*

D: Where was the Light Being?

M: *They hadn't appeared yet. The numbers came out and they danced around the room.*

D: Numbers came out and danced around the room.

M: *And then symbols came out – and last of all letters came out.*

D: Can you remember any symbols, any letters?

M: *Yes. Can you give me the pad? I need to do it with my eyes closed.*

D hands over an A4, spiral-bound notebook and a biro.

D: You need to do it with your eyes closed?

M: *Yes.*

D: You've got the pad there.

FN: Mike proceeds to draw 14 pages of symbols with the pad and biro

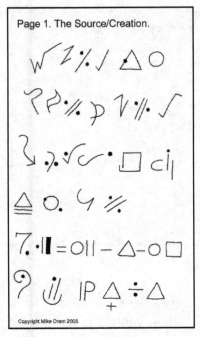

Page 1. The Source/Creation.

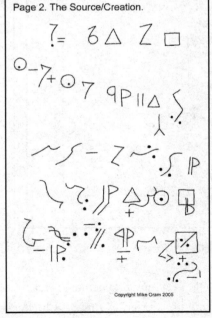

Page 2. The Source/Creation.

Fig 6   Fig 7

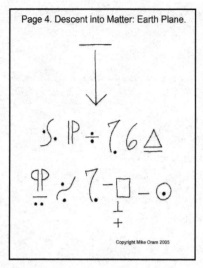

Page 4. Descent into Matter: Earth Plane.

Copyright Mike Oram 2005

Fig 8

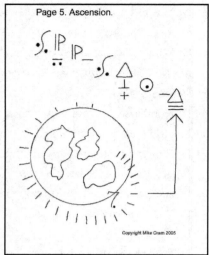

Page 5. Ascension.

Copyright Mike Oram 2005

Fig 9

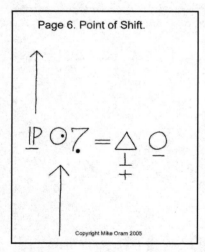

Page 6. Point of Shift.

Copyright Mike Oram 2005

Fig 10

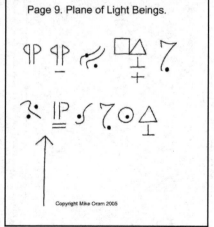

Page 9. Plane of Light Beings.

Copyright Mike Oram 2005

Fig 11

held in an upright position. (Figs 6 to 11). He draws neatly and precisely, with no overlap of rows. As he draws, he feels with his fingers for the correct place to write. He writes for over an hour. The biro, which should dry up held at that angle, lasts the whole time.

D: Would you prefer to sit up while you're doing that?

M: *No!*

D: Can I stop you for a mom.....

M: *No! It cannot be stopped!* .... (Pause) *I'm going into the Light!*

D: That's good!

Pause while Mike draws.

D: Ask the person what these symbols mean.

M: *I know what these symbols are.*

D: Can you tell us please.... tell us in your own words what these represent.

M: *These symbols represent Universal Love....*

D: ....Universal Love.....

M: *.... that comes from The Centre. All we need to know is in these symbols... nothing else matters...*

D: All we need to know...

Pause while Mike continues to write.

D: Would you ask a question for us? The question is: How do we interpret them or who can interpret them for us?

M: *They're saying that I can interpret them.*

D: You can interpret them? Would you write down your interpretation? Anything you like that will help us to understand your interpretation of the symbols. Just write it on top of there. You can open your eyes if you wish....

M: *... No! I'm in the Light...*

D: ... You're in the light?

M: *I'm in* The *Light!*

D: Thank you. Is there anything you'd like to tell us about how you feel in the Light?

M: *There is nothing else left to feel because you are in touch with The Source.*

D: When you say 'you', you mean...?

M: *Me.*

D: Does The Source want to give you any guidance?

M: *How can I commune with The Source?*

D: You cannot commune with the Source?

M: *I commune with the Light Beings.*

D: Will you commune with the Light Beings and ask them... will you send our greetings to the Light Beings.

M: *They send their love.*

D: Would they like to communicate to you now?

Silence

M: *They're seeking permission about these symbols............* (Pause) *These symbols are The Source. These symbols are what have created us and everything. This is The Source! On these two pages* (Fig 6 and Fig 7)... sobs... *This is The Source!......* (Pause) *The symbols have always been here! We are like children – we can't access them.....*

D: When you say...

M: *... I can access them...*

D: You can access them?

M: *I* can *access this but they are seeking permission – it may not happen tonight. This is the point we're moving to* (indicating symbols in Fig 10)

D: This is the point we're moving to?

M: *This is where we're moving to – soon!*

D: Right.

M: (Writing more and then pointing to symbols on the next page – still with eyes closed). *That's where the Light Beings are. This is where the*

Light Beings are. (Fig 11)

FN. In between Figs 10 and 11, Mike drew two pages, each with one long arrow pointing upwards. He pointed to these:

M: *That's how far we are away from the Light Beings and if we need to touch the Light we've got this other...* (Turning to Fig 10*)... this is our leap.*

F: And is this what...?

M: *This is the global consciousness. This is our next leap.*

F: Right – and can we make it?

M: *We can make it, but to live with The Source.... That's the next leap.*

F: How do we make it?

M: *A shift of electromagnetism.*

M: *Is this my page?* (Turning back pages and feeling the sheet with his fingers, eyes still closed)

F: Yes.

M: *That's where the Light Beings are. We don't need to know any more than that.*

F: Will they let you remember this when you are awake?

M: *I can access this information but they've got to ask for permission.*

F: For you to access it consciously?

M: *No – to release interpretations.*

F: To release it – in what way?

M: *To people.*

F: OK.

FN: At the time of writing this book, the Light Beings have not yet come back to give Mike permission to release interpretations of the symbols. This can feel frustrating but there are at least three factors to consider here:

1. During Mike's contacts with the Light Beings, it has been definitely inferred or implied that they take their instructions more directly from Source and it may be that they have not yet been given permission to

facilitate the interpretation from Mike's subconscious to his conscious mind.

2. If Time, as we are told by both off-world visitors and our own physicists[4], is a construction limited to 3D reality, then, living beyond that construct as they do, they may not be fully aware of how time passes for us and from their perspective may return 'in the moment'.

3. They said, both to Mike, and specifically in answer to Fran's question, that the symbols and their meanings are locked in our DNA and to unlock them we need to go within. They may be holding back to allow us to do this.

Cont:

D: Are the Light Beings with you now?

M: *Yes.*

D: Can you thank them....

M: *I have done.*

F: Can I ask them questions through you?

M: *Yes.*

F: Can... will we also be able to understand this?

M: *If I'm given permission to release the information, it will be done so that we can understand it.*

F: And this will affect our consciousness?

M: *Yes. This is the Shift..... it's in our DNA – it's here – we have it.*

FN: Scientists decoding the human DNA molecule discovered it had its own language of 3 billion genetic letters. According to molecular biologist, Michael Denton, the storage capacity of DNA is such that a teaspoon of DNA could contain all the information needed to build all the organisms that have ever lived on earth. Such sophisticated databanks could not be the result of a process of evolution but would need intelligent design.

In her book *The Convoluted Universe, Book 1*, Dolores Cannon tells of a client who also received symbols in a similar way to Mike. Under hypnotic regression 'J' says that the information is coming into her 'everywhere' and that she 'feels like a sponge'. If this information goes directly into the DNA, then it would be 'everywhere'.

F: How do we access it? If we don't understand how to access it, how can we access it? *How* do we access it?

M: *Because we have to be at peace with our self inside.*

F: So – quietness and balance would activate it?

M: *It would be a start.*

D: Would there be a name of a person on the Earth plane who can help us with this?

M: *If I'm given permission, I can help you with it.*

D: Could you ask when the permission will be....

M: *They won't say.*

F: They're doing that now, aren't they? Going to find out.

M: *Yes, they're going to seek permission – but it's in our self. We can activate it our self – by going within and by letting go.*

F: I don't understand. I mean, I understand the words but I don't understand how. Is there any way they can help?

M: *We are made up of these symbols. The symbols are what we are; it's a part of our journey. There's a part of our mind that can access this.*

F: But how do we find that – how do we tap into.....

M: ..... *By going within and reflecting on it.*

D: Is there a particular time, a particular place....?

M: *There will be a time when, if it is needed, it will be released. If people can't access it, it will be released.*

D: Do we know when that is likely to be?

M: *They won't say – not at the moment.*

F: Would studying Sacred Geometry help, or are these things a waste of time; you've just got to go within?

M: *Sacred Geometry could help because you do actually meditate on symbols and a part of those symbols is in this....is in.....is in........* (Trails off, long pause, starts to draw)

FN: Sacred Geometry maps the journey from the single energy origin-point of Creation through line and plane to solids and dimensions. The first solid to develop was the sphere and from this (and able to fit into this) came the tetrahedron (relating to Fire), cube (relating to Earth), octahedron (relating to Air), icosahedron (relating to Water) and dodecahedron (relating to Ether, Spirit and the DNA molecule). These shapes and solids are found in the basic building blocks of all life, including us. For example: the atomic structure of oxygen has a small tetrahedron inside a larger icosahedron.

The study of Sacred Geometry reveals a ratio or proportion that is known as the Golden Mean or Golden Section[5]. This is obtained by dividing a line in such a way that the whole line is longer than the longest section in the same proportion that that section is longer than the small section, for example: (Fig 12)

AB is to AC as AC is to CB

Fig 12

This ratio is 1.618 and is found throughout Nature. Human fingers, toes and bones are constructed on this ratio. It is found in animal skeletons, leaves and plants, and the spirals of sea shells and galaxies. Ancient buildings, especially temples and churches, were designed using these proportions, for example: the Parthenon at Athens, the Giza Pyramid, Chartres Cathedral, Notre Dame and Salisbury Cathedral. The Eden Project's Education Building in Cornwall has been designed using the Golden Section. It shows the harmony, connectedness and order of all things. The Greek philosopher, Heraclitus, called it 'Unity in Diversity'.

cont:

M: (drawing, eyes closed) *Here is a huge craft.......* (Is this the craft that the two fishermen saw?) *That's my mattress and that's where I'm lying. The Light Beings come out and go back through the funnel. They are male and female energies. It's like a massive electrical charge – when they leave my body I feel like I've been plugged into the mains and the whole room is buzzing, even though they have now left. The whole room is like electrically charged and I'm buzzing. I feel inside what touching The Source does to you inside. You feel like absolutely everything has been scrubbed pristine clean. It lasts 36 hours – this charge.*

D: 36 hours from now?

M: *When it happened.*

D: Is the charge still with you now?

M: *There's always a bit of it there. I can feel that – that's why I feel very close to The Source.*

F: Have you seen these beings before or since?

M: *I've seen them ever since a child. Seen them three times since that experience and it's all been here in this flat.*

F: In this room?

M: *In this flat. Twice in this room and once in the bedroom.*

F: Can you tell us about those experiences?

M: *Not now.*

D: Can you give any idea as to how long or when the Light Beings will be back with you?

M: *No. That's not up to me. I can't command the Light Beings. I can command certain Space People but I cannot command the Light Beings.*

D: Can you talk to the Space People now?

M: *Of course. I'm one of them.*

F: In what way are you one of them?

M: *Because I don't come from here. Never have done.*

F: Where do you come from?

M: *I can't tell you.*

F: Why not?

M: *It's not important – not relevant!*

D: Can you tell us how many and how often do you meet with other space beings like yourself?

M: *On this Earth? That are incarnated do you mean?*

D: Yes.

M: *10.*

F: Is **** one?

M: *You'll have to ask me another time.*

D: Does Fran know of any other space beings in her neighborhood? In her general area?

M: *You won't catch me out!*

D: I have no intention of catching you out!

M: *I can't reveal who they are. They have to reveal themselves.*

D: That's fine.

M: *It's not for me to reveal them.*

D: That's fine

F: In your conscious life here do *you* know them, who they are?

M: *Yes. I know who they are.*

F: And that would be reciprocal – they'd recognize you?

M: *They should do.*

F: Did you choose to come here?

M: *Yes.*

F: And do you know – I'm not asking you to reveal it – but do you know why you chose to come here?

M: *Yes. And a part of that – and I can only tell you a part – is to get this message out – is to do what I've been doing all my life: opening people's minds to the other realities, to what is real.*

D: May I gently say that we are not trying to catch anyone out; we're just trying to further our knowledge.

M: *That's OK. You won't catch me out and I can only reveal to you what I'm allowed to reveal...*

D: .... We're not trying to....

M: *....I can't be caught out.*

F: Well, you know me – I've got to be honest – I'm just basically curious and want to know as much as I can.

M: *So do I!*

D: We want to further not only our knowledge but the knowledge of all the people who are capable of assimilating and acting on this knowledge. We don't intend and we don't wish to catch anybody out.

M: *It's all in control. It's being taken care of.*

F: How does one find out one's purpose?

M: *Well, we can't have instant enlightenment. To find out one's purpose you have to go inside yourself because it is your decision to come here. You have made this choice. This is your journey and you have the answers.*

Pause

M: *This is why I didn't go through that star gate when I was told I could go home.*

FN: Below is Mike's account of what he calls his 'Star Gate' experience:

Synchronicity - 8 November 2003

I received an email this morning from my friend Laura, she informed me that today was Harmonic Convergence Day, a time when all planets are in a line, and that this was a good opportunity to ask for changes in your life. She said she had been in touch with her spiritual guide and he advised her that the best time for me to do this was between 3 p.m. to 5 p.m. in the afternoon but he insisted I had to be very careful what I asked for. I wasn't too sure what to think of this and continued working on the computer.

When at the computer, time seems to pass by at an alarming speed and when I next looked at my watch I was astonished to see that it was already 3.40 p.m. and four hours of my life had simply disappeared in a moment! I needed some fresh air fast and thinking about what Laura had said earlier in the email, I decided to take a stroll along the lane. It is a most beautiful, quiet country lane. An occasional car may pass but usually I am left alone to listen to the birds and sheep, while generally tuning-in to the solitude and peace that such a place conveys. I reached the bench at the crossroads, which is half-way along the journey, and sat down. It was now 4.10 p.m. and thinking about what Laura had said, I closed my eyes and tuned-in. After about five minutes I suddenly felt a presence to my right-hand side and opened my eyes. I was astonished to see Tellos, my Space Brother, standing beside me. He was glowing with energy and I could feel the Universal Love that he seemed to carry with him as part of his own self. He pointed to the other side of the lane and my vision followed. Then, to my amazement, what looked like an energy portal opened. It was oval in shape, about seven feet (2.13 meters) in height and five feet (1.52 meters) in diameter and hovered about one foot off the ground, if 'hovered' is the word. It rippled with energy. (Only three months later I was to see a similar device at Area 51 in Nevada!). Tellos looked back at me and, with great compassion, said that I could walk through this energy portal now and leave this life forever and return to my true homeland. I thought for a moment and then wondered about Fran, my partner. How could I just disappear without telling her what had happened? And anyway, I really felt that I had more to do here on earth, such as writing this book and talking to people, and Fran is also a part of that journey. I looked at Tellos and started to tell him what I was feeling but he already knew and smiled that smile that melts a million suns. Tellos moves me to tears without doing anything. I told him I had to stay and finish off what I came here to do. He said that if I stayed, then I would experience the coming changes and be of great help to people but there was a downside. He told me that I would have an unpleasant death, due to the conditions of the planet, and suffer much personal pain. (I am in constant daily pain anyway, as I suffer both from damage from a back injury and with peripheral neuropathy). I thought about this for a while but kept to my original decision. "But," I said, "I want a sign. I want a sign so obvious that I cannot fail to see it and that sign will tell me that I have made the right decision." Shortly after that the doorway closed. The entry to my home world was gone and I felt pain as it did so. For just one moment I wondered if I had done the right thing but on reflection, I knew I had.

I turned back towards Tellos and found him looking back at me. The Universe was in his eyes and I wondered how many marvels those eyes had seen. "I'm never far away," he said. Then, as I watched, he started to fade and in a few seconds was gone. The lane was back to 'normal'. Whatever normal is! I scanned around at the view and opposite me was a lone sheep, looking directly at me through the metal gate. I wondered if it had seen Tellos or the portal. Perhaps it was Tellos in one of his many disguises! Who knows?

I decided at that point to close my eyes and tune-in and see if anything would happen. It is relevant here to note that this is a quiet country lane, with only a few cars and the odd tractor passing along it each day. Within five minutes I heard some footsteps approaching and in the next few seconds they were quite close to me. I opened my eyes to see a man with his dog. The dog immediately went round to the back of the bench and lay down underneath. The man said that his dog was scared of cars and she felt safer under the bench. I replied that I had been here for 45 minutes and not one car had passed and then he said the strangest thing. He said, "At 5 o'clock it can get very busy! I normally come out at four in the afternoon to miss the traffic but for some reason I kept getting delayed." I looked down at the dog, which seemed quite at peace under the seat and didn't seem worried about all this impending traffic. He then went on to tell me that he had traveled all over the world but there was nowhere as beautiful as this lane. I agreed with him and told him that I had lived here for nearly 15 years and never get bored walking up and down this lane. He agreed and told me that he had lived here for 25 years and felt the same way. "Where do you live?" I asked him, there are only nine houses there and I have walked the lane a thousand times and never seen him before. He told me that he lived in the bungalow.

He then went on to say that in the winter this lane can get very icy and it is difficult to drive a car along it. Once again I agreed with him and remarked that only last winter I got stuck on the bend on a sheet of ice and ran to the farmer's house for assistance, but his wife had told me that he was out at an auction. She said, "He doesn't get paid for salting the lane and does it out of the kindness of his heart!"

The man smiled, then said, "Twenty-five years ago I got stuck in the lane at twenty minutes past midnight, in snow and ice, and I said to my wife that I would get out of the car and see if I could push it into the farmer's field because, if another car comes along, it will skid and run right into my car. Once I got out, I realized that there was nothing I could do as the snow was too deep. All of a sudden, three young girls appeared out of nowhere. They looked to be in their late teens, and said, 'Can we help you, Pop?' At first I was startled. Where had these girls come from? I told them that I needed to get my car back along the lane and into the field so that it would be out of the way and safe. 'Okay,' they said, 'get back in the car and we'll push you.' I got back in the car and they pushed me back down the lane and into the field. I immediately said to my wife that I would get out and thank them, but when I got out of the car they were gone! I could see right along the lane both ways as it was bright in the snow and the frost was twinkling. I said to my wife, 'They are not here!' 'What do you mean?' she said. 'Of course they are there! They have just pushed you into the field!' He looked at me and gestured with his arms, "But they were nowhere to be seen and I've never forgotten it!"

I told him what a fascinating story that was and he agreed. Then he stood up, said goodbye and walked back along the lane. Once at the top of the small rise he turned and shouted back, "I'll see if I can see the girls!" Then he disappeared over the hill-top.

I sat there for another ten minutes, wondering what all that was about. I had asked for a sign. Was that it? I was sure this man lived in the lane and that it was only pure coincidence that our paths had never crossed before. It was the timing and the stories he told that were baffling.

Perhaps that is the way that synchronicity works? It uses events that may already be set in motion as a way to confirm what you are asking for. It may be like, 'Yes, we have heard you and this is our proof. This is the synchronistic answer!' Somehow, in this case, it used a normal event, like a man taking his dog for a walk but making him later then he would normally have been. Then, for emphasis, he made a strange remark about traffic in a very quiet and rural lane! Then, an even stranger tale about the girls! Weird enough to perhaps register that this is not quite normal, i.e. the perfect timing. String all this together and it was enough to make me wonder if that was my sign.

I have been along the lane another five hundred times since then and still not seen the man with his dog, but I do believe that he lives in one of the nine houses.

Cont:

F: Because you've got other things to do?

M: *Because I've got things to do. Although they said I'd be in a lot of pain, that doesn't come into it because the message is far greater than any pain that I have to endure.*

F: In the space you are in now, can you see, or is there any way you can ask them or find out, if you can be healed?

M: *I asked earlier. I'm waiting to hear. I asked the Light Beings.*

F: And they have to ask about that as well?

M: *I'm afraid so. Perhaps Jason's right.* (Jason Andrews. The son of Ann Andrews, authoress of *Abducted,* 1998 and *Jason, My Indigo Child,* 2005).

F: That you can heal yourself?

M: *Yes.*

D: Do you personally feel now that there is anything else that you'd like to tell us?

M: *There are a lot of sleepers on this planet. By sleepers, I don't mean the people whose minds would be very difficult to open, I mean, there are sleepers here waiting for this shift in consciousness, so that when this time comes, for a lot of people it will be very straight forward. The sleepers are waiting in the wings.*

F: They are not aware that they are waiting in the wings, or they are aware?

M: *They're aware inside, they are not aware in their earthly mind, but they are ready.*

D: Are there many of these sleepers or only a few?

M: *No, there's a lot. There's a few thousand. A shift in consciousness and awareness is a natural thing for our divine self. It really is no problem – when the time is right. You know what it's like because you've done it many times before. You know inside. It's all inside. That's why I like to sit alone sometimes, because that is your key to who you are. You have to be at peace in yourself. It's very easy. We think it's difficult, but to sit in silence and to tune into your inner divine being is very easy.*

D: You do it many times?

M: *Every day.*

D: Do you do it consciously or subconsciously, or both?

M: *Both. I've done it since a child.*

D: How do you feel this helps you?

M: *Because it keeps me in tune with The Source and if you are in tune with The Source you're in tune with yourself. You are in tune with your journey and your journey is all that matters. We have to continually enrich our soul. Don't reflect on the negative and don't have fear.*

D: Do you feel it is important for you, yourself, to spread the understanding of the knowledge that you have?

M: *It has been my life. Of course it's important. It's what my life is all about. That's why I'm here. Of course it has to be important.*

D: How are you actively doing this now?

M: *By opening people's minds. You only have to open their mind a tiny, tiny bit to let the Light flood in and once that Light floods in, the door may not open for some people any wider but that Light will never then go – but for most people, once that Light comes in, the door will always widen – and that's what I've done all my life. You might only need a few words to somebody, just to shift their awareness, and you can do it in very indirect ways. You don't have to blow their mind. You just help them to shift their awareness – and that's what has to happen for this change.*

D: How much shift of awareness or how much will we measure this by before the shift in consciousness takes place with everyone?

M: *You can't put a figure on how much. The thing is, it's gaining momentum and has been for the last hundred years. It is like the famous exponential curve that we often talk about and, of course, the hundredth monkey syndrome.*

F: Do you think that 2012 is a significant date?

M: *When is eight years time?*

D: 2013.

M: *Well, let's say eight years time.*

D: Eight years time?

M: *Eight years time could be an important moment – or it may not! It's difficult to put a precise date because it is down to how quickly people change and that's where the hundredth monkey comes in. It could happen next week. It won't; but it could.*

D: Were the Light Beings with you, with us, in this room tonight?

M: *They were – didn't you feel them?*

D: I felt them through you. Will they come again?

M: *They will come when they know they have to come. We can't command the Light Beings to come. They will be here if they have to be here. There are certain things we have to do on our own. That's a part of our growth.*

F: Do you want to go and look at anything else now?

M: *No, I think that's it for tonight. I'll come back from this place. Perhaps we can have a look tomorrow?*

End of Session.

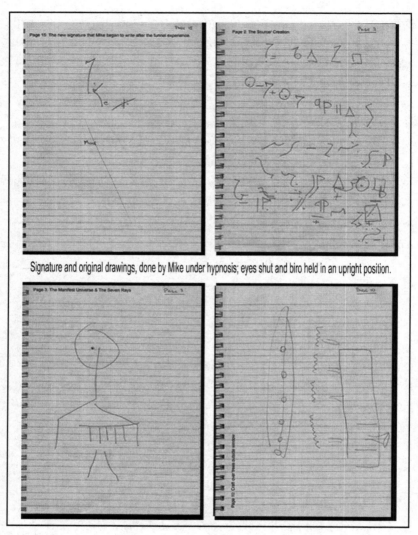

Signature and original drawings, done by Mike under hypnosis; eyes shut and biro held in an upright position.

Fig 13

As we looked through the symbols I had drawn, Fran commented that two or three of them were very similar to the components of my (rather flourishing) signature. Soon after the night of the original experience I had felt compelled to change the way I signed my name. As you can see from Fig

13, it now includes elements of those symbols given to me during my experience. Until Fran pointed it out, I had not realized where my new signature came from; I only knew that from the time of my experience in 1994, I had been compelled to change it.

FN: Signatures contain the energetic pattern of a person. Handwriting experts can tell much about a person's character traits, personality bent, strengths and weaknesses, from their signature. Police forces in many countries have employed graphologists to give them added information about suspects and many businesses and large companies will have a candidate's handwriting analyzed before considering them for employment. Psychics and psychometrists will 'read' a signature with their fingertips to gain information relating to the signee. The *Hygeia Method of Colour Therapy* uses a spine chart signed by the client to 'dowse' for imbalances and areas of disease. It is not unlikely therefore, that, after such an intense experience as that with the Light Beings, Mike's own energy pattern was changed and this was unconsciously expressed in his changed signature.

Fig 14

The symbols given by the Light Beings have a resonance, a dynamism; almost as if they should be dancing. Obviously they are important. Symbols are a higher form of communication and our subconscious mind, in particular, relates to symbols. Some, such as the spiral (Fig 14) and the cross (Fig 15) are archetypal, relating to universal patterns and processes stored in the collective consciousness. Some are personal coded images, created from our daily experiences, and our dream world, in particular, will use such symbols to help us problem solve or point us to areas of our life that need attention. Some symbols are both personal and archetypal, for example: a snake traditionally

Fig 15

represents energy, creation and transitions (two snakes entwined around a central pole is the symbol for the healing profession), but if you are afraid of snakes, then in your subconscious archetype it could also represent fear.

Symbols are powerful and can link directly and indirectly to objects, elements, attributes, emotions and stored knowledge. For example: if, in the middle of summer, you are sorting out a cupboard and come upon a card with an image of a traditional Christmas tree, immediately, without any words spoken to you, you know what festival this represents, you may get visual images of Christmases you have experienced, by association you may recall tastes and smells of food, mulled wine, crackling log fires; you may hear carols in your head or recall the feel of cold, crisp snowy days – all instantaneously from one symbolic image.

If you consider that everything on Earth (and in the Universe) has a frequency, a vibration, whether it be a thought, a word, an image or a sound, then it follows that a symbol will also have a vibration; one that affects our body cells. Each frequency has a correlating frequency and so the symbols, on a dynamic level, probably also have color, sound and shape. The science of Cymatics (from the Greek *kyma* or *wave/ frequency*) uses sand, liquids and filings to show how shapes form when sounds are played or words spoken. The final chord of Handel's *Messiah*, for example, produces a five-pointed star. People who suffer from (or are blessed by) synaesthesia, see these overlapping frequencies. They may see colors when music is played or hear sounds when they see flowers, etc. Each body cell communicates with other cells with pulses of light, and liquid crystals in our bodies transform one type of energy into another, for example: sound into form. In his book, *Cymatics,* Hans Jenny tells how the Creative process requires three fields: two poles, one of form, one of motion and in-between vibration and frequency. Cathie E. Guzetta, in his work, *Music Therapy: Nursing the Music of the Soul,* says:

"The forms of snowflakes and faces of flowers may take on their shape because they are responding to some sound in nature. Likewise, it is possible that crystals, plants, and human beings may be, in some way, music that has taken on visible form."

Fig 16

Interestingly, the Christian Bible states that Creation began with a 'word' i.e. sound vibration. (New Testament, Gospel of John: *In the beginning was the Word, and the Word was with God, and the Word*

Fig 17

was God. The same was in the beginning with God. All things were made by him; and without him (i.e. The Word – Vibration) was not any thing made that was made.) It is a reasonable postulation, therefore, that the symbols given by the Light Beings can affect the vibratory rate of our cells on many levels and so enable or help us to effect change.

Fig 18

It is quite feasible that symbols can carry knowledge of Universal Truths, of our creation and origins and of the relationships between our selves, the Earth and Nature, our cosmic neighbors and The Source. Is it coincidence that these symbols appear in the fabric of the Universe? For example:

Spirals appear in spiral galaxies (Fig 16), shells (Fig 17), the inner ear and a cabbage. They are often depicted in ancient art and structures, as seen on the curbstone at the entrance to the tomb at Newgrange (Fig 18). We are being given such symbols again in the many crop glyphs that appear across the planet? For example: (Fig 19). The spiral archetype permeates our world.

At first we tried to correlate the symbols with known ancient and other symbols, for example:

 (Fig 20) Supreme Being, beginning. Fig 19

 (Fig 21) Unity, infinity, wholeness, eternal, all possibilities.

 (Fig22) Sun / hydrogen, creative spark of divine consciousness, fire.

 (Fig 23) Frequency, wave form energy.

 (Fig 24) Earth.

 (Fig 25) Matter, physical plane of existence, perfection (| = spirit, – = material).

 (Fig 26) Fire, upward flow, masculine.

 (Fig 27) Water, downward flow, feminine.

And with symbols that were similar, for example:

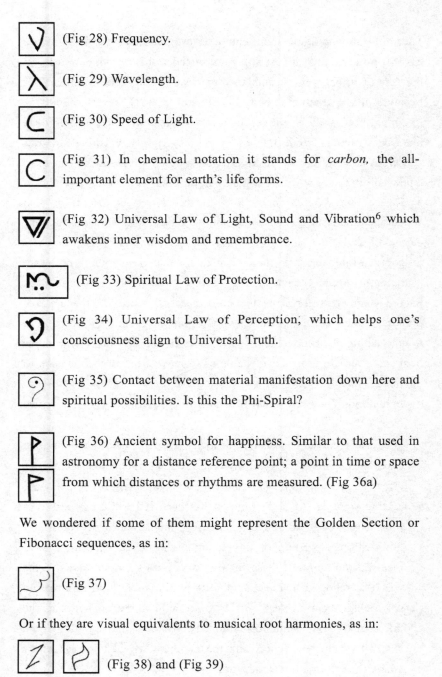

(Fig 28) Frequency.

(Fig 29) Wavelength.

(Fig 30) Speed of Light.

(Fig 31) In chemical notation it stands for *carbon,* the all-important element for earth's life forms.

(Fig 32) Universal Law of Light, Sound and Vibration[6] which awakens inner wisdom and remembrance.

(Fig 33) Spiritual Law of Protection.

(Fig 34) Universal Law of Perception, which helps one's consciousness align to Universal Truth.

(Fig 35) Contact between material manifestation down here and spiritual possibilities. Is this the Phi-Spiral?

(Fig 36) Ancient symbol for happiness. Similar to that used in astronomy for a distance reference point; a point in time or space from which distances or rhythms are measured. (Fig 36a)

We wondered if some of them might represent the Golden Section or Fibonacci sequences, as in:

(Fig 37)

Or if they are visual equivalents to musical root harmonies, as in:

(Fig 38) and (Fig 39)

Those of you who know about computer programming will know that a page of programming is just a page of coded words or symbols that, on the face of it, bears no resemblance to what appears on the screen. For example: the instruction '<body bgcolor="#0F00CD" text="#FF000 "> in simple html coding will result in a web page with red writing on a blue background. What if these symbols, rightly absorbed by our consciousness or our cells, result in either a newly-programmed 'us' or in a new ability to see reality. They may re-program our consciousness.

In the end we felt that while all this might be useful, it also encouraged the left-brain approach and we should follow the instructions of the Light Beings and go inwards for the answers. This process is on-going. Moreover, it is more than likely that the symbols represent a dynamic process that also involves movement and sound; as Sacred Geometry represents the movement of Source in the creative process within the Void, so these symbols may represent the movement of Source within us or movements our own spirit needs to make within our own cell structure in order to enable us to move from this dimension to the next.

In her book *The Convoluted Universe, Book1*, Dolores Cannon writes:

"I have received letters from many readers who have strange experiences of receiving information through symbols that seem to go directly into their brain. This sometimes occurs after, or while having, a UFO sighting. At other times it has occurred while the person is lying on a bed or sofa, and geometric symbols appear to enter their brain through a beam of light coming through a window. I have received too many of these reports to dismiss them as fantasy. This was also reported in *The Custodians,* as the aliens said information was being imparted very quickly on a cellular level. They said the information would come forth into the conscious mind at a future time when it would be needed, and the recipient would not even know where the information came from."

It might be worth noting here that while, generally speaking, the mass of humanity has become so left-brain dominant that it has lost touch with its deep, instinctive, spiritual attunement to the essential energy and power of symbols on our psyche, there are those who have not. They know that powerful symbols bypass our rational, conscious-mind filter and that many of these ancient symbols are locked deep in our 'Race Memory', our collective consciousness. Ignorance of these symbols and their meanings makes us vulnerable to their influence. Advertisers, in particular, use symbols to entrain us to respond unthinkingly to their persuasion techniques.

In the 500s BC, Confucius said, "Signs and symbols control the mind, not phases and laws." In 1992, Robert Morning Sky revealed the ancient history of the Hopi People and shared some of their ancient truths[7]. His overall and urgent message was: 'Do not give away your personal power.' Perhaps one way of rebalancing ourselves, reconnecting to who we are, would be to use the symbols given by the Light Beings as a way of re-activating our inner power, our 'selves'. To that end we have included the symbols in this book, so that those of you who feel so inclined may use them as visual aids on your journey inwards to find your Self.

Addenda: Shortly before going to print, we read of the discoveries by Russian scientists concerning what was previously thought to be 'junk' DNA. Molecular biologists, linguists and geneticists have revealed that the alkalines of human DNA follow regular syntax and grammar rules, as does spoken language. Therefore: "human languages did not appear coincidentally but are a reflection of our inherent DNA." It follows, therefore, that there is no need for physical genetic engineering (cutting and splicing) as cellular metabolism can be changed and reprogrammed by sending information through sound and light frequencies. Russian scientists transformed frog embryos to salamander embryos by transmitting the DNA information patterns through modulated radio waves and laser rays. As we know, everything has a frequency, including thought, so this current scientific breakthrough adds weight to the Light Being's instruction that meditating on the symbols (a type of language) would change our DNA and help us raise our consciousness. In their translation of the original research papers, Fosar and Franz Bludorf say: "The individual person must work on their inner processes and maturity in order to establish a conscious communication with the DNA." Did not the Light Beings tell us to 'go within and meditate'?

Within this whole body of research, the Russian researchers also found that: "Our DNA can cause disturbing patterns in a vacuum, thus producing magnetized wormholes! ....These are tunnel connections between entirely different areas in the universe through which information can be transmitted outside of space and time. The DNA attracts these bits of information and passes them on to our consciousness. This process of hyper-communication (telepathy, channelling) is most effective in a state of relaxation...... Modern man knows this only on a much more subtle level as 'intuition.' But we can regain full use of it."

1 See14/1 in *Suggested Reading* section.
2 See14/A in *Suggested Reading* section
3 See14/B in *Suggested Reading* section
4 See14/C in *Suggested Reading* section
5 See14/D in *Suggested Reading* section
6 See14/E in *Suggested Reading* section
7 See14/F in *Suggested Reading* section

CHAPTER 15

THE NEVADA UFO CONFERENCE AND MISSING TIME AT AREA 51, PART 1

There is a reason why we came -
An angelic spark of consciousness
Moving through the planes.
Yes, the elements clothed our ways.
Particles of light from the Eternal Flame.

On 4 February 2004 we took a flight out of Manchester to Las Vegas, changing in Chicago. In Las Vegas we hired a Mitsubishi Outlander for the duration of the trip, which was 16 days, and through the darkness we navigated our way from the airport, onto the main drag and, with tired bodies and minds, we started the last leg of our journey, the 90 mile drive to Laughlin. We arrived at the Flamingo Hotel at midnight and I dropped Fran by the main entrance with our suitcases while I drove into the hotel's multi-story car park and eventually found a place on the fourth floor. By the time I got back to the main entrance fifteen minutes later, Fran jokingly suggested that she thought I had been abducted.

We had talked about making this trip for several years and now we were finally here. We pulled our suitcases into the main entrance and up to the booking-in desk, where we were instantly hit by the noise of hundreds of fruit machines. Bells were ringing, money was rattling out for some lucky punters and girls were walking around in skimpy dresses shouting out in American drawl "Cocktails!" At first it was a shock. I wasn't expecting a conference on UFOs and consciousness-changing subjects to be held in such a vibration but I must admit, you do eventually adjust to such an atmosphere! I stood once for almost an hour by a Blackjack table and totally failed to understand the game. I observed people who were too afraid to leave their particular fruit machine in case someone else went on it and won the jackpot and so they had all the food and drinks that were necessary for a long stay brought to them on a tray. They also had, around their neck on a chain, a card that plugged into the machine, to use instead of money. This, I imagine, was to make their life easier and more comfortable. I dread to think how much money some people lost over a long weekend. Using one of those cards must have acted much like a credit card in the sense that you do not always realize how much money you are spending until you receive the credit company's bill! These businesses are certainly not stupid and they prey on the weaknesses of the human race. One man told me that a lot of poor people save up for a few weeks and then take a weekend trip there, in the hope of changing their lives. Well, they do in a way; they change their lives by making themselves even poorer.

The UFO conference, held in the upstairs conference suite, was excellent. The presentations, visuals and organization were spot on and the hotel buffets were incredibly cheap. I don't know what the Americans must think when they eat in England, as the cost and quality here in the UK mostly leave a lot to be desired. The hotels in Laughlin are very 'tacky' but the gambling is what brings people in and because they want 'bums on seats' so to speak, then the hotel costs are relatively cheap. As always, you get what you pay for.

The fun of UFO conferences is 'connecting'. Connecting to new people, connecting to long-time friends and connecting to people you know well but only meet at these conferences. The book stalls always have a great magnetic pull and last, but certainly not least, are the speakers, some of whom, experiencers like myself, bare their souls to an audience that, one hopes, at the very least, have open minds. Back in the seventies there were many 'Ufologists' that had no problem believing that we were being visited by extraterrestrials, yet their minds were totally closed to any suggestion that those 'Visitors' were in any way interacting with us. Even in the slightly more enlightened times in which we are now living, we still find this illogical anomaly of belief in 'nuts and bolts' craft but not that beings from elsewhere may be, and long have been, also part of our reality. Why ever not, for goodness sake? We are space people as much as they are! It is just that they are further down the technological and in some cases, spiritual road, than we are. Experiencers for a long time got a very bad deal and in some corners of ufology they still do, but thank goodness that people such as Raymond Fowler, Budd Hopkins, John Mack and Whitley Strieber, amongst many others, have come on the scene and made our lives a whole lot easier.

Conference registration was on Sunday 8 February and so we decided to make the 240 mile drive to Rachel and Area 51 on Saturday, the day before. We left Laughlin at 8.15 a.m. and made our first stop at Alamo, at 11.50 a.m, for a coffee and donut. Alamo is 48 miles from Rachel and 25 miles from the Groom Lake Road that would lead us for 14 miles down to the restricted, three-million-acre, 'secret' military base. There is no gate into the outer perimeter of the restricted zone, but a natural barrier is formed by hills and at the entrance to the narrow pass between the hills there are signs that tell you deadly force will be used if you attempt to cross the 'line'. There are also closed-circuit surveillance cameras, mounted on tripods, just a few feet away, pointing down and looking at your position. In addition, there are two armed guards in a   military truck on a low hill just off to the right. If you made an attempt to step over this imaginary line you would be fined $600 (in 2004) and if your car happened to venture too far it would be impounded with a $1000 retrieval fee. That is, if you were not shot dead in the first place! I have read that Area 51 is the size of Switzerland and, up to recent times, was not shown on any maps and its existence was denied by the US Government. Most of the mountains that gave a reasonably long-distance view of the inside of this establishment have, in recent years, been taken over by the military and only Tikaboo Peak remains for any visible access. The distance from Tikaboo Peak into the base is around 26 miles and this, along with heat haze, makes viewing almost worthless.

We left Alamo at 12.15 p.m. and drove the 25 miles to Groom Lake

Extra-terrestrial Highway, Nevada.

Little A'Le'Inn, Rachel, and trailers.

Start of the Groom Lake Rd.

Notice at the entrance to Area 51.

Fig 40

Road (Fig 40). We stopped to take a couple of photographs and then started the 14-mile journey along the dirt track to the infamous sign and imaginary line. We arrived at 13.10 and parked the car. It was just as we had expected and read about. The cameras, signs and military truck up on the right were all there for us to see. I walked up to the sign and read it:

'WARNING! TOP SECRET RESEARCH FACILITY.
USE OF DEADLY FORCE AUTHORIZED.
Photography Prohibited.

It is unlawful to make any photographs, film, map, sketch, picture, drawing, graphic representation of this area or equipment at or flying over this installation.

'USE OF DEADLY FORCE AUTHORIZED'.

I looked up at the cameras staring down at me. I looked up at the military truck off to my right. I looked straight ahead to the imaginary line and the dirt road turning to the left behind the hills and I wondered what was beyond. I had, for so many years, read hundreds of stories of crashed space craft and Aliens that were captured by the military[1] and also about Aliens supposedly working with the government on clandestine missions. I recently read the Charles Hall trilogy of books[2], telling of his time as a weatherman back in the early 1960s, out on the 'Ranges' and coming up against the Tall Whites; Extraterrestrials that had been living in that area for centuries and using it, amongst other things, as a stop-over place for this part of the galaxy. Is that why Area 51 was originally chosen? As the human race modernized and personal transport became widely available, travel and exploration for ordinary families was now no problem. Did the Tall Whites now need some protection to stop them from being discovered? Was a deal done in return for certain technologies?

In the couple of minutes that I stood by the imaginary line, all these questions raced through my mind as I tapped into the memory banks of my brain, which had collated 40 years of UFO knowledge. I made my mind up there and then that I had to take at least one photo. I had not come all this way from England without collecting one small memento of my epic journey to Area 51. You have to understand the situation here: this is not a shopping centre in the middle of some big city where there is safety in numbers; you are in the middle of absolutely nowhere. You are on your own, looking up at a sign that is talking about deadly force. Although I felt sure it was okay to take a photo from where I was standing, (I was, after all, on the side of the line where the land is owned by Lincoln County and not the military), there was no one around you could turn to and discuss exactly what the risk factors were. I wanted to take a photo of the cameras, the signs and the military truck but in the end decided to just take one shot of the sign and then head off to Rachel and Little Ale'Inn. I walked back to the car and explained to Fran that I would take this one photo, then do a quick three point turn, put my foot on the gas and head back the 14 miles to Nevada Highway 375. (Now officially known as The Extraterrestrial Highway. In fact it mentions in the official tourist brochure that if a dozen cars traverse the 98-mile stretch of Highway 375 in a day, it qualifies as rush-hour traffic!)

I got my camera from the back of the Mitsubishi, glanced at the military truck and took one quick shot of the sign. I then jumped in the car, turned it around and hit the pedal. After about 600 yards I noticed in the rear view mirror that we were being followed by the military truck. I mentioned it to Fran and she confirmed that. After about another 200 yards, I had just remarked they were getting closer when then there was a loud sound. Fran immediately exclaimed, "What was that? It sounded like we were shot!" I hit the brake, saying, "I think the tire has exploded!" I got out, walked to the back of the car and saw that the off-side rear tire was flat. I looked up and immediately noticed that the military truck was nowhere to be seen and yet there was nowhere for it to go! This was the first anomaly. We arrived at the sign at 13.10 and left 15 minutes later. No more then 5 minutes after that we had the puncture, so this would have made it around 13.30. I was out of the car in 15 seconds and yet the military truck was gone. How could this be? How could it have disappeared in flat, open desert in 15 seconds? (*See Fig 40*)

The second anomaly was the decision I made on where to change the tire. It would have made much more sense to have jacked the car up right where we were, on the flat dirt road. There was also the chance that some other 'ufologist' might venture down the track and help us. Something else has to be taken on board here also. That is that consciously we were totally unaware of anything strange at this time. We were not looking for anomalies, and yet I made a decision to drive the car for six miles along a smaller, bumpier track to Medlin Ranch and change the tire there! We had a more detailed map in the car, downloaded from the internet, and this clearly showed the Medlin Ranch road. Driving on the flat tire for six miles ripped it to shreds and by the time we reached our destination we were driving on the metal rim!

It should have been around 13.50 p.m. by the time we arrived at Medlin Ranch. A journey which should have taken no more then 15 minutes. Yet as soon as we arrived I said to Fran, "Look, it's ten to four, it's getting dark! We have to get this tire changed!" We did not question the fact that we had lost possibly two hours from the time of getting the puncture to arriving at Medlin Ranch.

I jacked up the car, loosened the nuts of the rear wheel and lifted it off. I placed the spare wheel into position and started to re-tighten the nuts. The spare wheel was an emergency tire, much like you have with new cars these days. It was a lot thinner, with a different tread and was a tire only for an emergency and not to be used for too many miles and not above 50 miles an hour, according to the handbook. In the US they call them 'donut' tires. Just as I was tightening the last bolt, a truck suddenly appeared. To this day we are not sure where it came from because it just seemed to be there! It was similar to the military truck but buff in color, whereas the other one was gray. Inside the truck were two men who looked like ranchers, along with a small boy about the age of ten. The three of them got out of the truck and the taller, slimmer one smiled and said, "Looks like we have arrived too late?" I replied that they had, believing they were talking about changing the wheel. Then he said "What do you think of our weather?" and I replied that it would be very similar to England right now as both countries were coming out of their winters. I have been to the US before and have always found Americans very keen to talk to anyone from the British Isles and they would immediately ask if you were enjoying yourselves or where have you been or what have you seen, even something about England itself, yet these two men asked just said: "Looks like we have arrived too late," and

"What do you think of our weather?"

There was something distinctly odd about the little boy. He spent the whole time just staring over my left shoulder towards Fran and several times I thought to myself what a strange lad he was. I ended up coming to the conclusion that he probably lived way out here in the middle of nowhere and now was standing next to two complete strangers so perhaps he was just shy or nervous.

The shorter, stockier man then went up to Fran and took the old wheel from her. "Let me help you with that, Ma'am," he said, and took the wheel to the back of our car. He stood for a while staring into the boot. I had my camera equipment laid out in the back and had an awful thought that we might be just about to get robbed, but he carefully placed the wheel in the back and returned to his original position, next to the other two.

I enquired if they knew where we could get a new tire and the tall man replied that we could go into Rachel but the person there would not have the type for our vehicle and so our best bet was to go back to Alamo. I then asked him the quickest way to Alamo and he pointed up a track and said, "That way!" They then all got back in their truck and shot off in a cloud of dust (or so we thought!). The track they sent us on was not the quickest way to Alamo and we actually came out onto Highway 375 at the famous black mailbox, which is now painted white. So we were now nearer to Rachel than we were to Alamo. I took some photos of the mailbox and then we made a decision to drive on to Rachel.

We wanted to visit Little Ale'Inn and we thought that we could at least get accommodation for the night and try to get the vehicle changed with the hire company. The elevation here is around 6,000 feet (1,828.80 meters) and on the way to Rachel we drove through a snow blizzard. Rachel has had several names down the years but became known as Rachel in 1979, in honor of Rachel Jones, who was the first baby to be born in the town in 1978. Sadly, she passed away in 1980, due to breathing problems caused by the dust from the eruption of Mount St Helens. Rachel began life as a mining town in the early 1970s and at one point had almost 200 residents. Today there are around 80 people living there in trailers and some of those people do work at Area 51.

The first building you come to in Rachel is the Quik-Pik Store and we arrived just before closing at 16.50. I asked the lady if I could use her phone to ring Hertz Vehicle Hire, a free phone number, and she readily agreed. I explained the situation to the Hertz contact and told her where we were. She said that she had the map in front of her but couldn't find where we were located and said that we would have to drive into Las Vegas and get the tire changed there. I told her I was concerned about driving that far at night on the donut tire, but she wouldn't listen. So in the end, I agreed and put the phone down. The lady in the Quik-Pik Store looked quite concerned and went on to explain that it is too dangerous to drive out there at night in the winter and especially on a donut tire. She stressed that if I got another puncture there would be no one around to help and added that one could die out there on a cold winter's night. She explained that television and mobile phones cannot get a signal and went on to tell me that only three weeks prior to our visit she broke down in her car and waited by the side of the road for four hours until eventually a military truck came along and stopped to help her out, but that in the night time there would be no one. I saw that she was quite serious and I asked that if I rang back Hertz, would she speak to them and explain the situation. She did this and the Hertz staff agreed to send out an exchange vehicle on the back of a low loader. This, I was told, would take over six hours and would arrive around midnight.

The Quik-Pik owner then locked her store up for the night and asked us to follow her car and she would book us in at Little Ale'Inn, (See Fig 40). We parked the cars and followed her into the building. She went straight to the counter and started to look in the reservations book. I asked her if she worked there as well and she replied that she did not but that she helps anyone out. She was, in fact, a very nice-natured and helpful person. There was a young lad behind the counter and while looking at the book she said to him, "Why have you put them in there?" He replied,

"I was told to put them in there!" She then asked, "Why can't they go in there?" (Pointing to another line in the book) Again he replied that he was told we had to go in there! *Who told him this prior to our arrival in the Inn?* This gets even more odd because she then took Fran across to the mobile home and on the way over told Fran that a stranger had turned up just ten minutes before we did and they did not know who he was but he had been booked in the other half of the mobile home allocated to us. She said that the bathroom was in the middle and we both had connecting doors to the bathroom. She then told Fran that there was a bolt on our connecting door and suggested that we keep it bolted!

We dropped our bags off and went back to Little Ale'Inn, to have something to eat, look around and buy some presents. We were both excited that we were finally standing in Little Ale'Inn. I took some photos and then our food arrived. The lady from the Quik-Pik Store stayed and chatted to us and another man, who was sitting at the bar and who was apparently a Rachel resident. The strange thing was that this was a Saturday night and there was nowhere else to go to in the evening and Las Vegas was 150 miles away yet we were the only people there all evening. There was, after all, no television reception, so a quick drink at the 'local,' one would think, would be a must. Yet it never happened.

We never again saw the young man who was originally behind the counter when we arrived and, soon after that, the owner of the property, Mrs Pat Travis, took over the reins. At around 10 p.m. we called it a night and went back to the mobile home. We borrowed a couple of videos to play and settled down to wait for the new car to arrive. It was not long before we became aware that the man that had been booked into the other half of the mobile home was coming out of his room and standing outside our door! This went on two or three times and eventually Fran knelt on the floor to look under the rather large gap and see if he was there. He was! By now I had had enough of this, so I drew the bolt quickly and opened the door. Sure enough, he was standing there, with a dog. Fran said that the odd thing was, he looked like me! He was tall and about my stature, with silver hair tied back in a ponytail and a silver beard. I asked him if he was all right and he replied that he was. I bent down to stroke the dog, we talked for a few more minutes then we bolted our door again. We still heard him outside a couple more times but, in the end, just ignored it. We settled down again to watch the videos and at 23.50 the low loader pulled into the car park and I went out to meet him. It made me feel a lot better when he told me that I had made the right decision not to try and drive to Las Vegas on the donut tire as he had not passed a single vehicle for the last 120 miles. He unloaded the new Mitsubishi Outlander and put the other one on the back. I signed some papers and he was gone.

It was now about 10 minutes past midnight and I decided that I was going to get into bed and try and get some sleep. Fran said that she was going to lay on top of the bed fully clothed and even keep her shoes on to be ready for a quick exit, but we never discussed why such odd behavior or what the quick exit was for! Neither of us wondered why she would even say such a thing!

I awoke abruptly at 1 a.m. and told Fran that I was going to be sick and that I had to get out of the mobile home straight away. I hurriedly got dressed and went outside. The sky was clear and there was almost a full moon. It was bright and very cold. My first thought was not to be sick right outside the front door, as we would be walking out here in a few hours to drive back to Laughlin. I went round to the back of the mobile home but at the end I noticed a small window and thought that it might be the other guy's bedroom and I did not want to wake him with my 'retching' sounds. Eventually I went to the side of the mobile home. I was sick four times and all the time I was vomiting there was a huge light in the sky, right above me. I was being sick then looking up at the light, being sick again then looking back up to the light.

After my sickness finally ended, the light moved away. I instantly ran around to the front of the mobile home and burst through the door. "Quick!" I shouted to Fran, "Come and look at this light before it disappears!" Fran came to the door, looked out and saw the light in the distance. It was now above the horizon and in some low morning cloud. You could see it clearly enough but not as I had seen it, hovering above me. I turned to Fran and said, "Well, you might have come out to at least see if I was all right!" "What do you mean?" Fran responded, "I did go outside and I couldn't find you!" I replied that I was round the side of the mobile home and that was why she had not seen me but, in an agitated voice, she said that she had gone to both the side and the back of the trailer and called out my name but I was not there. She had even gone across to Little Ale'Inn and to the front car park where, as anyone who has been there will know, you can see for miles, and called from there, but I was nowhere to be seen. She said that she thought to herself, "I hope he hasn't wondered off and his back has gone and he is now lying somewhere unable to move, because that is the sort of thing he would do!"

(I should mention here that I have permanent back damage due to an injury caused while saving someone's life in my late teens.)

Then she said she looked around some more and thought, "I hope 'they' haven't taken him!" Again, with no conscious, logical reason as to why that thought came into her head. In the end she went back to the mobile home and went into the bathroom. In the mirror she noticed that the tip of her nose was very red and wondered if she had walked into something. She then sat on the bed and went into a controlled panic. She couldn't find me and she was there, a non-driver, in the middle of nowhere, and although we weren't yet discussing any of the strange happenings, she had felt unsettled ever since we first went along the Groom Lake Road. She sat on the edge of the bed for quite a while and tried to contain herself. "Suppose he never comes back!" she thought. Then, I walked through the door and asked her to look at the light. What went on there, again rather disturbingly, we never discussed. Fran had lost total track of time but felt that it must have been at least 30 minutes that I was missing, possibly more. Whereas I was only aware of going outside and being sick, looking up at the light and then coming back in. In all, about five minutes. We then agreed to go to bed but as soon as one of us awoke and saw that it was light, we would go, even though Pat Travis had promised us a full breakfast in the morning! We still did not discuss why we needed to get away so hastily!

It was starting to get light at 4.15 a.m. and so we loaded up the car and pulled around to the front of Little Ale'Inn where I stopped to take some final shots of the place. Then we pulled once more onto Highway 375, 'Extraterrestrial Highway' (See Fig 40), and started along the downhill road and the long drive back to Laughlin. For some reason, we began talking about the two ranchers that had pulled up when we were changing the wheel and at some point in that conversation I said to Fran, "Yes, and that little boy was really odd!" Fran exclaimed in surprise, "What little boy? There was no little boy! What are you talking about?" Not realizing the full implications, I replied, "The little boy who was with the two men. I thought he was rather odd." Fran said it in a horrified tone, "What little boy? What did he look like? What did he do? Where did he stand? I would have seen him! There was no little boy!" I replied, "He was standing next to the two men and just staring across to you. I just thought he was very odd. He had a strange energy and I couldn't quite make it out." Fran asked, "How did he leave?" I replied that he left with the men. He got back in the truck and left with them. Fran excitedly said again that if there had been a boy then she would have seen him. "I am a trained Nursery Nurse; don't you think I would see a little boy standing six feet (1.83 meters) away from me?" I replied that you would think so and I decided to pull over and stop the car for a minute and rescue the situation. I went again through the scenario of where the little boy stood and what he did and how he left, in the hope of reassuring Fran that there was indeed a little boy. We then got back into the car and carried on our journey.

The little boy was the thing I most held onto that was telling me that something odd had happened but we did not fully take on board all that was happening to us until we got back to England. Fran told me some weeks later that she was not happy at all and during our stay did not feel safe until we landed back in England. As I said earlier, the strange thing about all this is that we never discussed any of these issues until we were back home. This 'missing' boy is what we kept turning over in our minds and while discussing it some weeks later, we started to talk about the time and how it could not have been 15.50 when we arrived at Medlin Ranch because we were at the bottom of Groom Lake Road at around 13.10 and we were only there for ten minutes. The more we started to talk about it, the more all these anomalies filtered into our reality. What surprised us most was the fact that, with sixty years of studying this subject between us and, when interviewing people, knowing what clues to look for, when it happened to us we totally failed to register any of these classic signs of Alien or Military abduction!

We finally arrived back at the Flamingo Hotel about 11 a.m. This was the day of registration and so we decided to first register for the conference and then go to our room and shower and then have a sleep for a couple of hours, then go back down to the conference and chill out. Fran went into the shower first and shortly after came running out, pointing to three long, finger-print bruises on the top of her inner thigh. She also noticed that she had a large, red triangle on the top of her right arm that felt rough, like sandpaper. I then checked myself and noticed three small, red puncture dots forming a triangle just above my right ankle. It had been an unprecedented twenty-four hours and there was still one stranger event waiting to encroach on our lives.

On Tuesday, 10 February, we went to the lecture hall to listen to Adrian Dvir. Adrian was born in Rumania in 1958 and had a B.Sc. in Engineering and an M.Sc. in Computer Engineering. He was involved in developing military computer systems for a company in Israel, a country he had lived in since 1965. In 1998 he published a book entitled *Healing Entities and Aliens*[3]. Adrian was a contactee himself and had set up around fifty clinics in Israel, working with Alien surgeons on an inter-dimensional level, and the medical teams were treating around 20 patients a week at his own clinic. He said that he was in the process of setting-up clinics in the US and UK. He then went on to say that while he was giving his talk the Alien surgeons would be in the etheric layer above the conference hall and if anyone put their hand up they would be given healing there and then. This was not really my cup of tea, so to speak, but as I was desperate to have my back healed, I raised my hand in the air and asked for help. I was not aware of anything happening at the time and there was no miracle cure of my back, but something happened. In the hotel room, later that evening, I started to feel sick. I was sick for two and half days and it was practically non-stop. This was no ordinary sickness; it was initially a white powder and then a clear liquid containing what looked like brown sawdust flakes, which was coming out of 'both ends'. I could not eat or drink and could not leave the hotel room for any length of time. I did not have an upset stomach or headache or fever. In fact I felt absolutely fine except that I dare not leave the room because of this strange liquid that was pouring out of me. The next day, Fran had the same thing happen to her, the only difference being that, with her, it lasted only one and half days. Once we were able to get back to the conference, several people, on different occasions, said that they thought it sounded like a cleansing or a 'de-tox'. Under regression, over one year later, that seems to have been exactly what it was and I was told that it was far more important for me to have been cleansed than for them to have dealt with my back at that time.

I do not know what to make of this, but in his lecture, Adrian Dvir said that the military had put an implant into him and his Alien friends had told him that the implant would eventually kill him but that they were unable to remove it because it was far too dangerous and to do so would kill him. A couple of months after giving this lecture, and when he was in the process of setting-up the new clinics, he suddenly died of a seeming heart attack. Make of this what you will!

1 See *Suggested Reading* 15/1 and 15/A
2 See *Suggested Reading* 15/2
3 See *Suggested Reading* 15/3

CHAPTER 16

THE NEVADA UFO CONFERENCE AND MISSING TIME AT AREA 51, PART 2

I will find a pattern in this plan.
Like Isis rising from the sand,
Nothing will remain of me.
Transformation therapy;
Conscious luminosity;
Fire from ashes I will be.
Fire from ashes I will be.

Transcript of Mike Oram's Taped Regression Session, Wednesday, 6 July 05.

© Mike Oram 2005

N.B. Transcript starts after D's initial process to relax Mike into the deeper level of consciousness.

Hypnotist = D
Subject = M
Questioner = F

D set the scene for Mike:

You are back on the dirt road at Area 51. You have been to the gate and now you are driving back along the dirt road. You see the gray pick up truck behind you. What happens next?

F comments: Mike could see a purple flower beside the car, on the driver's side. He remembered stopping, in real time, to photograph a cactus at the start of the dirt track and seeing this tiny purple flower beside it. As he watched the one by the car, it grew to around six feet (1.83 meters) tall and he commented that the petals looked like arms and feet.

M comments: Later in the regression, there will be mention of this six-feet-tall flower standing outside my driver's door, but in the regression, while looking at the real time event, I had stopped the car a short way along the Groom Lake Road to take a photo of a Joshua Tree (large cactus) and, in this deeper level of consciousness, I noticed a small white and purple flower growing on the desert floor. I had not remembered this in a conscious state but now found myself looking down at this flower and having a very strange feeling. The head of the flower seemed to envelop me and I was 'swooped up' in its essence. I could not understand why this tiny flower was having such a strange effect on me and it took my whole attention for that moment in time. I almost felt embarrassed to mention under regression that this was happening. "It was just a flower," I thought to myself. "What is happening here?" Eventually I pulled myself away from this powerful image and continued my journey. What I believe happened here is that this was just an ordinary desert flower but because of an event that happened afterwards, which was now in my deeper consciousness, seeing that flower then 'triggered' that event in my mind and made a connection.

As mentioned earlier, one of the anomalies that we consciously remembered was how on earth the gray military truck could possibly have disappeared in the 15 seconds that it took me to get out of the car. Under the regression we heard the noise and the tire went flat but before I could get out of the car we were surrounded by several armed military personnel who 'ordered' us out of the car. They were dressed in khaki and wore red berets. We were taken to the rear of our car, where a truck with a strange device on the back was backed up to ours. The truck held a long, tubular device which seemed to have two wheels attached (See Fig 41). At first, I thought this was a cannon. This was not the case, because when I managed to see the other side of the machine there was no 'wheel' device there. It was only on one side and seemed to consist of three raised sections that looked like a wheel (See Fig 42). In this deeper consciousness I said that there were three magnetic coils inside this wheel

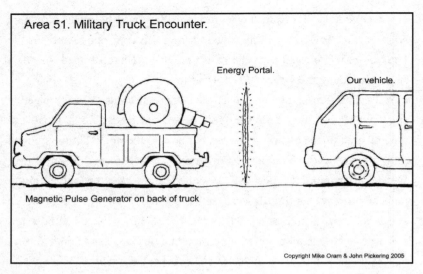

Area 51. Military Truck Encounter.

Energy Portal.

Our vehicle.

Magnetic Pulse Generator on back of truck

Copyright Mike Oram & John Pickering 2005

Fig 41

and that this device was known as a Magnetic Pulse Generator (I had never heard of such a thing but this was so clear in my mind that I just had to say it). I said that it could create a portal and that it was a 'Mobile Portal Creator'. (N.B. See Note[1] at end of chapter)

F: How did they pick up on you?

M: *I think they had technology that tells them who I am.*

I sensed here that they had technology, possibly with detectors along the Groom Lake Road, which somehow looked into my mind and retrieved information

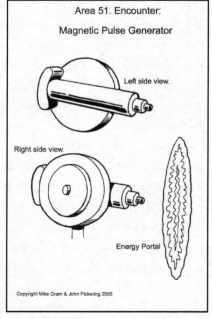

Area 51. Encounter:

Magnetic Pulse Generator

Left side view.

Right side view.

Energy Portal

Copyright Mike Oram & John Pickering 2005

Fig 42

about my communication with the 'Space Brothers'. They then knew that I was a contactee and they simply wanted to know what information I had regarding my 'Space Friends' and what I may have known about any future or past events.

F: Do you know, can you see, or could you ask, how I came by the triangle and the bruises?

M: *Manhandling was the bruises.*

F: In what way was I manhandled?

M: *Let's just say, resisting.*

F: I was resisting?

M: *Yes.*

F: Resisting what?

M: *Being taken.*

F: Do you know how or where we were taken and for what purpose?

M: *I think with me, it was to find out why I was there.*

F: OK. And with me?

M: *You were with me.*

F: How were we taken?

M: *With this machine that created the portal.*

F: And we were forced to step through the portal?

M: *We were told to; we had no choice - not with guns pointing at you.*

The portal was created in front of my eyes and it was about seven feet (2.13 meters) tall and just a couple of inches (5 centimeters) off the ground. It was an oval shape and very thin. It was unusual because you could see the desert around it as normal but the portal was like wavy lines of energy, or you could say like water rippling.

F: Where did we go?

M: *Into a military establishment.*

F: Which was where?

M: *Underground.*

We simply stepped into this 'energy' and immediately found ourselves in this large, underground room. This was actually quite confusing because one minute you were standing in the desert and the next, somewhere completely different.

F: Can you describe it?

M: *Just very busy, hectic.*

F: A large space, small space?

M: *We were in a largish room full of stuff, people.*

F: When you say stuff?

M: *Equipment.*

F: Equipment? Can you describe any of the equipment? Do you know what its purpose was, what it was used for?

M: *Well, it certainly doesn't look like the alien equipment.*

F: It doesn't?

M: *Too dense. Too 'here and now'.*

F: Do you have any idea what any of it was used for?

M: *Programming. I'm getting programming.*

F: Uh huh.

M: *Machines to, sort of, try and find out about consciousness.*

F: What happened to us there?

M: *I've just picked up that they've been told that I must be put back.*

F: Who told them?

M: *I don't know where it is coming from.*

This was incredibly clear in my mind and I do not understand what was going on here but there was a presence I detected very strongly and this intelligence was surrounding all the other minds that were in the room. What I am trying to say is that the 'mind' of this Being was so vast that it overshadowed all the other minds, so I could pick this up really strongly. It obviously was not human, of that I can be sure, and it was saying that I must not be harmed and that I must be put back in the same place I was taken. Why, I do not know.

F: Have you any idea how long we were there?

M: *One hour.*

F: Do you know.... were we, tampered with in any way?

M: *They were information gathering. They knew, they somehow knew, I don't know how, perhaps through these machines, that I was one of 'them'.*

F: One of whom?

M: *One of the Brothers.* (Referring to those he calls his Space Brothers).

F: So they wanted to find out as much as they could about you?

M: *Yes.*

F: But they were stopped?

M: *They had... somehow they'd been told no harm must come to me.*

F: And you have no idea why?

M: *No.*

F: When we went through the portal, what actually happened next? Where did we end up?

M: *Well, you literally stepped through and you're in the room.*

F: In the room where we were kept?

M. *Yes.*

F: And can you see clearly, do you know, exactly what happened when we got in the room? What happened to you and what happened to me? Were we together?

M: *They weren't too – and this isn't an insult - they weren't too interested in you, but obviously you had to be kept placid – but the thing is, that you know stuff about me. I don't know who this higher authority is that told them I had to be put back and no harm must come to me. I don't know where that is coming from.*

F: Could it be an off-world authority?

M: *Well, that's what I'm feeling.*

F: So did they ask you questions, or did they put you on a machine, or …?

M: *I can see you lying down at one point, but I mean you're not undressed or anything like that, it wasn't that sort of operation.*

F: Was I awake?

M: *At this point you're subdued, but at one point you obviously struggled.*

F: Do you know if I was frightened, or was I mad?

M: *A bit of both, but you knew I was there, so a part of you knew that no harm would come to you.*

F: And what did they do to you? Can you remember?

M: *They were trying to find out why I was in the area and was something going to happen. I think they knew that there would be a ship somewhere.*

F: So, did they try to find out just by questioning?

M: *I think they've got machines that can go into your mind.*

There were machines all around the walls of this large room and military men were sitting at these machines. Most of them were not concerned about me at all and were probably quite used to these 'portal arrivals'. They had their own agendas. Around six or eight men were responsible for us. These machines, I again felt very strongly, were to do with consciousness and messing around with the mind, but in what capacity I was not sure.

F: Was it that process they were told to stop?

M: *They weren't told to stop, but they were told that I had to be put back.*

F: How many personnel were in the room?

M: *There were quite a few milling around but a lot of them weren't to do with us.*

F: Was it a largish room?

M: *Yes.*

F: And were there any other humans undergoing......?

M: *No. Not where we were.*

F: But there were elsewhere in the complex?

M: *There could have been.*

F: Were the people in the room with us totally terrestrial?

M: *I'm just scanning around. Yes.*

F: What was the feeling of their energy? What sort of people were they? Were they sinister?

M: *Not sinister. They've got their own agenda. Let's just say they don't know any better.*

F: Right. So, were they fairly dispassionate about what they were doing?

M: *Let's just say that they don't warm to you. Let's just say that they've not actually got... they're not in touch with their divine self.*

F: Have they, themselves, been tampered with in any way?

M: *They're just under orders and they're controlled, as you are in military forces. You don't question.*

F.N.

In his book *Psychic Warrior*, David Morehouse, one of the CIA's remote viewing espionage team, says of the military and those involved in the intelligence community:

"Even the most seemingly sinister of those in the intelligence community do what they do because of their unfaltering belief in the 'Mission'. The mission is to protect our nation against all enemies, foreign and domestic. It is this passion that often drives them beyond the moral and ethical expectations of duty."

cont:

F: Were they American, or...?

M: *American. Yes.... There may have been an English General – may have been.*

For some reason I was picking up that there was an English general in the vicinity. I did not see him, but in this heightened mind state that I was in, I could detect his energy.

F: So, would you get the feeling, or do you know, if it was a multi... an international...

M: *Mainly American I think. In this part. I mean; I can't speak for the whole establishment.*

F: And is it a clandestine... to the extent that..... um... the American

Government would be unaware what is going on?

M: *I think they are briefed up to a point but I think, like on a need-to-know basis. If they can be kept in ignorance, they will be.*

F: This machine they used, do you, in the consciousness that you are in now, do you know if it can be activated anywhere and open a portal just to that place or to.....?

M: *It's moveable, isn't it? It's on the back of a truck. It's like a magnetic generator – a magnetic pulse generator.*

F: Would it always open a portal just to that Base?

M: *It's a portable portal.*

F: Just to the Base?

M: *Well, no, they could do it anywhere.*

F: No – is it a portal just to access the Base or can it be programmed...?

M: *It can be programmed.*

F: To access anything they want to access?

M: *More or less.*

F: Do you know....

M: *What did I say it was?*

F: A magnetic pulse generator.

M: *A magnetic pulse generator. Right. Look that up.*

FN: A cursory internet search revealed that there are indeed such devices. Pulsed magnets fall into two general classes: Non-Destructive and Destructive. They are, or can be, used for a variety of procedures, including breaking up kidney stones; lymph virus, microbe, fungi, and parasite elimination; effectively managing pain, sleep disorders, inflammation and improving joint flexibility; weather control, and destroying sensitive and complex electronic systems (from computers and microprocessors to (theoretically) the electronic systems of nuclear or electric power plants, banks, trains, or even a simple telephone switchboard). The most flexible pulsed magnets to date are "shaped-pulse" magnets in which the magnetic field shape can be specified to meet the particular needs of a given experiment. (i.e. create a portal?)

HAARP stands for High Frequency Active Auroral Research Program, which is an investigation project to "understand, simulate and control ionospheric processes that might alter the performance of communication and surveillance systems." The project started in 1993 and will last at least until 2013. Many scientists were worried that the HAARP antennas could be used as a weapon. A small group of American physicists aired complaints in scientific journals, in the mid 1990s, and these concerns were amplified by Bernard Eastlund, a physicist who developed some of the concepts behind HAARP in the 1980s. In September 1995, a book entitled *Angels Don't Play This HAARP: Advances in Tesla Technology*[1] by Nick Begich, Jr., claimed that the project, in its present stage, could be used for "geophysical warfare." It now appears that the technology behind Haarp has many uses.

Extracts from a paper reporting on the current status of HAARP, *HAARP's Covert Agendas—The Big Picture*, by John Quinn of NewsHawk Inc, written in 1998 and published on http://www.crystalinks.com/haarp.html:

"It is becoming very apparent that the radar systems are picking up electromagnetic perturbances which not only don't correlate to observed actual weather conditions but display totally unnatural formations like perfect circles (often concentric), perfectly straight lines, etc. This same phenomenon, often in conjunction with tremendous and historically unheard-of rainstorms, has also been observed in Western Australia, where the concentric electromagnetic energy pulses accompanying the fronts have been so severe as to totally knock out the power grids in the region—exactly what happened in Auckland, New Zealand earlier this year, when the entire heart of the city was without power for months after their electrical grid was literally fried by these EM pulse waves.

It bears repeating here that some scientists believe that HAARP, especially at its current extraordinary levels of power, is quite capable of generating such highly advanced, esoteric phenomena as gravity waves; the ability to implement interdimensional / time bending, distortion, shifting, rifting and the like would be along the same lines.

More and more, the emerging picture of HAARP is that of an extremely severe and very disturbing threat to our wellbeing here on Planet Earth; currently perhaps one of the very biggest threats technologically. This really seems to be their Big Gun, capable of being applied in nearly every imaginable and exceptionally undesirable way.

And

The more complete list of primary intended uses of HAARP now reads:

"*Enhancement of or interference with communications, as well as development of new types of radio transmissions;

*Manipulation of weather patterns;

*Weapons-related (physical/psychological disablement) and mind control uses;

*Earth-penetrating tomography — an X-ray like function which can reveal, for example, the existence of underground installations as well as oil or mineral deposits;

*Detection of electromagnetic seismic activity which may precede earthquakes — and triggering of such activity;

*Generation of gravitic waves, interdimensional/time "portals" and other highly esoteric, relativistic phenomena;

*Pushing the envelope" in terms of pumping electromagnetic energy into the ionosphere, just to see what happens;

*Drawing astronomical amounts of electrical power from the ionosphere."

On 14 February 2006, I emailed Alexander Frolov, head of the Faraday Lab Ltd, in St Petersburg, Russia. This is my email content:

'Dear Mr Frolov,

I realize you must be a very busy person but I am trying to find the answer to a puzzle occasioned by a personal experience and thought you may well be able to provide me with an answer. My question is: Is it theoretically possible for a magnetic pulse generator to be used to create a 'portal' from one place to another?

His response, dated 09:38 (his time) on 15 February 2006, was:

'Dear Sir, (*It is not always clear if unfamiliar names are masculine or feminine – hence him referring to Fran as 'Sir').* We worked to get confirmation of the conception about relation between aether density and time rate. It seems to be quite workable idea. Future results can be more interesting.

Best regards,

Alexander V. Frolov.'

Faraday Lab Ltd was founded on 14 March 2001, registered as a scientific research company. CEO and owner Alexander V. Frolov. Their main work is in R&D in the field of alternative (fuel less) power engineering and advanced propulsion systems for aerospace technologies, for example: electrogravities and other reaction-less propulsion systems, development of the new materials for the technologies, experimenting with permanent magnet motor-generators and others.

Some time after we had sent this book to the publisher we had the good fortune and pleasure to meet and spend some time with Paola Harris, the internationally-acclaimed, Italian investigative journalist. She told us of interviews she had done with Dan Burisch, the microbiologist who worked on black projects dealing with extraterrestrial races and technologies. In particular, he worked with one extraterrestrial entity called 'J-Rod', who was housed at Area 51. Burisch told Paola about a device they had in the early 2000s that created a time/space portal, through which they sent J-Rod home! His drawing of this device is reproduced in the Italian magazine *Area 51,* for which Paola writes. You can imagine how pleased we were to learn this, as it made Mike's recall of the portable device all the more likely. (http://www.paolaharris.it/italiano.html)

Continued:

F: How did we come back?

M: *Through the portal.*

F: We came back through the portal?

M: *Yes, they put us back in the car.*

F: In our four-wheeled vehicle?

M: *Yes, and by the time we had come round, they had gone.*

F: And how were we subdued, to be in that state? I mean, does the portal itself do it, or......?

M: *The machine will do it.*

F: The machine will do it?

M: *I think they might have some hand-held implement; I'm not too sure.*

One of the military men had a small device on his belt that he seemed to point at us and we would be put into this subdued state. They ordered us back into our car and used this device to subdue us. Once this was done, it would then take around ten minutes for us to come back to our full conscious state. This is why, to our conscious memory, when we got out of the car in supposedly 15 seconds, they were nowhere to be seen, whereas, it actually took us ten minutes.

F: There was some way that they suppressed our memories?

M: *Yes. That may be arranged as you go through the portal. There may be several functions to it.*

F: Right. Earlier in this regression, you felt that you saw beside the car, a six-foot flower with purple leaves tinged with white. In the consciousness that you are in now, what do you think that was? Can you see more clearly?

M: *It was a Space Brother.*

F: It was a Space Brother?

M: *Yes.*

F: So they arrived while we were still......

M: *The flower was there when we came back.*

F: Did the military see it?

M: *No.*

F: But it was one of your Space Brothers?

M: *Yes.*

F: So how... what happened from the point when we came back, the Space Brother was there......?

M: *We took a while to come round.*

F: Right, and what did he do?

M: *And the flower was there, but I think I'm seeing that on a different level.*

F: Right.

M: *It wasn't there physically.*

F: But they were aware of you? So, was it the beginning of the telepathic communication?

M: *It must have been, and that's why I drove to Medlin Ranch, just to be out of the way of that main track.*

F: Because you'd been telepathically told to do that?

M: *Yes. It wouldn't have been advisable for them to have appeared on that track, and that's why we drove on the metal rim to Medlin Ranch.*

So this is where the memory of this flower actually happened. Why I saw one of my Space Brothers as a flower I am not certain but, as we were slowly 'coming round' in the front of the car, I started to see a large flower just outside the window of my front driver's door. I described it as white and purple; similar to the one I saw earlier when I was taking a photo of the Joshua tree. The confusing thing about this imagery was that I described two large leaves where the hands would normally be and two large leaves where there would be feet. Then, I had a total realization that this was not a flower at all but that it was one of my Space Brothers and he was telling me to drive to Medlin Ranch as they wanted to meet me and it would be much safer there. That is why I was desperate to get to Medlin Ranch to change the tire – and ripped the tire to shreds in the process.

F: And it was daylight when we got there?

M: *Yes*.

F: So how did we lose that other segment of time?

M: *It was lost when they arrived.*

We got the puncture at around 13.30 and we were in the underground establishment for around one hour. Under regression I said that when they brought us back it was 14.30, so when we arrived at Medlin Ranch it was around 14.50, and not the 15.50 that we were aware of in our conscious mind. In our conscious mind we arrived at 15.50 and I said to Fran, "Look, it's ten to four, it's getting dark, and we have to get this tire changed." In actuality, under regression, I stated that when we arrived it was blue sky with some fluffy white clouds and that it was 14.50. This is because, as you will see, I spent one hour there talking to my Space Brothers. They were not two ranchers and the other was not a little, ten-year-old boy. They were my Space Brothers and the smaller ET was apparently on a training mission with them. He was learning certain techniques and he held Fran in a kind of stasis, as that was one of the things he could do. That is why, in my conscious memory, I was puzzled as to why he was just standing there staring at Fran and also why I thought he was a bit odd. The oddness was his energy, as I had not detected this type of energy before.

F: While they were communicating with you?

M: *Yes. When I looked up and saw this light.*

This, again while under regression, was a very powerful image. I was bending down undoing the bolts of the wheel when, all of a sudden, I turned to look over my shoulder and there, in front of me, was a blazing light. I watched this for a while, trying to work out what was going on.

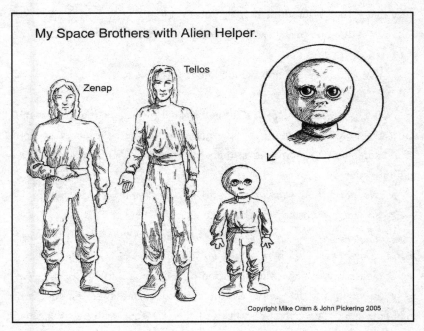

Fig 43

Then, out of the light walked my two Space Brothers, 'Tellos' and 'Xenap', along with the little boy, who was, in fact, a small, cute ET with a round orange face - as orange as an 'orange' (See Fig 43). He had a bald head and large, round eyes. He had three stocky fingers on each hand, which came to a rounded end. He was also wearing a one-piece ski suit, similar to 'The Brothers,' and had a very nice, innocent energy.

F: The shorter one of the two, who finished tightening the last two wheel nuts for me, called me Madam, and felt very comfortable. Do you think he really did help me with the wheel?

M: *Yes*.

My back was starting to ache and so I asked Fran to tighten the last two bolts on the wheel. She was, at this point, kneeling down and tightening the final bolt, while I was kneeling down beside her. That is when I started to look over my shoulder and notice the 'Light' and soon after that Xenap offered his help to Fran.

F: Was that one of the two you met later on the craft?

M: *Yes.*

F: Am I allowed to know which one it was?

M: *Xenap.*

F: Is he, in the physical..... in the way that they appeared to us at the time, as an older man and a younger man, would that be a representation of a discrepancy in their ages in their real state? You know, is one older and one younger?

M: *It's not got the same importance, if that's the right word.*

F: So why would they choose to appear like that?

M: *Just to look normal. To make us feel comfortable; that they were just American ranchers with a little boy.*

They are very much aware of intruding too much into our lives, as we have to live our life here under earthly conditions and laws. Our soul will incarnate here for various reasons and there is such a thing as karma, although this is not worked through our lives as we sometimes believe it is. It is not 'an eye for an eye' or 'tooth for a tooth'. It just doesn't work like that. It is much more subtle and much more complex. It is energy that is disturbed in such a way that that energy must, at some point in the future, come back into balance, and we work this out through our Higher Self. However much we may feel we can handle a certain situation in waking consciousness (in this case, meeting with the Space Brothers), it will have a tremendous impact on our lives and then we will have to try and bring that into our reality here and try to cope on an everyday level. I can assure you, this is not easy and is a decision that one should make with extreme caution. By working with our Higher Self, or in another part of our consciousness, the meetings can happen with as little conscious intrusion into our lives as possible. There will, I might add, be a time in the not-too-distant future when open fraternization with our Space Brothers will become the norm. Until then, we will have to accept that this is the way they work. There is always a part of the experience made available that will give you the necessary realization that 'something went on here'.

F: This, of course, would explain what we thought at the time was a lack of obvious questions on their part.

M: *Yes.*

When they first arrived, 'Tellos' said, "Looks like we have arrived too late" In my conscious mind I believed he was meaning about being too late to help change the tire, but in the deeper consciousness of the regression it was made very plain to me that what he meant was that they did not realize I was in the area and they arrived too late to stop me being taken by the military. Tellos actually told me that he cannot keep his eye on me all the time and that I have to stop putting myself in dangerous situations like this. The sickness, which I will touch upon later in this chapter, and which happened outside the caravan, was, he told me, a temporary cleansing for what the military had done when they were probing my mind.

F: When you felt that Xenap was looking in the back of the car, in the boot, and you were slightly suspicious of him looking at your photography equipment, what was he doing do you think?

M: *I think it was just out of interest.*

F: Would they have checked to see that we were safe? That the car was safe?

M: *I think they would have known that.*

F: Um…you being sick later was a form of cleansing?

M: *It was the start of it, yes.*

F: From what? Cleansing from what?

M: *Possibly from probing my mind.*

F: And later, much later in the whole Nevada experience, when we were both sick, was that a further part of the cleansing?

M: *Yes.*

F: Was that occasioned by them or by Adrian Dvir?

M: (Long pause) *They are different races and they have different agendas, but there's a lot of.... brotherly communication, if I can use that word, and they* (Adrian Dvir's contacts) *have got certain equipment available and it was agreed that would be satisfactory.*

F: Would it have happened – would we have been cleansed, if Adrian Dvir hadn't been there?

M: *They knew they'd be there.*

F: So it was pre-arranged?

M: *It would have happened.*

F: Was this pre-arranged – the whole thing – Area 51 – everything?

M: *Well, it's not necessarily pre-arranged but in, sort of, where their mind is, it can all be set in motion.*

F: Because they are beyond time?

M: *Yes.*

Fran then asked me about the truck that the ranchers had arrived in and I replied that there was no truck. This was all done for our benefit and that is why we were always confused as to why we never saw the truck arrive. It was just there and we could never explain that fact. Even though we saw them drive away in the truck, in this deeper state of consciousness they actually walked back into the light and the light just flew away and was gone from sight in a matter of seconds. As for Fran never seeing the 'little boy', he obviously put her into 'stasis' almost from the moment they arrived.

M: *The connection was made when we changed the wheel.*

F: Connection with what? With your brothers?

M: *Yes. The little boy, for some reason, had just put you on 'hold'.*

F: And who was the little boy? Was he part of your race or....?

M: *No. I'm just trying to find out why he was with them. He's totally different. I'm not too sure.*

F: Presumably he was with your brothers?

M: *He was a different energy and that's why I was feeling he was odd – but he's OK! He was with them. He might have been, actually... he's from another race, but he may have been, like, being schooled.*

F: But was he indeed a little boy?

M: *No.*

F: So that was, even for you.....

M: *He's an off-worlder.*

F: But he put a disguise on for you?

M: *Well, I was looking at him with earthly consciousness at the time, but I knew he was odd.*

In the regression, we then moved on to where I was feeling sick in the mobile home. I have gone outside and am standing at the side of the mobile home. I am being sick and looking up at this really bright light that is in the sky, directly above me. It is a huge white light and somewhere inside this light I can see a red light.

M: *It's moonlight. I'm being sick. There's a light above me. No, I'm in the light!*

In this expanded consciousness I actually saw myself being lifted up into the air in a beam that was directed down to me from this light. My legs were wide apart, my head had dropped back and my arms were down to my sides and I looked just like a lifeless dummy being lifted up.

D: You are in the light. What can you see? Tell us what you can see in the light.

M: *I'm in a room. There are other people here. They're not from Earth. They're from other star systems. They've got silver suits on. Oh, I know them! They're..... they're my Space Brothers!"*

The words here do not do justice to what I actually felt at that moment. The realization that I was with my Space Brothers was just simply overwhelming. There was also a massive revelation for me here that hit me hard on an emotional level. Tellos went on to explain that 'he' was the tiger that would come into my room as a child and would stand and watch me from the bottom of my bed. He also told me that it was he that came to my room in London and left the calling card and also that it was he that met me on the marshes after my friends had floated off in the boat, and made sure that I got to the main road and to safety. This is what I mean by Brotherly Love. I am incarnate here on Earth, helping in my own small way to open people's minds to who they really are, in preparation for the coming vibrational changes. It is not easy living here, especially when you have memories of your homeland. A place of such peace and universal love. A place where there is no such thing as violence. A place of freedom, whether in the world around you or freedom of your own mind. A mind that can greatly embrace the Universe. Tellos does not look after me in a fatherly way; it is more a brotherly connection. A connection that is bonded on a very deep and personal level.

Fran then asked me if I knew where they were from and for some unknown reason I replied: *R 67*!

Fran then noted the following:

At this point, the fingers on Mike's right hand began to move[2], each finger moving almost as if playing an invisible keyboard, with the whole hand arching and curving at times. He had done this once in the past in my presence, when he felt he was being given a communication whilst in a deeply relaxed state and, on that occasion, some of the fingers and especially the thumb, bent backwards over the back of the hand, in a way that would normally be impossible. I asked him now why he was moving his hand and he replied that it was a form of communication, that he was downloading information and telling them things. A two-way process that kept him in touch with his homeland and updated them on how he was doing here[2].

Mike comments:

Some years ago, I visited a local hypnotherapist, over an eight-week period, to look into some of my experiences. He was not versed in ET contact but was willing to help. At the start of the third session my hands started to move, as explained above, and it got to the point that as soon as I was relaxed enough the movement would start and would last the entire session. It had reached a point where that was all I was doing. I told him, while I was in this deeper state, that I was communicating with my Space Brothers. I stopped the sessions after that as I felt acutely embarrassed because this movement lasted almost the entire two-hour session.

F: Why are you moving your hand?

M: *Communication.*

F: With whom?

M: *My Space Brothers. Downloading.*

F: Downloading what?

M: *Information. It's two-way. I'm telling them things as well. They're giving me information, trying to help me while I'm here.*

F: Comforting you?

M: *Sort of, yes.*

F: May we know their names?

M: *Tellos and Xenap... Xenap... X –E – N –A – P, but I mean, that's not how they spell it.*

F: No, no.

M: *Tellosh.... Tellosh.... Xenap.... Zhenap* (repeating the names as if trying to get the pronunciation correct).

F: Are these beings... do they have gender as we do?

M: *Yes, they are physical but not dense physical.*

F: So, what gender are they?

M: *These two are male.*

F: And they are friends?

M: *Well, we'd say we are brothers, but not like we know brothers here.*

F: How... do you know why it is necessary for you to be given this information, or why this information exchange is taking place?

M: *Partly keeping me in touch with my homeland, so, in a way it's like a telephone call to a friend, asking how things are, etc.*

F: So it's catching you up on the news?

M: *Partly.*

F: And what's the rest of it?

M: *Why I'm here. How things are going.*

F: So you are, like, reporting in?

M: *Partly.*

F: Are they giving you instructions or more information….?

M: *Instructions come from above. We're on equal footing here. We're connected.*

F: You're connected? In what way?

M: *In our minds.*

F: So this information is coming mentally?

M: *Yes.*

F: Do you know if you will be able to access this information consciously or is there no need?

M: *Sighs. They're giving me a sort of a rose, and that is very important.*

F: Rose?

M: *Mmm. Type of rose, type of pink rose, but it's not a rose… it's a rose from their frequency.*

F: A rose from their frequency?

M: *It's like a rose.*

F: It's a flower, definitely a flower?

M: *Yes.*

F: What happens to that rose in this frequency?

M: *It's in the heart. It's an emotional… it's a…love…it's a connection…it's a love connection.*

F: For your benefit?

M: *For my benefit, yes. For being here.*

A short time after these regressions I was talking to a friend on the telephone and happened to mention this etheric pink rose experience. My friend is a long-time member of the organization 'The White Eagle Lodge', where she is involved as a healer and a teacher of Astrology. 'White Eagle' is the name given by a discarnate spirit teacher of great dignity, who gave his message through the instrumentality of Grace Cooke, from the 1930s right through till the mid-1970s. The White Eagle Lodge is now a very well-established centre for healing and spiritual teaching and has sister Lodges based in many countries around the world. See: http://www.whiteagle.org/we_home.htm. My friend did not comment much at the time but, two days later, I received a large, brown envelope through the post, together with a note explaining the contents. Apparently, White Eagle had said many things about the etheric pink rose and enclosed in the envelope were just a selection of them.

I cannot tell you how pleased I was to receive these writings from my friend, as this experience in my regression was so profound and strange it made me wonder if a very wild imagination had come into play, because I had never heard of such a thing as an etheric pink rose being placed within a person's heart. In the regression, I was sitting and talking to Tellos and Xenap when Tellos spread out the palm of his hand and I watched in amazement as a pink rose materialized in his hand. A beautiful, perfect pink rose. This had been formed out of the ether, as I said in my regression. Tellos then leant forward and placed the rose inside my heart. I looked down and saw his hand and the rose go through my physical body and into my heart centre. The 'Love' that emanated from him and the feeling that impacted my body from this rose was incredible. I could have died at that moment and would have been the happiest person in the Universe. That is how I felt for that moment in time. The rose, I sensed at this deeper level, was put there to increase the connection that we already had between us. It was strengthening the link, I felt, for the troubled times ahead. It was a way of saying, "Look, we will always be here with you. We are only a vibration away and this connection is just to reaffirm that you will never be alone."

White Eagle on the meaning of the rose:

"Can you believe that all souls at heart long for harmony, and so long for God? That is because all souls belong to God. Each one of you here tonight is a child of God. Within your heart is the Christ-child. You are yourself a potential Christ-child. The Christ-child is symbolized by the rose because of its fragrance and beauty. The old type of rose had to be protected by thorns, which caused anyone to handle the rose with great care. The rose then, is the symbol of the sweet Christ-love in the human heart, and this must be handled with great care. It can be a little prickly, as you are all finding out. You must learn to be tender with the heart of another, so that neither you nor he will be hurt. The rose is perfect in form and opens its petals to the sun. The human heart is perfectly formed in God's own image, and will always, always, respond to the sunlight of truth, to the sunlight of God." *(Stella Polaris Feb-Mar 1956 pp65-66)*

"Beloved brethren, will you hold in your mind the symbol of the soft pink rose; the symbol of the Mother love, Divine Love? Create the form of the rose in your mind, inhaling its fragrance, feeling the softness of its petals and looking into the centre and seeing there the sparkling jewel of the Christ-Spirit. This should release in you a beautiful spiritual power...This is a symbol of your own heart centre or chakra. To create this rose you have to create beautiful thoughts, you have to think softly, gently, radiantly, and the form of the rose comes on the etheric plane - because you are using etheric matter, which is so much more easily molded by thought. When you on Earth can create a perfect and beautiful flower, you are making a resting place, or a 'cave', for the birth of Christ; for in that heart centre, in that flower which your mind has created, the perfect jewel, the flashing jewel of Spirit rests..." *(Stella Polaris Feb-Mar 1973)*

"Beloved brother, try to visualize, as you read these words, a delicate pink rose, perfect in form and color, opening its petals to the spiritual sun which falls upon it. Try to become en rapport with that rose....inhale the spiritual perfume, absorb the delicacy of its life, its aura. It will raise you far above the earth into a world of silence, peace, love and truth...This rose is the symbol of the Christ life, the Christ sweetness and purity, of life untainted by the earth.

Withdraw into the consciousness of the rose as often as you can. Its fragrance will permeate your being and it will help you live

within the infinite Spirit of Love."
(Stella Polaris Aug-Sept 1972)
The Temple of the Rose:

"We visualize the symbol of the cross of light encircled by light. At its centre we see a perfect pink rose. Let us inhale its sweet perfume, and as we do so, receive renewed inspiration and courage to continue our endeavor to overcome all selfishness and the pull of materialism, and to work for brotherly love among men. We pray for understanding of our brothers' problems and for the vision to work together, side by side with them in greater harmony.

'As we meditate, the rose grows in size and we are enfolded in its fragrance - the temple of the rose; its walls are translucent, shining with rose-tinged light. We are surrounded by our spirit brethren and supported by their love. All things work together for him who loves God."
(Written by Grace Cooke. Stella Polaris Jun-Jul 1977)

I knew at this point that I would soon be returning back to Earth and more importantly, back to the mobile home and Fran. I then felt, quite strongly in my mind, to walk over to an oval window and look out. I saw the roof of the mobile home way below and in this altered state of consciousness I could see right through the roof as though it wasn't there and into the interior. I saw Fran sitting on the edge of the bed. She was motionless and her head was down and there was an overwhelming feeling of being lost, isolation and fear. Tellos told me at this point that Fran had got herself into an awful panic as she had been outside the mobile home, in the cold, searching for me for quite a while and had finally come to the realization that I was not there. She went back inside the mobile home and was at a loss what to do. It was at this point, he said, that they had to put her into a state of suspended animation for her own safety. Shortly after this, I returned back down the beam of light, to Little Ale'Inn.

M: *I have to get back to Fran.*

D: You can come back to Fran whenever you like.

M: *Fran's in the caravan. I'm somewhere else!*

After this regression Fran agreed that this is exactly how she felt and that she was sitting on the edge of the bed in quite a state of anxiety when I finally came back in.

Fran then continued the questioning.........

F: Are you aware, in any detail that you could share with us, of your purpose?

M: *To raise consciousness....... and to witness.*

In the first chapter of this book, you may remember, at the age of four, I told my Mother that something very important was going to happen on this planet and this was to do with the consciousness of all life forms, including the planet Earth. A shift in consciousness or awareness will become available for those who have the eyes to see what is going on around them or whose minds are, at the very least, open enough to see the true reality on this planet. Not the reality that is conditioned and laid out before us, that is controlled through the media, businesses, religions, schools, banks, etc., but the reality of who we really are and what we are truly capable of achieving. We are reaching a point in our evolution that will have a profound impact on our lives and our future existence and it is truly up to each and every one of us, as individual spiritual beings, to play our part. The future that is decided for you will be chosen by none other then yourself. We are not just physical bodies; machines that are somehow separate from God, 'The Source'. We are, in fact, multidimensional beings who 'are' the Source. We do not need to rely on some external force to connect us with 'The Divine' because we 'are' the Divine. We have our own personal space within the Divine and we are in control of our own destiny. There is no Heaven or Hell, no Purgatory or Original Sin; we simply do not need to carry such baggage. We create our own Heaven and Hell through the state of our own minds.

There are places on this earth that would seem like hell to the people that have to exist there and I am sure there are some people who have created their own little bit of heaven. There are planes of existence beyond this three-dimensional world of ours that would certainly feel like Heaven because, in those places, you would be much more in touch with your inner divine self and would be free to experience life on a deeper level then you currently can. You would then be fulfilling your true destiny. To have any chance of moving our consciousness to this 'higher level' we have to think 'outside the box'! We have to see the 'illusion' of what is happening around us right now. It does not have to be like this, but to have any hope of change we have to make the effort to change ourselves. We think we are free but we are not. We are trapped inside a bubble of false security. The system is set up to keep our minds so busy that all we can do is think about survival, financial survival. It takes all our energy and there is no energy left in the pot to actually take time out and quietly think "Is this right for me?" We have no energy left to even think about trying to change the way we lead our lives. Every time someone stops to think about where they are heading and decides to make a conscious change for the better, it will have an impact, somewhere, on someone else and they will then think about 'questioning what we never question' and make a change also in their lives. The future is 'bright' but to be in our rightful place, we have to make the effort to change.

F: Is this your first time here?

M: (Long pause and a few sighs). *I may not be coming back. Been here too long. I've done my stint. I can go home.*

F: Do you know how you'll go home?

M: *When I decide to leave.*

F: They'll come for you?

M: *Not necessarily. They'll be there… if I change form.*

F: If you died in this frequency, your consciousness would immediately be back home?

M: *I would be in my original form.*

F: Which is as they are?

M: *Yes.*

F: Is the lifespan on your home world longer than ours?

M: *Much longer, yes.*

F: So, did you, in fact, just take… were you already partway through your life span there when you chose to come here?

M: *I don't understand.*

F: Did you already have a conscious existence there before you came to this planet?

M: *It's my homeland. This is something I had to do.*

D: Where is your homeland?

M: *That's for no one to know.*

D: But you know?

M: *I know.*

© Mike Oram 2005

1 See *Suggested Reading* 16/1

2 On page 75 of *The Convoluted Universe, Book 1* by Dolores Cannon, a client under hypnotic regression also makes hand movements:

"After a few seconds of suggestions she relaxed and began making very graceful hand motions.

D. Why are you making these motions?

J. It's a greeting.

D. Who are you greeting?

J. A Being.

She continued with hand motions almost reverently and indicated that the Being in front of her was making the same motions."

CHAPTER 17

THE FLOATING CITY AND THE BIOMECHANICAL BEING

I rest in the bosom of my thought
And prepare for things unseen.
For all the future I have sought
Remains still inside my dream.

For over 25 years now I have been 'taken' in the middle of the night; usually between the hours of 1a.m. and 3a.m. It does, however, also occur in the daytime as well, but not as frequently. I know when it is going to happen and I prepare myself for the experience. I will get a feeling, a knowing in my head, either minutes, hours or even up to two days before the event. If I have only a few minutes warning, then I will immediately sit down in my recliner, tune-in and wait. If I have just retired to bed and feel that the experience is imminent, I will then lie back on the pillow and focus my mind on what is about to take place. Shortly after that, I will become aware of a presence and a buzzing sound will start in my head and move down through my body. This vibration through my body builds up and reaches a crescendo and at that point I simply lift off and go straight through the ceiling or closed window. I love this incredible, vibrational change and lift-off and if it has not happened for a while I actually miss it! I have been told that this process is to change the frequency of my body and this allows me to then pass through a closed window or ceiling. The actual lift-off and feeling of weightlessness is a very pleasant experience. The lift-off is quite gradual and the break in consciousness usually takes place once I have arrived on the craft and remains that way until it is time for me to return, although there have been many experiences where I have been allowed to remember much more than this. There is normally enough of the experience in my conscious mind to make me aware that something has happened and then that can be looked into at a later time, under regression. Whether this is arranged by, 'Them' or whether it is coincidental, I do not know, but I rather favour the first option. I have a feeling that enough of the experience is left available to the conscious mind so we can then make our own conscious decision to look into the matter further, if we choose so to do. This is how we grow as spiritual beings and also become closer to our galactic family and they, of course, then remain working within universal law.

Although I mentioned earlier that the 'take-off' is usually gradual, there was an experience back in 1990 that literally took my breath away.

I was now living in the Lake District, in the North of England, with my then girlfriend, Karen. It was New Year's Eve and we had gone to Karen's parents for the festivities. Karen's brother and his wife were also there, having driven up from Norfolk the day before. The evening went well, with a game of charades and some quizzes, and we retired about 2 a.m. We were all up by 10 a.m. the following morning and had a main meal at midday. We then waved goodbye to Karen's brother and his wife as they set off to make their way back South.

Karen's parents lived in a delightful, detached house in a small, quaint village. They had two living rooms at opposite ends of the house; one, for Karen's mother, so she could play the piano and listen to her classical music and the other for her father, so he could enjoy watching his sport on television. Karen and her mother retired to one of these rooms, to watch a film on television, while her father and I occupied the other. A log fire was crackling away, giving the room a cosy feel, and we were engaged in discussion. Karen's father was a very polite man and if he were about to leave the room, for whatever reason, he would excuse himself and tell me where he was going. We were part way through conversation when suddenly, without any warning, he stood up and left the room. I was very surprised at this and almost felt a little shocked, as this was out of character. I thought about it for a moment, then just rested my head back into the armchair and closed my eyes. Almost immediately, without any warning, the buzzing started in my head and coursed through my body in an instant and I shot up through the ceiling at the most amazing speed. I felt the change in temperature instantly, as I left the warmth of that cosy living room and was propelled into the cold air of a January day. I was travelling up into the sky so fast that I could feel the G-force on my face. My skin contorted and stretched back as I moved through the air at lightening speed. I could feel hands on top of my hands as they were resting on the arms of the chair. This had puzzled me for years, until the regression sessions in 2005, as I actually felt that the armchair had gone with me! I also felt hands on the tops of my shoulders.

When I was way up in the sky, the upward movement stopped. I then went along horizontally at the same breakneck speed. I passed over a pine forest and, with heightened senses, I breathed in the strong aroma of pine. Then over some hills and another pine forest with the same strong smell. Speedily I arrived at the coastline of Eastern England and carried on out to sea. I eventually stopped and could see, way below, the glittering water. I moved forward a little more and saw below me a huge, round object. It was a tremendous size and in the centre of it was an opening that was circular and flooded with the most intense white light. I descended into this light and immediately felt the change of temperature as I was once again out of the cold January air. I landed on a solid floor and the hands that had been on my shoulders, and the hands that had been resting on top of my own hands, were released. I cannot begin to tell you how incredibly excited I was about all this and felt that, at last, I would be fully aware of what was happening when, the next thing I remember was being lowered back down into the living room of Karen's parents' home!

I was bitterly disappointed but quickly pulled myself together and stood up. My shirt, for some unknown reason, was soaked in sweat. I ran through the house and into the other living room in time to see all three of them in suspended animation. Karen's father was sitting on the arm of the armchair while Karen and her mother were still on the couch. A few seconds later they suddenly animated and came back to life and I called to Karen to come and listen to what I had to tell her. I asked Karen's father why he suddenly left the room but he never really gave a clear-cut answer. None of them believed me of course, and for years I found this whole episode utterly frustrating.

This was one of the experiences I wanted to look at when David Coggins came to stay at my home, in July 2005, to conduct a series of regressions. Once in a relaxed state, I was taken back to the time when I shot off, through the ceiling at breakneck speed. Karen's father had just left the room. The buzzing flooded through my body and I found myself in the sky. Once again I travelled over the pine forests, over the hills and out to sea. Below me was the huge round object with a circular opening that was flooded with light. I was lowered into this light and landed on what seemed to be a long balcony. When I say long, I mean very long. It had a metal balustrade on the right-hand side and on the left were doors and other corridors. One door was open and there seemed to be a reason for that. I do believe that something went on in that room that was connected to me but, for some reason, we never explored that part of the experience. I looked over the balustrade and way below me was a massive hanger. There were 'V-shaped' craft and round saucers of different sizes that were either static on the floor or hovering and moving around this cavernous area. A voice in my head told me that this was a floating city and that it contained many different races from other systems, that were in alliance with each other. They were, what you might call, a Galactic Alliance. I had been here before. I recognized it. The doors. The hanger. The balustrade. In fact all of it!

A voice again spoke to me and told me to move along the corridor. I walked along and occasionally looked over the balustrade to view the strange craft below. Eventually, in front of me, in the distance, I saw what looked like a camera iris in a lens, at the end of the wall. It seemed to be an airtight door; perhaps leading to outside but I was not really sure. What had more impact on my mind was the tall, biomechanical being that was standing at the end of this corridor. To call him a robot would have been an insult. This was a highly intelligent being that could think and reason and also seemed to have feelings. I knew this 'person', because that is exactly what he seemed to be, a person. He seemed to be no different than you and I, yet much more intelligent. He must have been fifteen feet (4.57 metres) tall and highly complex (See Fig 44). There was a type of chair in his chest cavity and I knew that I had to sit in it. I also knew that I had sat in this very chair several times before. He bent his knees and that allowed me to sit in the chair. Three metal

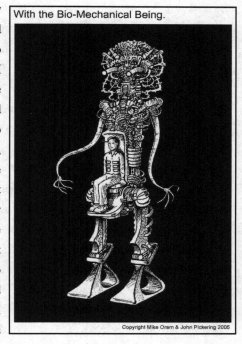

With the Bio-Mechanical Being.

Copyright Mike Oram & John Pickering 2005

Fig 44

strips wrapped round each side of my body and closed onto my chest. This was not a negative thing; it was just to stop me from literally falling out once he stood up. Then a very thin wire came around the right-hand side of my head and seemed to enter my temple. I knew instantly that this was a health check and I had the utmost faith in this wonderful being. It was almost like meeting an old friend that you had not seen for a while and, however strange this may sound, he seemed like a 'friend of the family!' Why this health check was carried out I am not sure and this was not looked at any further under regression but it is something I would like to look into at another time.

I think the half-memory of this chair led to my believing for years that I had actually left the living room still sitting in the armchair. Tellos has told me in the past that they 'stitch' together experiences so as to cause us the least stress and impact in this life. He has said that we may think we can deal with all this and easily amalgamate it into our conscious reality here on earth, but it is far harder then we realize. They live within universal laws and one of those laws is about interfering with evolution on other planets. So, they try and work behind the scenes to change or raise our consciousness, in the hope of giving us a greater understanding of who they are and who we are. They try and work with us by creating the least impact on our lives as is possible.

After about ten minutes the 'check-up' seemed to be over and the thin wire retracted from my right temple. Then this wonderful biomechanical being bent his knees again and the three strips of metal that covered both sides of my chest retracted. I then slid off the chair and onto the ground. I turned around and looked up at this amazing being and smiled. He looked down and somehow sent thoughts or feelings into my head that he was pleased to see me again and hoped that I was coping well back on Earth. I then heard another voice in my head, that told me to walk back along the corridor. I felt sad at saying goodbye to the biomechanical being but somehow knew that we would be meeting again. I turned around and started to walk back along the long corridor and, once again, found myself stopping and looking over the balustrade at the spectacular sight below. The huge 'V-shaped' craft that were parked and the smaller disc-shaped vehicles coming in to land or lifting off and making their way along the vast hanger to exit on who-knows-what journey. My mind was just flooded with all sorts of wonders. Where had these craft been? Where were the departing ones going? Why have we not been told by our governments that such wonders are taking place right under our very noses? Scientists theorise about the possible chances of finding other life in the universe or speculate on the possibility of other life when they detect another planet umpteen light years away that may have the right conditions to support life, yet here on Earth there are tens of thousands of people that are actually having contact on a daily basis, and they fail to take an interest! Am I missing something here?

I continued along to the end of the corridor and noticed a man waiting there for me. As I got closer, I once again recognized Tellos, my dear Space Brother. He seemed to pop up everywhere in my life and now I find him on this floating city. I was so pleased to see him again and we shook hands. A flood of energy shot through my being and for a while it made me feel quite inadequate because I am sure that my energy did not flood through him in the same way. He must have read my thoughts because he instantly smiled and impressed on my mind that I was not to underestimate myself. This energy exchange is, he said, a two-way thing and he was as pleased as I was that this meeting was taking place. He then led me through one of the many doors that were placed along the balcony and as soon as I stepped inside I started to feel a little faint and the air felt heavier. The buzzing started in my head and, in no time at all, I was back outside and hovering over the sea. At great speed I then headed for the coastline and inland, over the pine forests, over the hills, back to the small village where Karen's parents lived. I looked down below and recognized the top of the house and instantly found myself back in the armchair. The hands that were once again on top of my hands and shoulders immediately lifted and after a few seconds I opened my eyes and looked around the room, slightly disorientated.

In October 2005 I gave a talk at the 'Probe' conference in Blackpool and this gave me the opportunity to openly discuss some of these experiences for the first time. I had made some 35mm transparencies of the technically good and uncannily accurate drawings that John Pickering did for my book and these were shown also. I projected onto the screen the symbols, magnetic pulse generator, biomechanical being, etc. The talk went well, was generously applauded and seemed to be successful. At the start of the lecture, a step-ladder, that was leaning against the wall near me, decided at that point to leave the wall and suddenly toppled forward, crashing on to the floor. I turned around and thanked who ever it was that was late turning up from another dimension and in the rush knocked over the ladder! This was, of course, a joke and brought laughter from the audience and helped to settle people in.

Also during that day, whilst sitting listening to other lecturers, my right leg was repeatedly poked and tugged at. As Fran and I were on two chairs right at the back of the room, separate from the main audience, there was no one around to do this. Whilst in the 'speakers' room' at lunchtime, Fran was pushed so hard in the small of the back that she lurched forward and fell out of her shoes. This was witnessed by those present, including the organizers of the conference and again, there was no one behind her to do this.

A conference attendee, an old friend of mine who had experienced the early days in Warminster, as I had, asked for permission to video-tape my lecture and slide show and I was only too pleased to let him make a recording. He told me after my talk had finished that he had charged his batteries up to full charge the preceding evening and, to make sure that they were fully charged, he said he continued to charge them for another couple of hours. They should have lasted for almost three hours, he told me later. He was looking through the viewfinder of his camera while recording my talk and could see, in the top right-hand corner of the screen, that the batteries were fully charged but as soon as I put the symbols the Light Beings gave me onto the projector screen, the batteries drained in an instant. He said that one second they were showing full charge and the next second they were drained and the camera immediately shut down and so he failed to capture the symbols on the recording. Up to that point, my talk had lasted for 45 minutes, so he should have had plenty of battery life left. He told me later that he had never experienced such a thing before.

After the talk, a lady approached me, quite excitedly, and told me that she had also met this biomechanical being and had also sat in the chair! I was amazed to hear this and so pleased to get the confirmation. I was at conflict in my mind whether to mention this being at all, because of the strangeness factor, and only decided a couple of days before to go ahead and tell all. I am glad that I did so and this also goes to show that we must be brave with this stuff, because however weird some of this may sound, it is still important to get the information out there into the public domain. We are dealing with very advanced Alien races from other star systems, galaxies and dimensions and some of their technology is going to be so way in advance of our own that it may well be beyond our comprehension. Today's accepted knowledge was often someone's crackpot idea to yesterday's men of learning. Scientists today still make such wild assumptions, based on limited vision and faulty foundations. These faulty foundations hold up their entire life's' work and it would be financially and personally disastrous if someone were to take out one of the bricks from the bottom of the pack! If a UFO experiencer or Visitor contactee appeared on a television programme with one of these scientists or psychologists they would be pulled to pieces, simply because this subject is so open to ridicule and most people would prefer to believe the person who has degrees and letters after his or her name. Look what they did to Galileo, yet he was right! So, when we decide to bare our souls on stage and talk about these new aspects of reality, we must not end up basing our decision so to do on whether the public will think we are mad or not, because we may miss confirming for another that their experience is real and valid. If I had decided to not mention the biomechanical being then I would not have received confirmation from that lady about her experience with possibly the same being or one like it.

One month later, Fran and I went to Lincolnshire, to stay with friends whose son has had Alien contact all his life and claims to be an 'Indigo Child'. He had been giving a talk in San Francisco only the week before and, after the talk, a man from the audience came to speak to him and, to my friend's surprise, mentioned this biomechanical being and told my friend that he also had sat in the chair!

The third strange anomaly to happen in relation to this biomechanical being, was the following: When John Pickering was ready to draw this being I went to his home to sit with him and describe how this unusual being looked, as it was quite complex and I was worried that John may come up against problems depicting what was, to our eyes, quite bizarre. I had no need to worry; John immediately started drawing at breakneck speed. The image was quickly forming right in front of my eyes. I turned to John and asked him how he knew what to draw, as I had not yet explained it to that degree. John looked round, smiled, then turned back to the sheet of paper and continued. It was taking shape fast and he started to put in the thin wire that came around the right side of my head and entered my temple, before I had told him about this. I then noticed an odd thing happening. He began to rub the top of his head really hard, as if something was irritating him. I asked him what was wrong but he said, nothing, he was okay. I then asked him again how he could draw this being so well when I had not properly explained it to him and again, he just smiled and continued to rub the top of his head. I then said firmly: "John, do you know this being? Have you seen him before?" He did not answer, so I pushed the question at him once more, only this time even more firmly. He turned towards me and said that he had seen both the being and the chair before, but would say no more about it. He continued to rub his head until the drawing was finished and then no more was said about it and shortly after that I drove back home. I found out the following morning, through his partner, that a large, round lump had appeared on top of his head, as big as a large marble. His partner had told him that, if it was still there the following morning, she would take him to hospital, but in the morning it had completely disappeared! Whether this was a psychosomatic condition or not, I do not know, and John was reluctant to talk more about it, as he usually is with these matters.

What this all means I have no way of knowing but, in this elusive subject, confirmation is a wonderful thing and the more people that are brave enough to stand up and tell their stories, the better it will be for all of us.

CHAPTER 18

GENETICS, ORIGINS AND TULIP PEOPLE

Calm yourself my friend!

Why jump the spiky rail?

Walk through the gate

And mind that rusty nail.

The tears of wisdom run free.

Everything is known:

Understanding,

Purpose,

Meaning.

Be at peace.

Go home.

I had been feeling strange all day; something was going to happen but I was not sure what. This was not the energy of Tellos, my Space Brother, I knew that. I was now quite accustomed to his particular energy and this was not it. It felt okay and I was not apprehensive in any way, I just wanted to know who was around and what was going to happen. It was a fine, summer's day in 1997 and I had been reading and writing a new song. I was in a good state of mind. The sun had been sending its heat through my living room window all day and now the light was starting to turn golden as it set behind the mountains. 'What a beautiful place to live!' I thought to myself, 'and what a lovely day it has been!' Late in the evening I meditated for a while, then decided to retire to bed. It was around midnight when I finally turned out the light and this feeling that something was about to happen had not left me all day. I lay there, adjusting to the darkness, and finally went to sleep. At 3 a.m. I suddenly awoke. 'They are here!' I thought to myself. I quickly turned to look at the clock, to get an idea of the time. Then the buzzing started in my head and ran through my whole body. I was vibrating very fast and I knew that 'lift-off' was imminent. I prepared myself, as well as one can do in such situations, and soon after that I went up through the ceiling and into the warm, summer night air outside. I saw a powerful light above and ahead and was heading directly towards it. I entered the light and my conscious memory was put on hold. This is so frustrating but is par for the course for the many tens of thousands of us who have these experiences. I was dimly aware, through this experience, of children and emotions directed towards these children, and this was something that I had to look into when the opportunity arose.

About five years later, I discovered some books written by a lady called Dolores Cannon. She had, for several years, been regressing people who have UFO experiences and was now accepted as a world authority on the subject. At the back of her books are a contact address and email and, after giving it some thought, I decided to get in touch with her and explain some of my experiences. She lived in America, so it would not be easy for me to see her, as getting to America would be costly. I then found out that she constantly traveled the world, giving talks to various organizations and also doing regressions, so perhaps there would be a window of opportunity there at some point. In February 2005, I received an email saying that Dolores would be in London for a couple of days and had one session available. I would have to respond very quickly to let them know if I wanted to proceed, as it would otherwise soon be filled by someone else.

It is surprising how many people out there require this sort of help to understand what exactly is going on in their lives. How could you go to a doctor and say that you feel that Aliens are abducting you? He would send you straight to a psychiatrist who would have absolutely no understanding of the subject at all and would either give you pills or say that you are delusional or both! Anyone dealing with contactees also needs to understand the spiritual aspect of human beings. We are not just physical shells of matter with a brain and five senses; we also have an etheric body. This body is known as our health body and is the energy immediately surrounding our physical body, which is picked up by Kirlian photography. There is also our astral body, which is known as our emotional body, and any person that has gifted sight is able to see the many changing colors that this body emits as it reflects our moods. The astral body is also the body that we use when we travel at night. Most people leave their body when the physical shell is resting and while some of them may just float around the room or just above the sleeping form, some will venture further afield and visit other places or people. The astral body is also sometimes used when Aliens take humans aboard their ships. We also have a higher mind and higher self and this is the part of us that is eternal.

Tellos once told me, back in 1983, that I did not need to see their ships physically any more as it would serve no future purpose. He said that I was to now use my higher mind to tune-in and contact them. He said that 'we', as a race, had to reach up to them and that doing so would help us to raise the frequencies of our own minds and bodies. He said that they would be prepared to meet us halfway but 'we', as individuals and as a race, had to make some personal effort to reach up to them. Unfortunately, this does take effort, and a lot of people are not prepared to make that choice but unless it is done, there is no way forward to joining our greater galactic family. It is as simple as that.

He also told me about reincarnation and how we should look at ourselves as a pearl on a necklace. The necklace is the totality of our being and each pearl is a life in the ocean of life and how we live that life will, in some way or form, affect the totality of our being. It is just 'experience' I have been told, but an experience none the less that is important to the whole. The quality of our heart centre is what matters here. How we treat each other, how we treat the animal kingdom and how we look after Mother Earth who is, after all, a living, breathing Being who gives us sanctity. She offers us a safe place to be, to allow us to evolve and move on to higher realms and experiences. We must understand also that we do not own this planet; we do not even rent it and there will come a time when we will have to hand it back. Do we want to hand it back in the same condition that it was in when we arrived or do we hand it back 'trashed', like some irresponsible tenant? What would you like to do?

The sad thing is that it probably did not have to be like this, when we had people like Tesla and Wilhelm Reich who were on the verge of creating non-polluting, free energy. What happened to these people? I suggest you do some reading and see for yourself why Wilhelm Reich was thrown into a mental institution and most of his work destroyed. Was it just too much to bear for the controlling oil companies of the time? I mean, how can you tax free energy? A friend of mine dug a well on land that he owned, to produce clear water for his own use, only to be told by the water company that he had to pay for it. They told him that they owned all the water underground and even the water that fell from the sky! So, I suppose, if we had free energy, they would say that they also owned any energy that is produced from wherever, free or not! Mind you, even paying for 'free energy' would be better for the planet as a whole as it would, at the very least, be non-polluting.

Tellos has also told me that they would have helped us a long while ago if only we laid down our weapons of destruction. What is the point, he said, of giving us more technology that could then be used to create weapons of mass destruction, when we have already been driven mad by the technology that we already have. He said that if they gave us more technology now, it would not be put into the hands of the people, it would go straight to the military, who would then use it on other countries who 'step out of line' or on their own people, if they needed to. He said that what these people do not realize is that we are 'One People', living on a single planet and we should be working together as a whole. Governments should not be making decisions about going to war without the consent of the people. There are other agendas going on here and the scope of this book does not allow me to go into this.

Arrangements were made for me to take the train to London, where I would now have a four-hour session with Dolores, at the Theosophical Society Headquarters. She was staying there overnight, with one of her daughters, as she was giving a talk there the following afternoon. I have been interested in Theosophy since I was eighteen years of age and found, at that time, the Secret Doctrine a most interesting book to read. So, to be having this important session with Dolores at the Theosophical Society Headquarters was quite comforting. The session started with a general chat about some of the things I wanted to look into and when Dolores felt she had enough material, the session got under way.

After the ten-minute induction, I found myself in my living room, back in 1997. I went through images where I saw myself sitting in the recliner reading a book. Then I picked up my guitar and started to compose a song that 'appeared' in my head. Several times I got up from the chair and went to the window and looked out across the mountains and the tree-clad hills, to gain more inspiration. I also saw myself looking around the room, as though I were looking for someone. In the evening, I saw myself meditating and at midnight I went to bed. Before I turned the light out, I again saw myself looking around the room, as though I was aware of a presence. I eventually turned out the light and went to sleep. At 3 a.m. I awoke suddenly, turned the light on and looked at the clock. I was now aware, more strongly then ever, that something was to happen and it was imminent. I lay back on the bed and waited. The buzzing started in my head and pulsed through my whole body. I was nearing the point of lift-off. I knew this as my body had reached the point where the vibration is phenomenal. I just loved this frequency change and waited patiently for the lift-off. Moments later it arrived and I found myself shooting through the ceiling and into the night sky. I saw above me, a bright light and in no time at all I entered, and was immersed in, brightness.

Then there was blackness and I seemed to be stuck! Dolores had a job to move me forward. This is, I am certain, where the imposed block comes in and it requires a person such as Dolores to get you through this block. If you truly are not meant to see what is beyond this darkness, for whatever reason, then your higher mind will tell you so.

Dolores continued to try and move me forward and after a couple more suggestions I turned my head and noticed, on the other side of the room, a stainless-steel-looking bed. Someone was lying on the bed and there were two persons standing at the head of the bed. They each wore a white gown, cap and mask and reminded me of doctors in an operating theatre and that is who I thought they were. At the head of the bed were two stainless steel tubes that were either fixed to the bed or were a separate unit that, perhaps, stood behind the head of the bed. They stood about seven feet (2.13 meters) high and on top of them was a horizontal, flat piece of metal and on top of that were two more metal tubes, the same thickness (five inches (12.70 centimeters) in diameter) and out of them came two, narrow, flexible tubes. One of these flexible tubes came down and went up the person's nose and the other seemed to come down onto the person's body.

I could not see much more detail and so moved myself forward to then stand at the bottom of the bed. I could now see more clearly that there was, indeed, a tube going into this person's nose and the other tube seemed to come down near the person's belly area. I still could not see this person's face properly and so I made the decision to get even closer. I now saw that this person was not human. Well, there were human characteristics but her eyes were different. They were quite large and round and very liquid looking. I now looked up at the two medical people and although they had these masks that were covering their faces, the eyes were exposed and now I could see also that these people were not human either.

I was okay and was not afraid in any way. I was quite calm and looked around with great interest. Dolores asked me if the person lying on the bed had clothes on and so I looked down and said that her belly was naked and exposed but above and below that she was covered with a type of sheet. I now noticed that her belly was full; she was pregnant. I could see her belly clearly and I could see how the skin seemed stretched from the sheer size. It looked smooth and shiny. Things then started to happen and I saw what, at first, I thought was a pair of scissors, but they were long with flattened ends and they seemed to have one of the tubes clamped in them. As I continued to watch, I now noticed that it was not one of the tubes but it seemed to be clamped to an umbilical cord! Someone was talking to me inside my head and I clearly heard the word 'suture'. The scene was frozen once more, and after a while, Dolores told me to go to the next significant moment.

I now found myself in a different room and this one had a totally different energy. A most beautiful woman walked towards me, whom I could only describe under regression as a being with a star-shaped head. I later came to call them the Tulip People and when you look at the cover illustration you will see why. She seemed ancient yet young. Wisdom and love emanated from her. She was holding a baby in her arms and was no more then three feet (0.91 meter) from me. I was magnetically drawn to the Tulip Being's face, as it was hauntingly beautiful and totally beyond what my senses could imagine. I then looked down at the baby in her arms. It was human except for the large round eyes. This child had really fine, wispy hair; so fine that you could hardly see there was hair there at all.

Dolores asked me whose baby it was and I replied that I didn't know. She told me to ask the Tulip lady and I asked her in my mind. I was somewhat shocked when she replied that it was my baby! In amazement I told Dolores what she had said and Dolores asked me how the baby was conceived and again I replied that I did not know. Once more, Dolores told me to question the Tulip lady. I did so and she immediately started to send back really strong images and I felt slightly embarrassed to tell Dolores what I had seen and been told. The answer was 'intercourse' but I quickly stated quite firmly that this was nothing to do with me on a conscious level and I had had no control on this matter at all! The Tulip lady then handed me the child and I held her in my arms. I looked down at her fragile form and thought how beautiful she looked. I had such a lovely feeling holding this child; a strange feeling that I have not consciously felt before. In this life I have never married or had children and so would not know what it is like to hold one's own child. Dolores then asked me when this intercourse took place and I replied that it was in 1996.

Extract from regression:

D: Have you had other contacts with them?

Mike: *Yes*.

D: Have you had contact with them for a long time?

Mike: *17 years*.

D: Do you have other children or is this the only child?

Mike: *There are other children*.

D: Can you tell us why this has been taking place?

Mike: *Procreation*.

D: Why were you chosen for this?

Mike: *Genetics*.

D: Why are they interested in your genetics?

Mike: *It is to do with my origins*.

D: Have you asked them to explain this better?

There was a long silence at this stage and after further questioning it was made clear to us that no more information was to be made available.

The Tulip lady took the child from me and smiled. She could see that I was upset and no doubt read all the thoughts in my mind. The main one being, would I see this child again? I was lost in her eyes. There was so much love and wisdom there that I felt quite inadequate. She made it plain to me that I would see this child again and then turned and walked away. This was the end of this particular journey and I began to feel disoriented. I was led away to another room and soon after that the familiar sensation of frequency change moved quickly through my body until, in no time at all, I was back in my bedroom.

An odd thing happens sometimes when I return from these trips; not every time, but around 40 per cent of the time. I have an old-fashioned doorbell at my front door and often, just as I arrive back, the doorbell rings, or it is a sound that, for some reason, perfectly mimics my doorbell. Every time I hear the bell I go to the front door and open it. Of course, there is no one there, but I cannot stop myself from answering it. Why this happens, I do not know, but the only thing I can think of is that it takes my attention away from what has just happened and perhaps that process then takes my attention away from the experience and helps the memory of the experience fade. It may not be the reason but I can think of no other explanation that would make any sense. Then again, how do we make sense of this 'reality', because the reality that I live in, along with the tens of thousands of others around the world who experience similar things, is certainly not the reality we were told about at school!

This child was on my mind for years and sometimes I felt quite angry that I was not being given the opportunity of seeing her growing up. When this happened, I would sit down and meditate and try to send my thoughts to these Tulip People and demand that they allow me to see her.

Nearly eight years later, in late 2004, my wish was answered. I had retired to bed, again around midnight, and was already prepared for something to happen, as I had been sensing for two to three hours an energy change in my aura. My mind was also detecting a presence in the room. It felt good and I was quite excited and wondering what would happen in the night. I was in bed no longer then fifteen minutes when the familiar buzzing started and quickly ran through my body. Lift-off was imminent and did not disappoint. Once in the light, I found myself in a brightly-lit room. In these places you can never see where the light is emanating from, as it seems to just 'be there'. There is no direct source that you could look at and say, yes, *that* is where it comes from. Also, although the light is bright, it is not bright like our light is bright and is not harsh on the eyes. All my life I have been subject to light-sensitive eyes and on a bad day I even wear sunglasses to watch television or to read a book, much to the amusement of others. So, I know when light is too bright or harsh for my eyes but I never seem to have the same problem when on these ships.

This experience did not need a regression as I remembered it all quite clearly and that may have been because of how I had been demanding to see this child. Although I do not know if that was the case or whether there was some other factor at play. One of the Tulip People, whom I had seen back in 1997, appeared and stood by my right side. Then this small girl entered the room, with another about the same age. They looked about seven or eight years of age and were quite shy but at the same time seemed excited about meeting me and were childishly giggly. The Tulip lady then pointed to the one on my left and told me quite calmly that she was my daughter and made it quite clear that this was the child whose birth I witnessed all those years ago. This child knew there was a connection, but whether she knew that I was her father, I am not sure. She was wearing a blue and white dress that had smocking on the top part and reminded me of dresses that were around in the fifties, and I could not work that out at all. The two of them began to play and the one that was supposed to be my daughter playfully tried to climb onto the back of the other child but she toppled and fell to the ground. She was unhurt but just lay there, as though she did not quite know what to do. She had the most beautiful, large, dark, liquid, round eyes and her skin was as white as porcelain. It did not have an anemic look, as you would expect from a skin so white; it actually looked quite stunning. In fact, she looked just like a porcelain doll as she lay still, for that moment in time, on the floor. Then she stood up and walked over to me and I bent down and gave her a gentle cuddle. The Tulip lady then looked down at them and mentally told them that they had to leave now and off they went. Looking back now, there was not much time available at all and it was all over in about ten minutes but when it was happening I was so excited and bewildered that any time would have satisfied me.

The Tulip lady then motioned me to follow her and we left the room and walked along a long, curving corridor. We entered another room with the same white brilliance that seemed to be everywhere. We passed through this room and into another, much larger, room and I was simply amazed at what was before me. There, on a bed, was a child. He looked about four years old and had the really fine, wispy hair that I had seen on the baby back in 1997. The hair did not seem to have developed much at all, except that it seemed a bit more, curly (See Fig 45). Another Tulip lady was leaning over him and I was told that she was just checking him over to make sure that everything was going as planned. Across the room was a large opening leading into another, even larger, room and from where I was standing I could see what I thought, at first, were bee hives! (Fig 45), As I looked more closely, I could see that they were large, glass-type jars containing fetuses and the tops of the jars had a honey-combed effect that reminded me of bee hives. Tubes emerged from the tops of the jars and they joined a long, horizontal pipe that was fixed above them. These fetuses, I was told, were continuing development

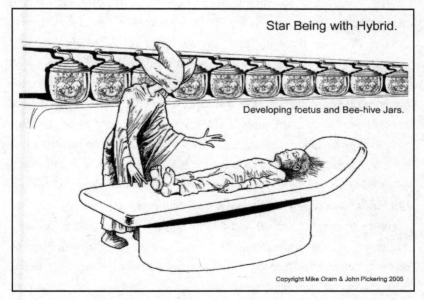

Star Being with Hybrid.

Developing foetus and Bee-hive Jars.

Fig 45

outside of the womb and they seemed to be floating in a liquid. Why this was being done to these particular children was not made clear to me and for some reason, I felt it best not to ask. If anything, I did pick up that there may have been complications, caused by more then one reason, relating to their premature birth and susbsequent placement inside these incubation chambers.

Why my extended trip to the beehive jars was carried out I do not know and this, again, is something I need to look into in a future regression. It was now time to leave and I followed the Tulip lady back along the corridor to yet another room. This was obviously the room I had arrived in and, once again, I started to feel slightly disorientated. The frequency change ran through my body and I lifted off. Next moment I was back in bed, with the front doorbell ringing. As always, I left my bed and opened the front door, to find no one there. I closed the door, climbed back into bed and lay for quite a while, running over in my mind what I had just experienced.

I still longed to see my child and once again found myself sitting in meditation and asking to see her. I wondered if my demands were starting to annoy them but then, almost one year to the day, I had a similar experience. It was now late in 2005 and I lifted off at about 4.30 a.m. This was an unusual time, as it would normally occur between the hours of midnight and 3 a.m. and sometimes even in the daytime, but not normally so late into the night. I arrived in what seemed to be the same room as before and, as before, my child was brought out to see me. I was now wondering if these visits were for her benefit as well as mine, as I felt a bonding was taking place and it must have been the same for her. She recognized me straight away and did not seem to be so nervous. She came up to me and smiled and I bent down as before and gave her a gentle hug. She spoke to me in my mind. "I like you," she said. I looked down at her and told her that I liked her as well. I liked her very much. This was no ordinary child; she was, after all, a hybrid; she was part of me and part 'off-worlder!' Whether this environment was ideal for her, I have no way of knowing, but it was far removed from how I remember my childhood of playing games in the street and football after school and a nice Sunday dinner. She seemed happy enough and who am I to know what the best environment is for a child to grow up in. The environment for children today in inner cities is one of danger and deprivation and kids are running around with guns and knives and live in a culture where you shoot first and ask questions later, if at all. We seem to be turning into an amoral society and if this is allowed to continue, then we will destroy what little love and respect we have left for each other. So perhaps this little girl is not in such a bad place after all?

The Tulip lady told me that the child was doing very well and was very happy, living here with other hybrid children, and I would see her again sometime soon, she assured me. The child, once more, was beckoned and she smiled and walked away and again, I knew it was time for me to return back to my home.

Before I returned, I mentally asked the Tulip lady about the little girl. What was her destiny on board this galactic ship? The Tulip lady looked at me with those amazing eyes and replied, "Future leader!"

CHAPTER 19

ARE THERE SHIPS IN THE BAY?

By Fran

The Christian Bible starts with the story of Creation and states that the first thing God said was, "Let there be Light!" Light is one of the most fundamental building blocks of the universe and the objects of the material universe, including ourselves, are light vibrating at different frequencies.

Light is composed of streams of energy, each moving at different speeds in a wave motion. Some of these streams of energy move too fast or too slowly for us to see. Those we can see we call the *visible spectrum*.

Below is a chart of the known electro-magnetic spectrum. The visible spectrum is the narrow white band. We can only see those things that vibrate on frequencies within that band (Fig 46).

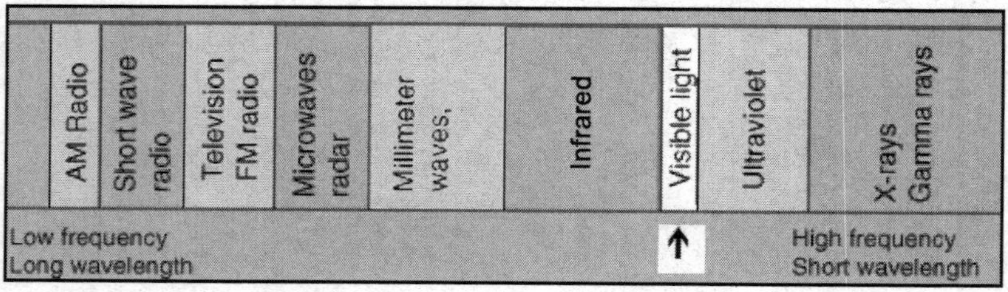

AM Radio	Short wave radio	Television FM radio	Microwaves radar	Millimeter waves,	Infrared	Visible light	Ultraviolet	X-rays Gamma rays

Low frequency
Long wavelength

High frequency
Short wavelength

Fig 46

The University of Washington website states:

'Humans can see only the wavelengths of electromagnetic radiation between about 380 and 760 nanometers...this is light. Our eyes do not have detectors for wavelengths of energy less than 380 or greater than 760 nanometers, so we cannot "see" other types of energy.'

We cannot even see our whole selves. The physical body that we see is only one aspect of our body/mind system. It is the densest layer and so comes within our visible spectrum. Beyond that, as with light itself, are layers of our energy self that we cannot see, or see so easily. Around the body is a thin band of energy that has the same shape as the physical body but vibrates at a higher rate and so is invisible to us. This is known as the *etheric body*. Beyond that is a band of energy called the *aura* or *astral body*. Extending outward from the aura is the *mental body*. Mystics say there are even more layers[1]. (Fig 47).

Some of these layers can be photographed using *Kirlian* cameras. Others we feel the effects of, even if we cannot see them.

Everything in the universe is energy and energy vibrates at different rates. Each person has a unique vibration, which is their energy signature. Everything that influences us and all that we think and focus our attention on affects that vibration. We know this in some part of our being

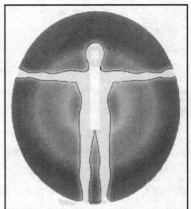

Fig 47

and show this by using expressions such as: 'The place had bad vibes' or 'He/she had nice vibes.' If you strike a tuning fork it will make any other tuning fork within hearing range vibrate at the same frequency. Romantic attraction, that frisson of energy and spine-tingling touches between lovers, is often based on meeting another person whose vibratory rate matches ours and, like a struck tuning fork, we vibrate in response. The higher a vibrational frequency is, the closer it is to the frequency of Light.

Is it reasonable to assume, as we are taught to do, that no life exists in the frequencies we cannot see and that there are no frequencies beyond those we know of; that we are the only Life in the universe? Even within our own frequency band, in the context of the Universe we know, that is a very arrogant and ignorant assumption. If we postulate the likelihood that Life, however similar or different to us, exists in other frequencies, that the whole of Creation, not just our wavebands, is teeming with life, then how strange is it that some of them visit us?

Across the planet, many thousands of people believe in, and even worship, an extra-terrestrial being who claimed to come from, and be part of, the Creative Source (as, in a sense, are we all). They readily accept this as fact yet scoff at those who also claim contact with off-worlders. None of the extra-terrestrials currently visiting us make such amazing claims as the one who claimed to be the Son of God. He has not been seen visibly for nearly two thousand years. The Visitors today come regularly. They interact with thousands of people right across the globe, yet those who claim such contact are treated as insane by people who believe in a being they have never seen.

The Bible mentions Jesus and Peter walking on water; it is claimed that the Buddha walked on water and these claims are believed worldwide by many thousands of people, none of whom have any evidence to back up their belief, which is based on second-hand testimony from many years ago. Why then, when claims such as these are accepted without evidence, do people clamor for 'evidence' when more cogent, recent and tangible personal testimonies to unusual experiences are presented? Why can reason extend to encompass possibilities in the one case and not in the other? Especially when the experiences associated with the contact phenomenon fall more easily within the parameters of known physics than does walking on water.

Some of the visitors' craft are seen in our skies and on the ground, reported by pilots, police officers, naval officers, and military personnel – people who are trained to observe and discount the known before making claims for the unknown.

The media of many countries (UK excluded) are open in reporting sightings of unknown craft and the experiences of those who interact with our visitors. Some countries, such as Mexico, Brazil, Chile, Turkey, India and Russia, are openly sharing information between the armed services, police forces and the secular groups that form to investigate this aspect of reality. Yet still the mainstream UK media continue to ignore these exciting, history-making, perspective-changing events and the mass of people are ignorant of what is going on or refuse to open their minds to it.

For me, the most perplexing aspect of all this is why people cannot accept that we are being visited! The Universe is vast from what we know and what we know is a drop in the ocean. Why are we afraid of that? It is the most exciting thing that can happen to us; a widening of our neighborhood and our experience and our knowledge. I also do not understand the rationale that limits travel to linear journeys across linear space. Why do we assume that what we know is all there is to know? Our science fiction programs, such as *Star Trek*, *Star Gate*, etc., have extrapolated and extended their science logically and feasibly from where we are now with our knowledge and they have faster-than-light travel and 'particle beam transporters', so why should not other beings have discovered laws in the universe that we cannot even dream of?

I think it was Jung who said that people are addicted to their belief systems. Now that we know more about the nature of consciousness, we know also that the reverse of the old adage, 'I'll believe it when I see it', is true. Rather, you will see it when you believe it. In 1519, Ferdinand Magellan, a Portuguese explorer, set sail to find the Spice Islands. Most times, when his fleet of five, tall-masted ships, sailed into the bays of small islands, the natives would be overcome with fear. On one island, however, they completely ignored the huge ships, because they actually could not see them. The ships were so far beyond their consciousness that none of the natives, apart from the shamans, could see them. The shamans explained what to look for and finally, one person saw a red flag flying from the mast of one of the ships. Once that happened, more and more of them began to see the ships.

It is our beliefs that limit us. Certain achievements are often thought impossible, for example: diving to a depth of more than 300 feet, climbing Mount Everest without oxygen. Once a record of human achievement has been broken *and the belief that such a thing is impossible* is broken as well, others go on to beat the original record. For example: we see athletic records broken almost yearly. We all know the person who is less talented than others but achieves more because they have confidence in themselves; *because they believe they can do it*. The secret of success is not in their talents but in their mind. A popular image for some years was a poster showing seagulls in flight with underneath the text: 'They can because they think they can.' Once you open your mind to other possibilities, to a reality that is larger, more colorful and much more diverse than the one you have been trained to see, then your mind will allow you to see that wider reality that is around you.

Most people have heard that an opera singer is often able to smash a glass by singing a note that vibrates at the resonant frequency of the glass, causing the glass to vibrate past the elasticity of the material and so shatter. Windows in buildings often rattle when a large lorry passes. This is because the glass in each frame has a vibrational frequency close to, or a multiple of, the revs per minute of the passing engine. In 1939, Dr Jarl, an Oxford University student, was in Tibet, where he photographed Tibetan monks levitating a five-ton stone slab purely by using the tones of 19 musical instruments, including drums and trumpets. The sound made in such instances is at, or close to, the resonant frequency of the stone slab and the molecules within the stone vibrate in such a way that the normal effects of gravity no longer affect the slab. The monks took up positions in carefully measured arcs, which could suggest that Sacred Geometry may also have been involved. Dr Jarl's two films were allegedly confiscated by The English Scientific Society, for which he was working, but a sketch he did can be seen on:

http://ourworld.compuserve.com/homepages/dp5/gravity2.htm

Austrian Film maker, Linauer, was at a remote monastery in northern

Tibet in the 1930s, where he was shown two strange instruments that could produce weightlessness in stone. One was a very large gong, made out of three different kinds of metals, including gold. The second instrument was shaped like a mussel shell and was also made from three metals. It was 6.56 feet (2 meters) by 3.28 feet (1 meter) wide, had strings stretched over it and was hung in a frame. The monks told him that this instrument was not played by humans, but reverberated in sympathy with the gong of its own accord. The two worked together to produce the required vibrations. The monks also told Linauer that their ancestors had used this method of levitation to build protective walls around Tibet, and that such devices could also disintegrate physical matter. The Bible tells of the walls of Jericho falling after being submitted to sound. The walls of the Greek city of Thebes were supposedly built by Amphion, a son of Zeus, who used the sound of his lyre to move the stones through the air. Maybe similar applications of sympathetic vibratory physics apply?

A NASA technical pamphlet (N0017488) in their category 'Levitation & Gravity', describes an experimental acoustic levitator in which stable levitation of a solid particle or liquid drop can be achieved by the application of sound.

In 1991, an American acoustics engineer, Tom Danley, filed a US patent for Acoustic Levitation and Positioning Devices, The patent states:

"An acoustic levitator includes a pair of opposed sound sources which have interfering sound waves producing acoustic energy wells in which an object can be levitated. The phase of one sound source may be changed relative to the other in order to move the object along an axis between the sound sources."

These devices were used for a process known as 'Containerless Processing' which has since been tested by NASA in two experiments on two Shuttle missions, which successfully melted and solidified ceramic samples from about 1000 deg C to about 1500 deg C and described on the

CSA information web site, thus:

'Many of the experiments to be carried out in the Space Shuttle will require containerless processing techniques that will provide manipulation and control of weightless (molten) materials without physical contact with container walls or other holding devices. The variety of containerless processing technologies now being developed for space - and ground-based materials processing facilities is surveyed. It is shown how the utilization of air jets or high-intensity acoustic.....'

Trial demonstrations of this can be seen in the TV documentary film *Mystery of the Sphinx*, made in 1993 and filmed inside Danley's laboratory.

These are examples of sound being used to change the vibratory rate of objects so that they can be manipulated more easily.

Many of those who have regular encounters with our visitors tell, as Mike has done, of the vibrations felt in their body before they are taken. Presumably a technique is used to change their vibratory rate so they can move through 'solid' objects and access a different electro-magnetic frequency wave to interact with those that exist there. We do not yet have (at least not in the mainstream) technology or the technique to achieve this but it is probable our ancient ancestors did. The Flower of Life School[2], amongst others, draws on ancient knowledge to teach a method of meditation, visualization and breathing that effects a change in vibration. Again, it is not unlikely that beings from elsewhere have long possessed the ability to alter their vibratory rate to access other frequencies or dimensions, including ours.

A large percentage of visitations involve beings just 'appearing' or 'walking through walls.' Once, when, unknown to me, Mike had off-world visitors in the room with him, I was walking along the hallway and, as I passed the wall of the room that Mike was in, I felt as if I walked through an area of resistance, like I would imagine it feels to walk through a gentle force-field. As I did this I heard a sound like a sigh but all around me. I have wondered since if it was the effect of a frequency change or a dimensional doorway.

It is an undisputed scientific fact that what looks and feels to us like a solid object, such as a table, is also, on an energetic level, a mass of moving, dynamic particles in a sea of energy. The study of the universe at that energetic level is called Quantum Physics. Quantum Scientists have discovered some interesting things:

1. Electrons can communicate with each other instantaneously, regardless of the distance separating them, however huge that distance.

That means that, theoretically, the electrons in your body, in your DNA, can communicate with electrons anywhere else in the Universe. The process of thought causes electron movement in your brain. Those electrons exist in two dimensions at once; they are a part of the physical world, and at the same time are part of the quantum world where Time does not exist and thought can effect change. So your thought can affect the fabric of the Universe. (See 4 below). The same would apply to any being within at least this dimension of the universe. Have we thought them into existence? Have we thought them out of our conscious reality? Have they thought us into existence? Has the nature of the phenomena i.e. types of crafts and beings, changed as the concepts in our collective consciousness have changed?

2. When they move, particles 'jump' from one place to another, seemingly randomly and seemingly without effort.

We hear of craft that 'jump' instantaneously from one position in the sky to another. Are they using physics not yet known to us, which our quantum scientists are working towards? Are some craft guided by thought? The German scientist, Werner von Braun, was taken to view the crashed alien craft at Roswell, New Mexico, in 1947. He later told Clark C. McClelland that "the craft's interior was bizarre; it was very bare of instrumentation, as if the creatures and the craft were of a single unit[3]."

Thought or intent is faster than light. Thought-guided craft would surely be feasible, given what we already know from our own science. Researchers at Emory University, Atlanta, Georgia, working to find aids for people who are paralyzed, have developed a neural implant that sends thought signals to a computer. The Functional Electrical Stimulation Centre, Cleveland, Ohio, produce prosthetics for quadriplegics that animate limbs by using thought-operated muscle-stimulant electrodes. The 2,000-year-old Indian epic *Ramayana* tells of a supersonic-type plane, the Pushpak Vimana, which could fly at the speed of thought.

3. Given a choice in which a particle can do one thing or another, it will do both simultaneously. To do this, the particle changes from behaving like a particle and behaves like a wave while traveling and changes back to a particle when it arrives. Scientists suggest that while in wave form, the particle creates a parallel universe, to enable both options to exist.

What if some UFO sightings, dream-like encounters, visitations of entities, etc., are experienced in a parallel universe? What if some off-world societies have the technology to create craft that can use this aspect of the nature of particles in order to travel from one dimension to another? Maybe they can do it without craft and just transport themselves interdimensionally?

4. Particles in experiments react to the thought of the observer. Quantum physicists discovered that every act of observation made of an atom by a physicist disturbed the atom. That whatever

methodology they used to observe the universe at a quantum level affected and determined what they saw.

In his book, *Taking the Quantum Leap*, Fred Alan Wolf says:
"Quantum mechanics appears to describe a universal order that includes us in a very special way. In fact, our mind may enter into nature in a way we had not imagined possible. The thought that atoms may not exist without observers of atoms is, to me, a very exiting thought. Could this fact concerning atoms also apply to other realms of science? Perhaps much of what is taken to be real is mainly determined by thought...... The order of the universe may be the order of our own minds."

In the mid-1960s, holographic images were developed. In these three-dimensional images, any tiny piece of the image holds the blueprint for the whole image and can be used to recreate the original 3-D image. In the same way, one cell of our body holds the blueprint for the whole body; a factor which has led to experiments in cloning animals and humans.

One of the current theories of physics is that the universe itself is like a hologram. Michael Talbot, in *The Holographic Universe*, says:

"To the naked eye, an un-illuminated piece of holographic film appears to have no order or meaning. Its order is implied within the apparently random interference patterns; illuminated by the proper light, the implicate order becomes explicate and the image appears. Our three-dimensional universe, likewise, is the explicate construction of a vaster and more mysterious dimensionless realm, illuminated by the light of consciousness."

The German mathematician and philosopher, Gottfried Leibniz (1646-1716) believed the universe is composed of countless conscious centers of spiritual force or energy, known as monads. Each monad represents the universe in concentrated form, exists in synchronous time alongside the others in the same reality and, although separate, each monad mirrors the whole universe, containing within it the pattern for the macrocosm. Sounds a bit like our conscious, holographic universe?

Many aspects of our reality cannot be explained by our traditional model of reality: telepathy, precognition, clairvoyance, astral travel, UFO sightings, encounters with off-worlders, time-slips, etc. What science and society cannot explain they treat with either fear or ridicule! What does that say about our level of intelligence and emotional maturity? What does it say about our desire to find Truth?

A holographic model of the universe goes a good few steps towards explaining and encompassing all those elements that society currently classes as 'weird', 'fringe', 'spooky' or 'supernatural'. It also helps to show what mystics have long known, what tribal shamans experience, what Sacred Geometry points us to and what Quantum Physics indicates, namely that at an energetic and deep consciousness level everything is connected. The carbon atom in us is connected to the carbon atom in all living matter. The electron 'here' communicates with the electron 'there'. Patterns repeat themselves, from the spiral in the inner ear to the spiral galaxy, from the human DNA helix to cosmic DNA helix[4]. A tenet of ancient mysticism and some philosophies is, 'as above, so below'. Patterns and interactions repeat from the microcosm to the macrocosm; all part of the same cosmic dance of life. It is not therefore unreasonable to assume that what we do on Earth affects the rest of the Universe and it might be well overdue that we wake up to that fact and behave more responsibly with our planet.

As part of this holographic universe; part of the essential, primal creative energy that sustains all and exists in all, does our DNA carry within it knowledge of the Whole? The Light Beings told Mike and me that the answers are in our own DNA.

In my opinion, the best source of information as to what is currently happening with and to humanity lies with those having the leading-edge experiences. Those who see, communicate with and interact with, life-forms that originate elsewhere in the universe. They are many. Hundreds of thousands from all countries, creeds and cultures. From peasants to pilots, housewives to military intelligence personnel, children in playgrounds to politicians; from the unemployed to business tycoons, from skeptics to scientists. In fact, this experience is not limited to any one nation or personality type. It is worldwide, ongoing, growing and very, very real.

Still today, scientists, psychologists and mainstream media ridicule, dismiss and otherwise censure the personal truths of those who are contacted. Why? What are they afraid of? Skeptics call for 'evidence' of these phenomena but consistently reject the greatest body of evidence, namely the personal testimony of those who see craft or experience contact. To me, it is evidence in itself that so many thousands of people from all cultures are claiming virtually the same, or extremely similar, experiences. However, when you link that with testimony from people who, if in a court of law, would be acceptable witnesses; people trained to observe and make rational deductions, such as pilots, police officers, military personnel, etc., then one is forced to accept that *something* is going on. Increasing numbers of testimonies to the alien presence on our planet are from military personnel, especially those within the intelligence sectors, who claim to have experienced sightings of unexplainable craft (even accounting for secret technology) or close-up encounters with landed craft or beings or to have knowledge of beings captured and kept /interrogated by the military or report that alien beings and the military are working together (MUCH corroborative evidence from diverse sources)[5]. Is it credible that so many trained and professional men would make up these tales or be the victims of frontal-lobe epilepsy, sleep disorders, or whatever other explanations are used to decry these testimonies? If it is mass hallucination, then I reckon we have an even more serious problem on our hands than if our neighbors (3D or other-dimensional) are visiting us.

The trouble with all this stuff is that we don't often have much 'nuts and bolts' evidence in the way that our society has trained us to desire. Maybe we have to find other criteria for measuring these experiences. The data is there if you look. Even though our UK press mainly suppresses publication of reported sightings and events, still the information is there: in written testimony, audio-taped interviews, camcorder tapes of sightings, etc., if you seek it out. There are plenty of videos out now, and some artifacts, and I guess these belie the 'mass hysteria' theory. Countries such as Turkey, Brazil, Russia, Chile, Mexico, etc., have regular TV programs on which video footage is shown. Even Belgium, years ago, released footage shot from RAF planes and the French are releasing their UFO records. There IS visual stuff out there in plenty, including logged radar recordings - it is just that in the UK you have to seek it out for yourself.

Another factor that puts material in the hard-evidence-skeptics' ball court is that, with numerous encounters, we are probably dealing with aspects of reality and consciousness not yet clear to us. Skeptics will gleefully seize on the fact that so often one person in a crowd will claim to see something or even have contact, while others see nothing. This has been reported so many times by experiencers that it is obviously part of the phenomenon, part of this aspect of reality and in itself is worthy of study, to teach us more about the nature of consciousness and time as we perceive it. I have also been in public places where craft have been visible overhead and most people have never looked up. I have pointed them out to folk and they glance up and say 'Oh yes, that's odd', or something similar, and dismiss it. Sometimes they won't look!! What does that say about the mindset in the UK? A few years ago I was at an open air play in the Rollright Stone Circle, Oxfordshire. It was a clear summer's evening and suddenly, very low over the fields came a small, light-filled globe. It virtually 'buzzed' the circle, it was so low, and went directly across the circle, almost across the diameter and over the heads of the audience. About six people watched it! No one else seemed to notice, though how they could fail to notice beat me. This is also part of the oddness of it all - often only some folk in a group will see the object. Why I don't know, but I think it warrants some exploration itself because I find that very puzzling indeed.

Throughout our history, mystics and ordinary people have claimed glimpses of the Divine; moments when Jesus, an angel or another being connected with our planetary religions, has appeared to them, to comfort or give a message, or times when they have been saved from disaster by divine intervention. Visions, transportations, extreme and instantaneous bodily changes and miraculous healings abound within a religious context and, in the main, these testimonies are accepted as real, personal experiences and some experiencers have even been awarded sainthood – why do we judge differently those who also claim contact with off-worlders, just not divine off-worlders? In an interview with Dr Steven Greer and journalist Paola Harris on 23 September, 2000, the Vatican's Monsignor Corrado Balducci said:

> "It is illogical and a bit arrogant to believe that we are the only beings in God's creation. *Since all of Christianity is based on witness-testimony, we must realize how important testimony is.* It would be a tragedy if we began to be suspicious of all the people who report that they have experienced something unusual, like seeing craft in the sky, because there are some very credible witnesses who have seen these and who have come forward."

This same attitude exists within the medical community who cannot, or will not, accept the evidence of healing success within alternative forms of healing. To take one example: Homeopathy, which has been used for thousands of years and has helped equal thousands of people heal, is largely excluded and viewed with suspicion by mainstream allopaths. (Did you know that in the UK you have a right to homeopathic treatment on the NHS? Yet how many practices and hospitals offer you that option?) The medical profession demand 'tests' and 'evidence' for the efficacy of homeopathic remedies yet gear those tests as if for allopathic drugs, when homeopathy is a science that deals with the body on an energetic level – on a different level of reality to that of mainstream medicine. Thus, the required 'proofs' are rarely found because they are set by people asking the wrong questions and looking in the wrong places for the answers and refusing to see other aspects to reality.

In chapter one, Mike tells of the tiger that appeared by his bed when he was a child and of the fairy he once saw in his garden. Of course children have imaginary friends, and that is a sound and obvious point to raise, but it does not stop it being true that some off-worlders, and the Grays in particular, also appear to children in the guise of animals or birds. If we turn that on its head for a moment - we always assume that a child's friend that we cannot see is imaginary because our society does not allow for invisible companions or beings that do not fit within certain material parameters, but what if that is not the case? What if children, nearer to their origins and the stream of cosmic consciousness, less programmed and conditioned by society's taboos, can still see what we cannot? Maybe they see the ships in the bay?

In some world cultures today, where the culture still allows for the belief in a planet populated by diverse beings, people see fairies or devas or tree spirits. Iceland is one such country, where elves and nature spirits live alongside the population. Colin Nickerson, writing in *The Boston Globe* on 26 December, 1999, said:

> 'Highway engineers in recent years have been forced to reroute roads around supposed elf dwellings. Similarly, builders of the country's first shopping mall took care to lay electrical cables and other underground installations well away from suspected abodes of gnomes and fairies.'

The Iceland Tourist Board reports:

'Couples who are planning a new house will sometimes hire "elf-spotters" to make sure the lot is free of spirit folk......The Iceland road authority typically responds with sensitivity, routing roads around hallowed boulders or delaying construction long enough to give non-human constituents time to find new accommodations.'

To the discerning mind, a vast body of evidence exists and grows yearly to show that we, as a planetary species, are undergoing change on a deep consciousness level. We are beginning, as did Magellan's natives, to see the ships in the bay. We are starting to perceive that consciousness is not tied to the body but can exist apart from the body and in a greater reality than this 3D one. We are breaking free from the illusion that we are alone and powerless and limited to 3D and emerging into the light of a glorious landscape, where the gates of the Universe stand open for those who can go forward in Love and Light and purity of intent, and our neighbors are waiting for us. The caterpillars are getting ready to become butterflies.

Science and Mysticism, long at opposite ends of a long pole, with UFO 'weirdoes' precariously teetering in the middle, are discovering that they are dipping their toes into the same water – that of the true nature of reality and consciousness.

As proof of the connectiveness of consciousness, there exists what scientists call 'the Hundredth Monkey Syndrome'. During the mid-twentieth century, a group of islands in the South Pacific were inhabited by monkeys. A severe drought caused the monkeys to begin to starve. A team of Japanese science researchers visited the islands to try to help and dropped sweet potatoes onto the sandy beaches. The monkeys fed on the potatoes, eating them as they found them, dirt and all. A young monkey washed her potato in a stream. Soon the rest of the monkeys on that island did the same. Then something unexpected happened. Monkeys on other islands, that were separated by miles of sea-water from the original island were also washing their potatoes. The scientists repeated this experiment elsewhere and decided that it took approximately 100 monkeys to learn a new skill before that skill passed, at a deep consciousness level, to others in the species group. The same thing happened with birds in the UK, when a few blue tits learnt to pierce the foil tops of bottled milk on doorsteps. After a few months, blue tits and sparrows across the UK had acquired this skill.

We must remember that what we see is governed by our brain not our eyes. Open your mind to other possibilities; to other aspects of reality than those you currently see. Look for the ships in the bay. Become one of the hundred monkeys that, by opening up their own consciousness, will help change the collective consciousness.

Be assured. We are not alone. We never were. We have just lost our ability to see the universe as it is.

As with a hologram, if the blueprint of the whole is within us, then is that why the Light Beings told us to go inside and find the answers in our own DNA? We may find, in the end, that we and our visitors are not so very different; that we are part of the same original spark of creative consciousness, still linked at an energetic level, and that what affects one affects all. How silly it would be to sit in a small, darkened room, by an open door, through which light flooded and people came to visit us, but to persist in believing that the small room was the sum total of the universe, when evidence indicated otherwise. Yet that is the mind-set of much of humanity today. Not very intelligent!

The Italian community of Damanhur[7] is well known the world over for its extraordinary work in bringing ancient, esoteric knowledge and skills back into everyday life. To quote from their website:

"By uniting spirituality, art and technology, Damanhur's research groups often succeed in carrying out experiments that contemporary science considers impossible."

"The Damanhurians have developed two separate ways of traveling in time. One involves the transmission of what they call the 'subtle body' of the traveler, which could be more accurately translated as the 'essence' or 'spirit' of that person. The other involves full dematerialization and materialization, of both subtle and physical body."

It would appear that many of the visitors that interact with people the world over travel in one of the above two ways.

The Damanhurian experiments include the use of sacred geometry, spiral energy, crystal energy, inner spiritual strength, thought, art and different-than-mainstream beliefs in the nature of space and time. Elements woven together in a way that mainstream science would scorn – but they work – and they travel through time and space without need of a 'nuts-and-bolts'craft!

Throughout our written history we have evidence that those who postulated new scientific theories not in agreement with mainstream thinking were vilified, ridiculed and at times imprisoned or killed. Elements of this closed-mind attitude exist today in the treatment of those who tell of their encounters with others not from this planet.

Copernicus and Galileo were right; that became evident in the end and today their 'fringe' claims are part of mainstream belief. Truth will out, no matter how much we may try to suppress it or how much we are afraid of new concepts. As Michael Schneider says: "The universe may be a mystery but it is not a secret!" Open the door in your consciousness to the possibility that reality is greater and more glorious than you have so far imagined – and wait to see what happens. You may be surprised!

1. See *Suggested Reading* 19/I
2 See *Suggested Reading* 19/B
3 See *Suggested Reading* 19/C
4 See *Suggested Reading* 19/D
5 See *Suggested Reading* 19/E
7 See *Suggested Reading* 19/F

INTO THE ARMS OF ANGELS

© Mike Oram 2005

As death escaped into life,
My bones eased from discomfort.
On gaining wings
I flew away,
Soaring into the night of a thousand stars.
From storm on troubled land
I fled for shelter in the arms of angels.

I left behind the shattered blow;
The curse of Man bent with age.
Thinking instead of youthful moments
In fields and valleys where I played;
We simply ran forever.
A land where petals never ceased to fall.
Nothing died.
Just a childhood with Eternity a game.

But Death,
Like wind that stopped the silence,
Drifted along and toiled with the child.
My life was like those leaves that fell.
I returned again and again
For more and more;
Hardly aware of my own innocence.
The laughter made it all seem worthwhile.
And the rocks that stood for centuries,
Grey and smooth,
Listened, and begged us to go no nearer.

But as a child
Fear is tossed into the sea
To rest upon the sand and stone of Time,
Which beckons with each incoming tide
To take it and lift it far away

Looking back now at my body of old,
I wondered about those eyes.
Are they the same eyes as the eyes of that child?
Is that the same body that ran with the wind;
That played with Forever?
I wished for peace now, in the arms of angels.

SUGGESTED READING

Books

1/1 Steven M.Greer, *Hidden Truth: Forbidden Knowledge.* Crossing Point, 28 April 2006. ISBN: 0967323827

In *Hidden Truth: Forbidden Knowledge*, Dr Greer provides his own personal disclosure based on years of high-level meetings with over 450 military and government-connected insiders and whistle-blowers and briefings with senior government officials, such as former CIA Director R. James Woolsey, members of the US Senate and senior UN officials.

7/1 Alan Baker, *The Encyclopaedia of Alien Encounters.* Virgin Books, 6 January 2000. ISBN: 0753504804.

7/2 Clive Harold, *The Uninvited.* W.H. Allen & Co Ltd, 1979. ISBN: 0352303506
And
Randall Jones Pugh and F.W. Holiday, *The Dyfed Enigma.* Hodder & Stoughton, 1 June 1981. ISBN: 0340266651

7/3 Ed Walters, *The Gulf Breeze Sightings.* Avon books, April 1991. ISBN: 0380708701

12/1 Budd Hopkins, *Witnessed.* Pocket, 1 April 1997. ISBN: 0671570315

14 /1A Bob Frissel, *Nothing In This Book Is True, But It Is Exactly How Things Are.* Frog, Ltd, January 2003. ISBN: 9583940677

14/1B Dolores Cannon, *The Convoluted Universe.* Ozark Mountain Publishing (AR), 1 November 2001. ISBN: 1886940827. On page 119, one of her clients talks of a funnel of light.

14/1C Jain, *The Book of Phi. The Living Mathematics of Nature.* From:

http://www.jainmathemagics.com/

15/1 Branton, *The Secrets of the Mojave*. Creative Arts & Science Enterprises, 1 December 1999. ISBN: 1881808440 and *The Dulce Wars: Underground Alien Bases and the Battle for Planet Earth*. Inner Light - Global Communications, 7 December 1999. ISBN: 1892062127

15/2 Charles James Hall, *Millennial Hospitality* trilogy: *Millennial Hospitality*. Authorhouse, November 2002. ISBN: 1403368740
The World We Knew. Authorhouse, January 2003. ISBN: 1403392048
The Road Home. Authorhouse, May 2003. ISBN: 1410733955

15/3 Adrian Dvir, *Healing, Entities, and Aliens*. Dvir, 31 January 2003. ISBN: 9657269008

16/1 Nick Begich, *Angels Don't Play This HAARP: Advances in Tesla Technology*. Earthpulse Press, September 1995. ISBN: 0964881209

19/I Robert Trundle, *Is ET Here? EcceNova Editions*, May 1, 2005. ISBN: 0973534125

Also:
Fred Alan Wolf, *Parallel Universes*. Simon & Schuster, 15 February 1990. ISBN: 0671096017 and *Taking the Quantum Leap*. Harper Perennial, 25 January 1989. ISBN: 0-06-250480-2-09105381
Michael. S. Schneider, *A Beginner's Guide to Constructing the Universe: Mathematical Archetypes of Nature, Art and Science*. Harper Paperbacks, 8 November 1995. ISBN: 0060926716

Joseph McMoneagle, *The Ultimate Time Machine*. Hampton Roads Publishing Company Inc, October 1998. ISBN: 1-7174102X and *Mind*

Trek. Hampton Roads Publishing Company Inc, July 1997. ISBN: 1878901729
(Remote Viewer for the US Military 'Star Gate' programme)

Murry Hope, *Time. The Ultimate Energy*. Element Books, November 1991. ISBN: 1852302372

David Morehouse, *Psychic Warrior*. St Martin's Paperbacks, 15 January 1998. ISBN: 0312964137

Paola Harris, *Connecting the Dots,* Wild Flower Press, July 2003. ISBN: 0-926524-57-7

Web sites:
1/A http://www.nicap.org/wnsdir.htm and
http://www.cufon.org/cufon/cia-52-1.htm

1/B Black Vault: http://www.bvalphaserver.com/

7/A http://www.ufoarea.com/events_bonnybridge_ufo.html

7/B See: Masters of the Stars video – available from http://www.amazon.com/gp/product/B00004S5JC

7/C Audio interview concerning UFO Disclosure in Brazil:
http://www.jerrypippin.com/UFO_Files_aj_gevaerd.htm
And
Article on UFOs and the Brazilian Air Force: http://www.cosmicparadigm.com/UFOs_and_the_Brazilian_Air_Force.html
Also: http://www.crowdedskies.com/tony
dodd_military_encounters.htm- article on military encounters with UFOs.

7/D http://www.ufocongressstore.com/servlet/the-Director-Presentations/Categories and
http://netmar.com/~maat/archive/mar3/akdogan.htm

7/E http://www.mufon.com/ - click on 'UFO Case Files'
And http://www.mufon.com/fastfacts.htm - for some myth busters
And http://www.stargate-chronicles.com/those_who_know.html - for statements by officials
And http://www.mufon.com/znews_kgb.html
http://www.rense.com/ufo6/boom.htm
http://www.ufodigest.com/china.html
http://www.rense.com/general65/cchin.htm
http://www.ufodigest.com/india.html

Also:
http://video.google.ca/videoplay?docid=-5210326345538570434&q=ufo+cylinder

http://video.google.ca/videoplay?docid=-4468185100897567649&q=ufo+cylinder
for video footgae of Soviet MIGs chasing UFOs
and
http://video.google.ca/videoplay?docid=-6489758600806134101&q=ufo+cylinder
for a UFO filmed from an F16

13/1 http://www.experiencefestival.com/mayan_calendar

14/A http://www.edenproject.com/about/1523.html. Eden Project building based on Phi Spiral
14/ B http://www.marxhowell.com/Articles/articles.html

14/ C http://www.sciencepub.net/0101/01-ma.pdf and
http://arxiv.org/ftp/physics/papers/0310/0310055.pdf

14/D
http://www.mcs.surrey.ac.uk/Personal/R.Knott/Fibonacci/fibInArt.html

!4/E http://www.enlightenedbeings.com/star_symbols.html
http://www.star-knowledge.net/index.htm
http://www.v-j-enterprises.com/sksymbs.html

14/ F http://www.v-j-enterprises.com/hopigrey.html

15/A http://www.v-j-enterprises.com/mojave.html

19/A http://en.wikipedia.org/wiki/Subtle_body

19/B http://www.floweroflife.org

19/C http://www.stargate-chronicles.com/case_von_braun_at_roswell.html

19/D http://www.unexplained-mysteries.com/forum/index.php?show-topic=64395

19/E http://www.disclosureproject.org/

19/F http://www.damanhur.org/time/html/time_physics.htm and
http://www.damanhur.org/time/
The Federation of Damanhur is well known all over the world for its extraordinary experiments, which border on science fiction. By uniting spirituality, art and technology, Damanhur's research groups often succeed in carrying out experiments that contemporary science considers impossible.

BOOKS

O is a symbol of the world, of oneness and unity. In different cultures it also means the "eye," symbolizing knowledge and insight. We aim to publish books that are accessible, constructive and that challenge accepted opinion, both that of academia and the "moral majority."

Our books are available in all good English language bookstores worldwide. If you don't see the book on the shelves ask the bookstore to order it for you, quoting the ISBN number and title. Alternatively you can order online (all major online retail sites carry our titles) or contact the distributor in the relevant country, listed on the copyright page.

See our website **www.o-books.net** for a full list of over 500 titles, growing by 100 a year.

And tune in to myspiritradio.com for our book review radio show, hosted by June-Elleni Laine, where you can listen to the authors discussing their books.

MySpiritRadio

SOME RECENT O BOOKS

Back to the Truth
5,000 years of Advaita
Dennis Waite
A wonderful book. Encyclopedic in nature, and destined to become a classic. **James Braha**, author of *Living Reality*
Absolutely brilliant...an ease of writing with a water-tight argument outlining the great universal truths. This book will become a modern classic. A milestone in the history of Advaita.
Paula Marvelly, author of *The Teachers of One*
1905047614 500pp £19.95 $29.95

Beyond Photography
Encounters with orbs, angels and mysterious light forms
Katie Hall and John Pickering
The authors invite you to join them on a fascinating quest; a voyage of discovery into the nature of a phenomenon, manifestations of which are shown as being historical and global as well as contemporary and intently personal.
At journey's end you may find yourself a believer, a doubter or simply an intrigued wonderer... Whatever the outcome, the process of journeying is likely prove provocative and stimulating and - as with the mysterious images fleetingly captured by the authors' cameras - inspiring and potentially enlightening.
Brian Sibley, author and broadcaster.
1905047908 272pp 50 b/w photos +8pp colour insert **£12.99 $24.95**